MW00333987

Alterations of State

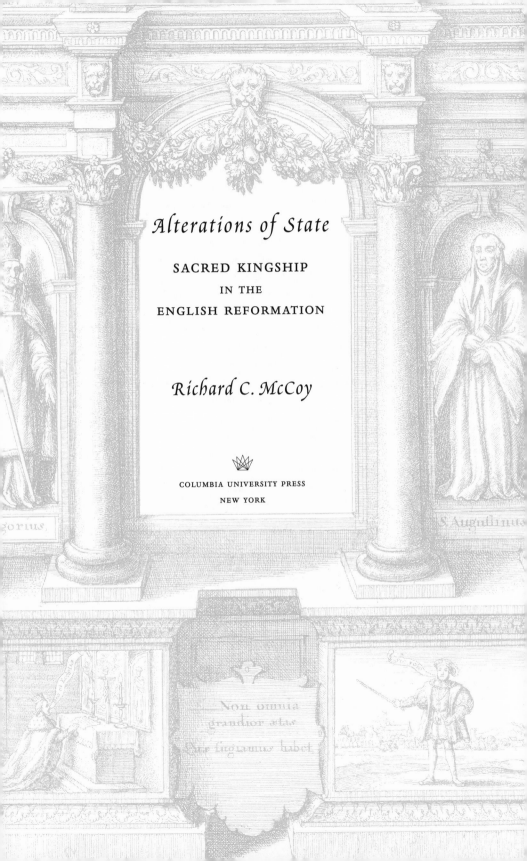

Alterations of State

SACRED KINGSHIP
IN THE
ENGLISH REFORMATION

Richard C. McCoy

COLUMBIA UNIVERSITY PRESS

NEW YORK

Columbia University Press

Publishers Since 1893

New York   Chichester, West Sussex

Copyright © 2002 Columbia University Press

All rights reserved

Library of Congress Cataloging-in-Publication Data

McCoy, Richard C., 1946–

Alterations of state : sacred kingship in the English Reformation /
Richard C. McCoy.

p. cm.

Includes bibliographical references and index.

ISBN 0–231–12616–6 (cloth)

1. English literature—Early modern, 1500–1700—History and criticism.
2. Kings and rulers in literature. 3. Christianity and literature—Great Britain—
History—16th century. 4. Christianity and literature—Great Britain—History—
17th century. 5. Kings and rulers—Religious aspects—Christianity. 6. Politics
and literature—Great Britain—History. 7. Church and state in literature.
8. State, The, in literature. 9. Holy, The, in literature. 10. Monarchy in literature.
I. Title.

PR428.K55 M34 2002

820.9'352351—dc21   2001047739

∞

Columbia University Press books are printed on permanent and
durable acid-free paper.

Designed by Chang Jae Lee

Printed in the United States of America

c 10 9 8 7 6 5 4 3 2 1

Parts of chapter 3 first appeared in the article "A Wedding and Four Funerals:
Conjunction and Commemoration in *Hamlet*," *Shakespeare Survey* 54, 2001,
copyright Cambridge University Press. Reproduced with permission.

To Sarah,
who waited even longer

Contents

Preface

> What an Earth-quake is the Alteration of a State!
> —Thomas Dekker, *The Wonderful Year* (1603)

FIGURE I

Thomas Hobbes, *Leviathan*, frontispiece
By permission of the British Library; 522.K.6

$\mathcal{K}$ings were sacred figures for centuries in Europe, perceived as the Lord's anointed deputies on earth. The Church and its sacraments were considered holier than the monarchy, but medieval rulers were still thought to have sacerdotal, spiritual, and even miraculous powers. Coronation was seen by some as a sacrament, akin to ordination; the royal touch was thought to have healing effects; and the mystical conception of the king's two bodies implied that kingship never died. Moreover, rulers from Charlemagne to the Hapsburgs had claimed imperial autonomy from the papacy, causing tension between kings and clerics. The Reformation intensified this conflict while vastly expanding older notions of sacred kingship, making them simultaneously more grandiose and more problematic. In England, Henry VIII's break with Rome was justified by new theories of royal supremacy that made the king the head of the church and clergy as well as the spiritual embodiment of the realm. As the Reformation advanced, even the sacraments themselves were diminished and the Mass suppressed. These developments caused what John Bossy calls "a migration of the holy" in which "the socially integrative powers of the host" were transferred "to the rituals of monarchy and secular community."[1] Under the Tudors, the royal presence acquired some of the awesome sanctity of Christ's real presence in the Eucharist and at times even threatened to replace it. Rood screens were dismantled and sometimes replaced with the royal coat of arms under Edward, and the feast of Corpus Christi was eventually suppressed and superseded by a cult of Elizabeth and its annual royal processions.[2]

Both old and new ideas of sacred kingship still provoked increasing ambivalence and even hostility, and challenges and conflicts intensified throughout the Reformation. "Because Protestantism rejected physical holiness," as Paul Kléber Monod says in *The Power of Kings*, ". . . it could easily clash with a kingship that made the body sacred."[3] More zealous Protestants found veneration of the monarchy as idolatrous as adoration of the host and repeatedly criticized the shortcomings of godly rule under the Tudors. Under the Stuarts, Puritan opposition increased, helping to fuel the Civil War and leading to the execution of Charles I in 1649. The English Reformation's struggle over sacred kingship was hardly resolved by regicide and republican rule. To John Milton's horror, the blood shed by Charles I only increased England's tendency toward "a civil kinde of Idolatry in idolizing thir Kings."[4] The king proved more popular in death and defeat than he ever had in life, inspiring support for the restoration of Charles II in 1660. Nevertheless, the Stuarts' papist sympathies became increasingly unpalatable, and James II was deposed in 1688. By challenging hereditary divine right, the Glorious Revolution seriously damaged more traditional ideas of sacred kingship and inaugurated a new era of constitutional monarchy.

As this brief summary indicates, conflicts over the English monarchy grew more tumultuous throughout the early modern period. It was a time, in the words of different contemporary accounts, of "many great changes, and terrible alterations," marked by "days of shaking."[5] Even a relatively smooth transition could arouse dire fears. In his chronicle of 1603, ironically entitled *The Wonderful Year*, Thomas Dekker conveys the anxieties surrounding the death of Elizabeth and the succession of James by exclaiming "What an Earth-Quake is the Alteration of a State!"[6] Any change of regime could arouse acute anxieties because, throughout the English Reformation, political change often entailed religious changes as well. King James understood these fears and tried to assure his new subjects that such drastic alterations were behind them when he spoke at Hampton Court in 1604: "in this land, King Henry VIII towards the end of his reign altered much, King Edward VI more, Queen Mary reversed all, and lastly Queen Elizabeth (of famous memory) settled religion as it now standeth. Herein I am happier than they, because they were fain to alter all things they found established, whereas I see yet no such cause to change as confirm what I find settled already."[7] However, James's own hostility to Puritans aggravated sectarian conflicts throughout his reign, and his heirs only further inflamed them. Charles I's religious policies helped provoke the Civil War that cost him his head, and James II's conversion to Catholicism caused the Glorious Revolution that cost him and eventually the Stuart dynasty the throne. For many in England, these alterations must have felt like earthquakes indeed.

I have adapted Dekker's phrase for my book's title because it suggests the monarchy's increased importance when the rule of *cuius regio, eius religio* pertained. By disrupting both temporal and spiritual arrangements, alterations of state threatened to alter the conditions of existence itself, shaking England to its very foundations. These words also suggest the traumatic impact of the death or deposition of a monarch. A far more famous work from Dekker's period, Shakespeare's *Hamlet*, shows how "the cess [or cease] of majesty" jeopardizes the entire social and cosmic order, rendering time itself "out of joint."[8] The play also dramatizes the deep ambivalence aroused by notions of sacred kingship in the English Reformation. Among many other paradoxes, the resonant claim that "There's such divinity doth hedge a king/That treason can but peep to what it would" (4.5.123–124) is attributed to a regicide and usurper, rendering kingship's divinity dubious. At the same time, the ghost of Hamlet's father suggests possibilities of a more mystical alteration of state in which the legitimate ruler somehow survives assassination and returns to bring ruin to his enemies. This mysterious, supernatural royal presence acquires, at least for a time, the force of a real presence outlasting even the "cease of majesty."

That phrase is itself ambiguous, since it appears in a speech addressed to Claudius by Rosencrantz and Guildenstern. Hamlet's former friends are worried about the well-being of the murderous usurper, and they cloak their own selfish apprehensions with unctuous piety just as Claudius does when he speaks of the "divinity" hedging a king:

> *Guild.* Most holy and religious fear it is
> To keep those many many bodies safe
> That live and feed upon your majesty.
>
> *Ros.* The single and peculiar life is bound
> With all the strength and armour of the mind
> To keep itself from noyance; but much more
> That spirit upon whose weal depends and rests
> The lives of many. The cess of majesty
> Dies not alone, but like a gulf doth draw
> What's near with it.
>
> (3.3.8–17)

In addressing Claudius, their monarch and master, each speaker is primarily concerned with his own "single and peculiar life," yet, for all their hypocrisy, their speeches really do express a "most holy and religious fear."[9] The venerable concept of the king's two bodies informs the claim that the monarch's well-being preserves his subjects' "many many bodies," an image emblematically shown fifty years later on the title page of Hobbes's *Leviathan*, where all those many little bodies make up the body of the king (figure 1). As in Hobbes, the common "weal depends" on the safety of the king. At the same time, the royal presence becomes a sacramental real presence: the idea of the king as the collective body politic transforms an otherwise revoltingly parasitic image of those who "live and feed upon your majesty" into a form of holy communion. A comparable symbol of Christike sacrifice appears in 1649 on the title page of *The Princely Pellican*, one of the many hagiographic tributes to Charles I, the martyr-king (figure 34).[10] This implicit comparison of the monarch to the host evokes a more salutary alteration of state or condition, namely transubstantiation. As Ernst Kantorowicz points out in his classic study of *The King's Two Bodies*, these two doctrines had been linked from their inception by a shared belief in the redemptive presence of an immortal corporate body that miraculously survives "the cease of majesty" and holds the bereft community together; the successor is presumed to incarnate that immortal mystical body.[11] As the traditional response to the monarch's death proclaims, "the king is dead, long live the king," a formula assuring continuity from one reign to the next.

In *Hamlet*, that continuity is undermined, of course, by the villainy of the successor and his disruption of the rightful succession, but the play briefly holds out the prospect of an even more miraculous royal survival. The ghost of the legitimate king returns "in his habit as he lived" (3.4.137) to expose his murderer's treachery and demand retribution. The appearance of this majestic figure at the beginning and the midpoint of the play allows a kind of reunion of the king's two bodies, giving the supernatural spirit a visible shape and form. Hamlet is thrilled at this possibility that seems to promise miraculous effects: "His form and cause conjoined, preaching to stones/Would make them capable" (3.4.126–127). In a realm where so much is "out of joint," such a conjunction might very well be "a consummation/Devoutly to be wish'd" (3.1.63–64). Unfortunately, it does not hold. The ghost proves evanescent, confusingly sinister, and only partially visible. Though others see it on the ramparts, Hamlet alone hears its shocking revelations, and Hamlet's mother does not see it at all.

The ghost's unsettling appearance in *Hamlet*'s closet scene resembles, in some ways, the image of the king and queen in Velasquez's *Las Meninas*. In that painting, the royal couple are placed at the back of the room while the Infanta and her entourage occupy the center and the painter works off to one side. Because the two sovereigns are so far removed from the vivid foreground, according to Michel Foucault, "they are the palest, the most unreal, the most compromised of all the painting's images; a movement, a little light, would be sufficient to eclipse them . . . in so far as they are visible, they are the frailest and the most distant form of all reality. Inversely, in so far as they stand outside the picture and are therefore withdrawn from it in an essential invisibility, they provide the centre around which the entire representation is ordered."[12] Perceived thus from perspectives of "incompatible visibilities," this peculiar royal portrait is, like *Hamlet*, a "pure representation of essential absence."[13] In both works, the monarchs' absence is keenly felt as a longing for their presence. Paradoxically, they acquire more importance by their "essential absence" than they would by greater prominence. To some extent, this paradox still pertains even today. Foucault maintains elsewhere that "the representation of power has remained under the spell of monarchy. In political thought and analysis, we still have not cut off the head of the king."[14] When the English cut off the head of their king, they certainly found it hard to escape from the spell of kingship. The extravagant guilt and hagiography prompted by the execution of Charles I made him into something like an "essential absence" in the course of the interregnum. The British monarchy was restored and survives to the present day, despite scandals and declining popularity. Moreover, as I shall suggest in my conclusion, the immediate reaction to the death of Diana, Princess of Wales indicates that a royal absence remains a compelling phenomenon.

Monarchy's enduring power derives in part from a vague but persistent desire for a real presence in the face of an "essential absence."

This ambivalence has its origins in the early modern period, when struggles over Christ's real presence in the Eucharist launched the Reformation.[15] These struggles divided Protestants from the beginning and were never completely resolved. Martin Luther rejected the Catholic doctrine of transubstantiation, but he still believed in a real bodily presence that others tagged "consubstantiation." By contrast, Ulrich Zwingli argued for a purely spiritual and symbolic presence in the sacrament. Luther and Zwingli debated these issues at a theological summit meeting in Marburg in 1529, but they parted confirmed in their opposition. Other reformers sought a solution to this impasse, striving for a third or middle way, and, as Brian Gerrish explains, Martin Bucer was initially "the chief spokesman of mediation" until "later, the leadership passed" to John Calvin.[16] Calvin objected to both the Lutheran and the Zwinglian positions, condemning consubstantiation for positing "the sort of local presence that the papists dream about" while criticizing Zwingli's failure to acknowledge "the reality and efficacy" of the sacraments and demoting them to symbols, allegories, and parables.[17] Calvin's disciple and successor, Theodore Beza, charged them more succinctly with reducing the Eucharist to "either transubstantiation or a trope."[18]

Most reformers were intent on finding an alternative to this bleak binary, and one preferred solution is particularly intriguing in light of Hamlet's desire to see his father's "form and cause conjoined." Some of the most influential theologians describe the Eucharist as a "conjunction." After the accession of Edward VI, Archbishop Thomas Cranmer invited Peter Martyr Vermigli, along with Martin Bucer, to help rectify "corrupt opinions about the *Eucharist* in the Universities as well as elsewhere," and he appointed Martyr Regius Professor of Divinity at Oxford and gave Bucer the same post at Cambridge.[19] In a public debate on the Eucharist at Oxford in 1549, Martyr asserted that Christ was present "by a sacramental conjunction, which is the most effectual signification."[20] The concept was taken up by Calvin, whose *Short Treatise of the Lord's Supper* describes the sacrament as "the presence and conjunction of reality and sign."[21] Beza elaborates on the term's implications, explaining that Christ's "body is truly joined (*coniungi*) with the bread and the blood with the wine, sacramentally and not otherwise, [and] this is not in a place or location, but because they efficaciously signify (*efficaciter significant*) what is given by the Lord to all participating with faith, and truly received by believers through faith."[22] Beza's conception of the sanctity of the Eucharist and the grace it bestows is intriguingly minimalist: in his view, communion establishes relationships among believers and God. He concedes the intellectual modesty of this concept but emphasizes its interpersonal validity: "*Relata* have, I confess, the least of Being, as they say in the schools, but they are nevertheless maximally efficacious according as they have true and solid subjects and objects in wholly natural things, as father and son, Lord and servant."[23]

The relevance of these theological disputes over a real presence to Hamlet's emotions in the closet scene and to our own continuing unease at "the cease of majesty" is a major subject of this book. Stephen Greenblatt has convincingly shown how *Hamlet* is "charged with the language of eucharistic anxiety" in its desire for spiritual liberation from fleshly corruption.[24] In his eagerness to see his father's "form and cause conjoined" in the closet scene, Hamlet yearns, as I shall suggest, for something like a Eucharistic miracle. He wants his father's "essential absence" to become a palpable and potent real presence through a kind of transubstantiation of the king's two bodies. No such miracle occurs. Nevertheless, something takes place in this scene and in the play that permits the kind of contact described by Beza. Hamlet and the ghost and the audience all enter into a relationship resembling those having "true and solid subjects and objects in wholly natural things, as father and son, Lord and servant." Seen from this less transcendent perspective, conjunction permits a connection with things absent even if it does not make them a real presence. While true communion with God or his saints or even with one another may prove an impossible hope for many, relationships between the living and the dead and with the actual and the imaginary are, willy-nilly, inescapable—and the source of much that matters in literature and in life.

There is considerable reluctance to claim such relationships in much contemporary literary criticism. Deconstruction has succeeded brilliantly in demolishing naïve ideas of presence, but in doing so it risks reducing truth to a trope while reifying and even fetishizing absence. Paul de Man sets out to complicate the "assimilation of truth to trope," but he reaches the now banal conclusion that truth is power.[25] Geoffrey Hartman contends that "the 'work' of art, then discloses Being as this absent presence: it allows us to stand on absence, as it were"; the qualifying "as it were" does not diminish a certain complacency in taking such a bravely precarious stand.[26] Hartman's more recent work expresses the somewhat wistful hope that "Learning . . . can . . . recover history as a more complete kind of memory," but absence and emptiness still prevail: "Writing, in seeking to capture the unique, or to image what is absent, hardens it, so that we are left with a consciousness of language incorporating the void."[27] New Historicism, in turn, seems uneasy and even embarrassed about claiming too strong a connection with the past. Stephen Greenblatt acknowledges his own "desire to speak with the dead" as if it were slightly bizarre, the "familiar, if unvoiced motive" of an aspiring clairvoyant, and by drolly describing "literature professors" as "salaried, middle-class shamans," he makes literary scholarship sound like a branch of magical thinking.[28] Greenblatt acknowledges that he does not need to resort to shamanism to make contact with the dead since they "contrived to leave textual traces of themselves," each containing "some fragment of lost life."[29] Nevertheless, New Historicism remains no less determined than Deconstruction to escape delusions of presence, emphasizing gaps in records, the inevitability of bias, and the alien strangeness of the past. Leah Marcus is intent on spurning illusions of "communion" supposedly suffusing Machiavelli's fictive dialogues with ancient Greek and Roman authors, and she emphasizes "disjunction" over "universality, intellectual continuity, and transcendence."[30] Yet Renaissance writers were no less self-conscious about such complications. Francesco Petrarch undertook a comparable correspondence with the great writers of antiquity, but his letter to Homer clearly recognizes "how far removed you are."[31] This recognition of our remoteness from the past was a crucial Renaissance discovery, but distance and contingency do not preclude relationships with older authors or render them inscrutably strange.

In *Alterations of State*, I focus on four authors from the English Reformation whose texts allow a particularly vivid connection with struggles over the real and royal presence: John Skelton, William

Shakespeare, John Milton, and Andrew Marvell. They lived and worked at the beginning, middle, and end of the early modern period, and they approach monarchy and the sacred from radically different perspectives. Skelton is a staunch defender of the English monarchy and traditional religion, Milton a radical opponent of both; and Shakespeare and Marvell are, characteristically, harder to place. Skelton and Milton each took on the role of religious and political propagandist, writing verse or prose on official commission. Each ended his career as a fierce opponent—and, to some extent, casualty—of the age's varied alterations of state: Skelton denounces the onset of the Reformation in his last poem, and Milton laments its reversal throughout his late verse. Marvell eventually, and somewhat reluctantly, joins in these struggles. He assists Milton and his "good old cause" both before and after the Restoration and subsequently writes a denunciation of *The Growth of Popery and Arbitrary Government*, but he began his writing career as a royalist. Shakespeare, by contrast, detaches himself from the perils of opposition even when he is implicated in the most dangerous alteration of state of his own time. When *Richard II* was performed in 1601 on the eve of the Essex revolt, Shakespeare and the other players were still deemed innocent of any complicity in the rebellion.[32] Two years later, the peaceful accession of James I was happily acclaimed, and Shakespeare's company secured the new king's patronage. In contrast to many other writers, Shakespeare kept his distance and his footing amid the tremors caused by alterations of state.

The long-running succession crisis of Elizabeth's reign still had a discernible impact on Shakespeare's life and work, as did Tudor and Stuart theories of sacred kingship. He was a brilliantly adaptable man of his moment, and long before he became the principal playwright of the King's Men, he composed paeans to Tudor sovereignty. He concludes *Richard III* with an effusive tribute to the providential union of Henry VII and Elizabeth of York:

> O now let Richmond and Elizabeth,
> The true succeeders of each royal House,
> By God's fair ordinance conjoin together,
> And let their heirs, God if Thy will be so,

Enrich the time to come with smooth-fac'd peace,
With smiling plenty, and fair prosperous days.

(5.5.29–34)

Yet his later history plays show English monarchs beset by guilt and doubt and staggered by the prospect of their own mortality. In *Richard II*, the king collapses in defeat, resolving only to "sit upon the ground / And tell sad stories of the death of kings" (3.2.155–156). In *Henry V*, on the eve of a victory proclaimed miraculous, the king bleakly repudiates all the props and trappings of sacred kingship in a soliloquy addressed to "thou idol ceremony," dismissing "the balm, the sceptre, and the ball / The sword, the mace, the crown imperial" as the wrack left by "the tide of pomp / That beats upon the high shore of this world" (4.1.246–271). Here and elsewhere, Shakespeare powerfully dramatizes the desolation of disenchantment with regal objects once adored.[33] The other writers I consider are no less astute in their representation of the paradoxes and contradictions of early modern sacred kingship. The verse and prose of Skelton, Shakespeare, Milton, and Marvell bring old struggles over the real presence, ruined choirs, royal supremacy, and ancient rights back to life. Thus, as we shall see, these works can help us understand the origins of our own enduring sorrow at "sad stories of the death of kings" as well as our persistent uneasiness with "alterations of state."

Acknowledgments

*T*his book took a long time to complete because its scope kept expanding over the course of the last decade. It started modestly enough as a study of the succession crisis of 1603. However, during a year's sabbatical partially funded by the Guggenheim Foundation, my notion of my subject and its historical horizons grew dramatically, extending from the late Middle Ages to the Restoration and the eighteenth century. For providing me with the opportunity to think big, I am very grateful to that organization and its director, Joel Connaroe. A National Endowment for the Humanities grant from the Folger Institute allowed me another year to do some of the reading necessary to substantiate and support my expanded approach, and the NEH also provided funds for me to participate in a summer institute, "Religion and Society in Early Modern England," at Claremont College and then to direct another, "Redefining the Sacred in the English Reformation," at the Folger Shakespeare Library. For their support, advice, and instruction I want to thank David Cressy and Lori Anne Ferrell, Kathleen Lynch and Barbara Mowat, as well as the participants in both programs. The staff of the Folger Shakespeare Library and Folger Institute are paragons of academic hospitality, and, to name only a few, I want to thank Carol Brobeck, LuEllen DeHaven, Martha Fay, Richard Kuhta, Betsy Walsh, and Laetitia Yandle for their help during my year there. Grants from the Professional Staff Congress of the City University of New York Research Foundation enabled me to travel to England to conduct additional research.

A number of good friends and colleagues have read some or all of the manuscript, and they have helped me to pound its disparate parts into a more coherent account. I am acutely aware of the need to exempt them from any responsibility for the book's errors or shortcomings, and I am very grateful for their thoughtful and valuable assistance. These scholars include David Bevington, Rachel Brownstein, Joseph Connors, Morris Dickstein, David Kastan, Peter Lake, Ron

Levao, Diarmaid MacCulloch, the late Jeremy Maule, Luke Menand, Nancy Miller, Michael Murrin, Wayne Proudfoot, Debora Shuger, Joseph Wittreich, and two anonymous readers. Jim Shapiro has been an especially astute reader and supportive friend, and I want to single him out for special thanks. I have also really appreciated the prompt responses, intelligent advice, and thoughtful support of my editors at Columbia University Press, Jennifer Crewe, Jennifer Barager, and Leslie Kriesel; and designer Chang Jae Lee. Part of chapter 3 appeared in *Shakespeare Survey* 40 (2001) as "A Wedding and Four Funerals: Conjunction and Commemoration in *Hamlet*," and I am grateful to Cambridge University Press for permission to reprint this material here.

Did I mention that this book took a long time? My wonderful wife, Marsha Wagner, was a steadfast and affectionate companion throughout this project, putting up with my absences and distractions, listening to my ideas and arguments, and then reading and re-reading the manuscript as it took shape. I dedicated my first book to her and to our first daughter, Kate, who thoughtfully delayed her arrival into the world until the day after that manuscript's submission. Our second daughter, Sarah, missed out on the second book, which I dedicated to my beloved parents, so now it's her turn. A student of English literature at Columbia and Oxford, she is certainly a fitting recipient. Like her sister, Kate, Sarah has been an extraordinary daughter and great companion over the years—smart, funny, thoughtful, and kind—but, for this dedication, she had to wait even longer.

Illustrations

Alterations of State

Real Presence to Royal Presence

How ran we from post to pillar, from stock to stone,
from idol to idol, from place to place, to seek remission of our sins,
and to make God amends for our sinful living!
—Thomas Becon, *The Jewel of Joy* (1553)

FIGURE 2
Henry vs. Pope; John Foxe, *Acts and Monuments*, 1201
By permission of the Folger Shakespeare Library

The Reformation began with a determination to eradicate old ideas of sacred space—what Calvin derided as papist fantasies of God's "local presence."[1] Early Tudor reformer Thomas Becon fairly spits out his disgust at the snares and delusions of traditional Catholicism: "How ran we from post to pillar, from stock to stone, from idol to idol, from place to place, to seek remission of our sins, and to make God amends for our sinful living! How called we upon dead mawmets [puppets] for relief and succour! How gilded we images, painted their tabernacles, and set up candles before them!"[2] The benighted are compulsively bound by their attachment to locales and objects in their futile passage from "place to place." Becon continues denouncing his former errors, declaring, "What confidence we had to be delivered out of the pope's pinfold [i.e., Purgatory] after our departure, though we lived never so ungodly, through the popish prattling of monstrous monks, and the mumbling masses of those monstrous lazy soul-carriers. What trust we reposed in the masking masses of momish mass-mongers."[3] Becon's scorn for icons and images, shrines and sanctuaries, and, most shockingly, the Mass itself is all part of what Christopher Haigh calls a broader Protestant attack on "Catholic symbolism and the sacralization of physical things."[4]

Resistance to that sacralization began long before the Reformation—indeed, it divided Christianity from the start. A dualistic opposition of spirit and matter had been part of the Hellenic legacy accentuated by St. Paul. Groups such as the Gnostics, Cathari, Waldensians, and Lollards recurrently inveighed against sanctifying material objects. By contrast, orthodox Catholicism has been aptly described as "incarnational" in promoting its church and its sacraments as a "perpetual extension of Christ's incarnation" and a means of achieving holiness on earth.[5] For most of its long history, the Catholic Church suppressed its opponents as heretics, until Protestants achieved unprecedented victories in the sixteenth century.

Nevertheless, even Protestants remained reluctant to dislocate the sacred entirely from ecclesiastical and worldly institutions. Notions of a real presence proved hard to detach from a God who made himself incarnate, and traces of that belief persisted in the liturgy of the English Church. A more basic religious concern proved even more intractable. Ideas of the sacred have always been closely linked to specific locations in many religions; as Jonathan Z. Smith puts it, "sacrality is, above all, a category of emplacement."[6] As for holy objects, Claude Lévi-Strauss maintains that "it could even be said that being in their place is what makes them sacred for if they were taken out of their place, even in thought, the entire order of the universe would be destroyed."[7] Reformation iconoclasm stirred up fears of this magnitude, as we shall see, but the prospect of chaos was countered to some extent by the assertion of royal supremacy. Tudor theories of sacred kingship made the monarch the sovereign reformer and embodiment of the realm's temporal and spiritual health. The sacred was thus relocated through what John Bossy calls the "migration of the holy."[8] In Becon's terms, it moved from "place to place," from the real to the royal presence. Some reformers accepted the new Tudor version of sacred kingship as part of their alliance with the monarchy, but others opposed it, continuing to object to locating the sacred anywhere. The historical origins of these conflicts over the real and royal presence are the subject of this introductory chapter.

Late medieval Christianity was, according to Carlos Eire, "a religion of immanence. Heaven was never too far from earth. The sacred was diffused in the profane, the spiritual in the material. Divine power, embodied in the Church and its sacraments, reached down through innumerable points of contact to make itself felt."[9] In the Middle Ages, the Eucharist became the Church's "supreme sacrament" and its sacrifice in the Mass the primary means for "the communication of grace."[10] The profound significance of the Mass and the Eucharist for pre-Reformation Christianity is eloquently described by Eamon Duffy in *The Stripping of the Altars*:

> The liturgy lay at the heart of medieval religion, and the Mass lay at the heart of the liturgy. In the Mass the redemption of the world wrought on Good Friday once and for all, was renewed and made fruitful for all who believed. Christ himself, immolated on the altar of the cross, became present on the altar of the parish church, body, soul, and divinity, and his blood flowed once again, to nourish and renew Church and world. As kneeling congregations raised their eyes to see the Host held high above the priest's head at the sacring, they were transported to

Calvary itself, and gathered not only into the passion and resurrection of Christ, but into the full sweep of salvation history
as a whole.[11]

As Duffy indicates, the Mass and Eucharist were regarded as a recurrent reenactment of Christ's redemptive sacrifice, and this belief was
officially formulated at the Fourth Lateran Council in 1215 as the doctrine of transubstantiation. That doctrine became for Catholicism
the "definitive statement of the doctrine of the real presence," asserting that "the body and blood [of Jesus Christ] are truly contained
in the Sacrament of the Altar under the outward appearance of
bread and wine," and it was categorically reaffirmed at the Council
of Trent in 1551.[12]

The medieval emphasis on "the miracle of the Mass" led to a
growing devotion to the sacrament and the host itself, culminating in
the feast of Corpus Christi, established in 1264.[13] Within the Mass, the
elevation of the host was the literal high point for many in the con-
gregation, a glimpse of the deity that excited even more fervor than
the reception of communion. This visual veneration was the purpose
of the Corpus Christi ritual. The solemn procession through the city
streets with the host in an elaborate display case or monstrance under
a canopy was a kind of sustained elevation allowing the entire popu-
lace to gaze on the "comely corse" of Christ. As Duffy points out, the
iconography of Corpus Christi focused on both the actual corpse of
the crucified Christ, "his woundes bleding day and night," and the
host in order to emphasize the equivalence of both sacrifices and the
reality of transubstantiation.[14] The doctrine was sometimes drama-
tized in pageants and tableaux incorporated into the procession itself,
such as the one witnessed by Pope Pius II at Viterbo in 1462, where
"Christ was represented by a man naked except for a loincloth with a
crown of thorns on his head, painted so that he seemed to be exud-
ing blood, carrying the cross on which he seemed to have hung. He
was borne in a chariot from the church of San Francesco to the cathedral and while mass was being celebrated and the assumption of the
Mother of God represented, he stood motionless as a statue."[15] Albrecht Dürer may have witnessed a comparable Corpus Christi procession in Antwerp in 1521. His drawing shows a deposition scene

with Christ attended by Mary and John sitting astride his grave while blood spurts from his chest into a chalice held by his mother; the figures are carried in a large canopied litter borne by burghers in contemporary dress (figure 3). Alternatively, Dürer's drawing may be an allegorical and visionary image of Christ as a real presence rather than a documentary depiction of performers in a procession.[16] This juxtaposition of Christ's actual sacrifice with its quotidian celebration is often the point of such art. Dürer depicts a somewhat similar scene in his drawing of the miracle of St. Gregory, in which only the viewer and the pope see Christ risen from the altar to display his wounds and the instruments of his torture (figure 4). These grisly yet ecstatic visions of the crucified Christ or bloody hosts were designed to overcome the doubts of those who did not believe in transubstantiation. Through such miraculous revelations, the real presence acquired the force of flesh and blood, and the grace imparted by the sacrament was rendered palpable.

Among the most compelling Renaissance renditions of these eucharistic beliefs are the frescoes done by Raphael for Pope Julius II early in the sixteenth century. Of these Vatican *stanze*, the *School of Athens* is the most well known, but Raphael's *Disputa* is its celestial counterpart, depicting an allegorical tableau of theological wisdom (figure 5). Despite its name, the painting is more of a theophany than a dispute; it shows an assembly of patriarchs, prophets, and apostles encircling the vault of heaven with the Trinity hovering above the midpoint, while down on the earth below, doctors of the church are joined by popes and artists and poets, including Fra Angelico and Dante. At the center of the picture and the exact focal point of everyone's gaze is a luminous host enclosed within a monstrance with the image of the crucified Christ stamped upon it. The painting's perspective makes a strong theological point, as several art historians have noted: "To focus attention on the material object also underlines the way in which man's perception of God is not direct. Very few of the earthly participants are privileged to look up."[17] In fact, given the divinely instituted resources of the Church militant, those on earth do not need to look up. Christ himself looms above the sacrament and the altar, but for these learned and saintly believers, as for the more humbly devout (including those who view this scene from

FIGURE 3
Albrecht Dürer, Drawing of a Procession-Bier
with an Allegory of the Triumph of Christ
Copyright: Bildarchiv Preussischer Kulturbesitz, Berlin.
Photograph: Jörg P. Anders

FIGURE 4
Albrecht Dürer, Mass of St. Gregory
The Metropolitan Museum of Art

FIGURE 5
Raphael, *Disputa*
Musei Vaticani

beyond the picture's frame), the exalted vision of the host suffices. Indeed, the host, with Christ's image imprinted upon it, takes center
stage, assuring access to the mystery and miracle of faith. Raphael's
architectural details reinforce the importance of the Church's liturgical and institutional mediation. The vault of heaven resembles an
apse made up of living members, but the painting also depicts the
ambitious rebuilding that Pope Julius undertook by showing the vast
architectural base of St. Peter's under construction as well as the ar-
chitect, Bramante.[18] The letters of Julius's name are inlaid in the altar
supporting the host, indicating yet again that the papacy is the rock
on which Christ built his church and its sacraments.

In another powerful fresco, Raphael shows his papal patron witnessing a historic eucharistic event, the miracle of Bolsena (figure 6).
In 1263, a German priest who doubted the recently promulgated doctrine of transubstantiation discovered bloodstains on the corporal, or
cloth, on which he placed the host immediately after consecrating it.
His faith restored, he carried the cloth bearing physical evidence of
the real presence to the cathedral at Orvieto, where Urban IV was in
residence, and the next year that pope established the feast of Corpus
Christi to honor this miracle.[19] Raphael shows the thirteenth-century
priest and other contemporary witnesses stunned by the bloodstains
on the linen as he unfolds it, while on the other side of the altar, from
another point in time, Julius II and his newly established Swiss
Guards calmly and devoutly behold this variation on "the miracle of
the mass."

Raphael's picture of the miracle of Bolsena, like Dürer's drawings
of Corpus Christi and the miracle of Gregory, are stunningly beautiful renditions of what has been called "vulneral sacramentalism."[20]
This involves a literal belief in Christ's bleeding wounds as a source
of sacramental efficacy, a belief that is also manifest in late medieval
English art. Bishop John Fisher, an ardent defender and martyr of
Catholic orthodoxy under Henry VIII, emphasizes grace's sanguinary sources in a sermon on Psalm 51: "th'effusion of the moost precious blod of cryst Ihesu upon a crosse plenteously" was shed for all
sinners, who "receyue the vertue of this precious blode by the sacramentes of crystes chirche. . . . They are sprencled with the droppes of
the same moost holy blode."[21] The point was driven home in church

9

FIGURE 6
Raphael, *Mass of Bolsena*
Musei Vaticani

architecture and prayer books by sculpture on baptismal fonts, stained-glass images, and crude woodblock prints that traced the flow of Christ's blood directly into all the sacraments while giving preeminence to the Eucharist. As Ann Eljenholm Nichols explains in her account of this phenomenon, "vulneral sacramentalism" was largely a response to Lollardy, the heresy embraced by John Wycliffe and his followers in the late fourteenth century. The Lollards' rejection of the doctrine of transubstantiation prompted the orthodox to affirm the real presence by making it more palpable. Eucharistic miracles in which the body of Christ materialized or the host bled were intended to dispel such doubts, and they were a staple of late medieval tales and homilies.[22] Similar miracles abound in the fifteenth-century Croxton *Play of the Sacrament*, in which the Jews, apparent surrogates for the Lollards, repeatedly profane the host, making it bleed profusely until Christ himself appears as a bleeding babe. Sacrilege only confirms the sacred presence, and the play's climactic theophany prompts the conversion and forgiveness of these infidels.[23] Yet, despite such presumably "happy endings," Lollard resistance to belief in the powers of the sacraments and the priesthood continued throughout the fifteenth century.[24]

By the early sixteenth century, a kind of perverse dialectic prevailed in which orthodox efforts to make the real presence more palpable only increased nonconformists' skepticism and revulsion.[25] These conflicts soon exploded in the Reformation, and Martin Luther's opening salvos were the most incendiary. After promulgating his 95 theses in 1517 criticizing the sale of indulgences and other mercenary abuses, Luther published *The Babylonian Captivity of the Church* in 1520. This influential attack on "the whole pageantry of outward things" in the church, including "vestments, ornaments, chants, prayers, organs, candles," condemns Purgatory as a manipulative fraud. Most shockingly, it rejects the belief that "the mass is a good work and a sacrifice" as "the most wicked abuse of all."[26] Moreover, Luther also rejects the doctrine of transubstantiation, redefining the real presence as a matter of faith rather than a scholastic "*opus operatum.*" Nevertheless, Luther still believed in the coexistence of material and spiritual elements in the sacrament, and Lutheran doctrine retained vestiges of traditional ritual beliefs. These are manifest somewhat ironically on the title page of one of his early sermons on baptism; appended to a tract actually reducing the number of sacraments, this conventionally pious depiction of "vulneral sacramentalism" still depicts Christ's blood flowing into all seven sacraments with the Eucharist at the center (figure 7).[27]

Ulrich Zwingli soon advanced a more radical challenge to Catholicism's sacramental system, arguing for a purely spiritual and symbolic presence: "The sacraments we esteem and honour as signs and symbols of holy things but not as though they themselves were the things of which they are the signs. . . . Thus in the Lord's supper the natural and actual body of Christ in which he suffered on earth, and is now seated in heaven at the right hand of God, is not eaten naturally or literally but only spiritually, and the papist teaching that the body of Christ is eaten in the same form and with the same property and nature as when he was born and suffered and died is not only presumptuous and foolish, but also impious and objectionable."[28] Luther and Zwingli persisted in their differences at Marburg in 1529, with Luther chalking the words of consecration on the table and insisting on a literal interpretation of "*Hoc est enim corpus meum.*" Zwingli responded by invoking John 6:63 and arguing for a figurative rather than carnal understanding of the Eucharist: "It is the spirit that quickeneth; the flesh profiteth nothing; the words that I speak unto you, *they* are spirit and *they* are life."[29] Zwingli's radicalism had an impact on English reformers even as they searched for a *via media.* Thomas Cranmer was uncertain about the real presence for much of his career, but "Zwingli's favorite text (*John 6:63*) stands like a banner on the front page of the *Defence,*" Cranmer's treatise on the Eucharist, and the *Book of Common Prayer* eliminated the Mass altogether.[30]

Nevertheless, despite their eventual triumph, early Protestant attacks on the Mass were at first stoutly resisted by church and state authorities as unthinkable sacrilege. In his denunciation of Luther, Thomas More exclaims, "What was once celebrated with so much veneration as the most holy sacrifice of the mass? What has been so defiled by these pigs and trodden under foot and all but abolished?"[31] King Henry VIII himself joined the counterattack in 1521, writing the *Assertio Septem Septorum* (Defense of the Seven Sacraments), the work that earned him the title Defender of the Faith. The ironies of this

Ein Sermon von dem heiligen hochwirdigen Sacrament der Tauffe doctoris Martin Luther Augustiner.

FIGURE 7

Martin Luther, *A Sermon on the Sacrament of Baptism*, title page

By permission of the Folger Shakespeare Library

papal honor have often been noted in light of his subsequent break with Rome, but his belief in traditional religion's sacramental system remained unshakable.[32] Transubstantiation remained a key doctrine in Henry's church, and its denial was declared a capital offense in the Six Articles of 1539.[33] Moreover, his belief in the church as "the mystical body of Christ" is explicitly incarnational, for he asks why Christ, "who never abandoned the Flesh which once he took, should have cast off the Church, for whose sake he took that Flesh."[34] The king went to his grave insisting on Christ's presence in the Eucharist, and his will provided for requiem masses, annual obits, and chantry chaplains "to speed his soul through a Catholic (though now officially unnamed) purgatory."[35] As Christopher Haigh says, "Henry VIII had died a Catholic, though a rather bad Catholic."[36]

Henry's attachment to the Mass was consistent and genuine, but his critique of Luther was also motivated by other, more broadly conservative reflexes. He claimed in 1529 that, had Luther only "limited himself to inveighing against the vices, abuses, and errors of the Clergy, instead of attacking the Sacraments of the Church and other Divine Institutions, everyone would have followed him, and written in his favor. He, himself, should have been one, and instead of taking the trouble of refuting his arguments, would willingly have taken pen in hand in his defence."[37] Henry balked at Luther's attack on the church's "whole pageantry of things visible" because he saw these devotional practices as essential props of ecclesiastical *and* social order. Such political concerns were a major source of England's rooted resistance to radical reform, and other conservatives shared Henry's views. Germaine Gardiner argued that Protestants not only supported "the division and rending asunder of Christ's mystical body, His Church" but also promoted "the pulling down of all power and utter subversion of all commonwealths."[38] Thomas More insisted that, because both church and society were held together by "the mynystryng of the blessed sacraments of our sauyour Cryste," Lutheran heresies threatened "the very hole corps and body of the blessed fayth of Cryste."[39] Taking holy things out of their place threatened the entire cosmic and social order. As John Bossy explains, More worried that Protestantism's "radical dismissal of incarnate holiness" would lead to a "divorce between the sacred and the body social," and many, including Henry

VIII, shared More's belief that the "community of Christian Englishmen . . . was kept in existence by a complex of holy things of which
the most important were the sacraments and the most visible a certain
number of places and objects. The duty of a Christian king was to
offer these things a due respect himself and to inculcate it in others."[40]

Despite their agreement on the need for incarnate holiness, his sovereign's conception of the duty of a Christian king cost More his head.
Henry preserved the sacraments, but he also promoted a doctrine of
royal supremacy making himself responsible for "the cure of souls."[41]
In parliamentary proclamations of his imperial authority, the monarchy became the head of England's mystical body and the nation's unifying principle. The Act in Restraint of Appeals in 1533 denied authority to the papacy by proclaiming "that this realm of England is an
empire governed by one supreme head and king having the dignity
and royal estate of the imperial crown of the same, unto whom a
body politic, compact of all sorts and degrees of people divided in
terms and by names of spiritualty and temporalty, be bounden and
owe to bear next to God a natural and humble obedience."[42] Obedience to the sovereign was affirmed as a religious obligation by both advocates and opponents of radical reform, including William Tyndale,
translator of the vernacular Bible and author of *Obedience of a Christian Man*, and Stephen Gardiner, scourge of heretics and author of *De
Vera Obedientia*.[43] Some advisers embraced the principle for practical,
political reasons, but Henry's "notion of his imperial crown was a
much more mystical, even 'thaumaturgical' idea," according to G. R.
Elton.[44] J. J. Scarisbrick says that royal supremacy made the monarch
the embodiment and spirit of the realm and its people: "The king was
the vicar of God, and as Henry said of himself, his 'high minister
here,' the 'soul of the whole kingdom,' who, having overthrown the
blasphemous thraldom of the self-styled vicar of Christ, must 'ani-
mate, rule and save' his people."[45] Under the Tudor Reformation, this
immanent royal presence became an animating and redemptive real
presence, binding ruler and ruled together in a communion stronger
than any proffered by an alien papal authority.

Tudor notions of royal supremacy drew on ancient traditions of sacred kingship but redefined them and gave them a new ideological
force.[46] Royal claims to imperial and ecclesiastical authority predate

the break with Rome, and tensions between clerical and sovereign authority were centuries old, going back to Charlemagne and beyond.[47]
The old idea of the king's two bodies envisions the monarch as the
head of a mystical body whose immortality is ensured by an orderly
succession.[48] The thaumaturgic powers of a ruler entrusted with the
cure of souls are rooted in the medieval practice of the royal touch.[49]
Tudor propaganda expanded these ancient claims by assigning the
monarch almost messianic authority, describing the king as the "soul
of the whole kingdom" and identifying Henry VIII as the "Son of
Man."[50] "Based on the conviction that true Christian kingship had at
last been discovered after centuries of desolation and darkness," Tudor
notions of royal supremacy sustained what Scarisbrick calls a "powerful new national epic, indeed theology of History . . . of which Foxe
will later be the most fulsome exponent."[51]

John Foxe's *Acts and Monuments* certainly does present a "powerful
new national epic," but its "theology of history" is far more complicated than Scarisbrick suggests.[52] Moreover, Foxe's massive work reveals the inherent ambiguity and instability of Protestant notions of
sacred kingship. Tudor theories of royal supremacy finally could not
completely relocate the sacred in the monarchy, and Foxe and his
sources skeptically dismiss attempts to do so. Henry VIII eagerly embraced the role of supreme head up through the end of his reign.
When he addressed his last Parliament, in 1545, he presented himself
as a reformer determined to enforce and embody the communion of
"the spiritualty and temporalty." The theme of his speech was charity, and his text was Paul's First Epistle to the Corinthians, chapter 13,
which he used to rebuke his subjects for their enthusiasm for sectarian controversy. Exasperated by the spread of "variety and discord,"
he enjoins those preaching division to mend their ways "or els I
whom God hath appoynted his Vicare and high mynyster here, wyll
se these dyvisions extinct, and these enormities corrected, according
to my very duety, or els I am an vnprofitable seruaunte, and vntrue
officer."[53] Diarmaid MacCulloch sees the speech as a final vindication
of royal supremacy, transforming the king's last parliamentary appearance into "the perfect icon of the supreme headship of the
Church of England as Cranmer conceived it; it was the pictorial title-
page of the Great Bible come to life" (figure 8).[54] On top of that title

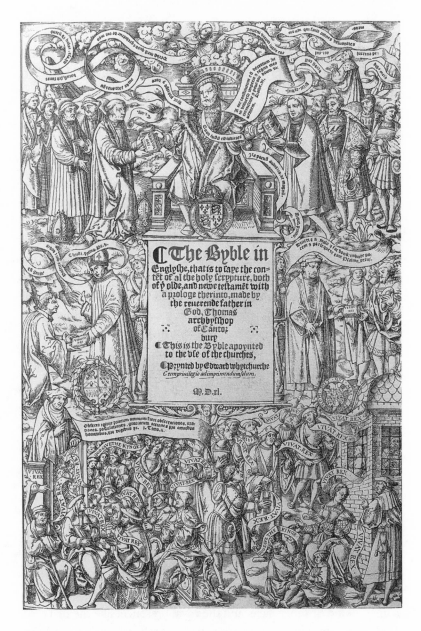

FIGURE 8

The Great Bible, title page

By permission of the Folger Shakespeare Library

page, the king sits enthroned just below a figure of God. Flanked by Cranmer and Cromwell and other representatives of the clergy and laity, he binds all together by distributing Bibles as his grateful subjects repeatedly proclaim "Vivat Rex" in this vivid illustration of a unified body politic.

Such majestic images became a mainstay of Tudor propaganda for the duration of the dynasty, and several illustrations in Foxe's *Acts and Monuments* promulgate a comparable vision of the monarch as the supreme embodiment of imperial autonomy crushing papal pretensions (figure 2). As Frances Yates and John King have shown, these images became icons of mystical imperialism and godly rule, culminating in the dedication of the first English edition of the "Book of Martyrs" to the new Queen Elizabeth.[55] There, Foxe compares her reign to that of Constantine, the imperial convert who ended the persecution of the early church.[56] The large capital first letter of the Roman emperor's name encloses an enthroned Elizabeth, and the pope's twisted torso, keys in hand, forms the C's lower half (figure 9). Continuing her father's aspirations, the last Tudor monarch made reverence toward royalty into a veritable "cult of Elizabeth," as Frances Yates, Roy Strong, and others have shown.[57] A major treatise on government composed during her reign, Sir Thomas Smith's *De Republica Anglorum*, advances a mystical theory of sovereignty in which courtly protocol verges on the liturgical: "The prince is the life, the head, and the authoritie of all thinges that be doone in the realme of England. And to no prince is doone more honor and reverence than to the King and Queene of Englande, no man speaketh to the prince nor serveth at the table but in adoration and kneeling, all persons of the realme be bareheaded before him; insomuch that in the chamber of presence, where the cloath of estate is set, no man dare walke, yea though the prince be not there, no man dare tarrie there but bareheaded."[58] In Smith's account, the presence chamber becomes a kind of tabernacle, and the royal presence, like the real presence, is venerated even in the monarch's absence. Such acts of homage became even more elaborate in the annual tilts and pageants celebrating Elizabeth's Accession Day; according to Frances Yates, they made her into "a symbol strong enough to provide a feeling of spiritual security in face of the break with the rest of Christendom."[59]

FIGURE 9

Elizabeth as Constantine; John Foxe, *Acts and Monuments*

By permission of the Folger Shakespeare Library

Nevertheless, the mystical pretensions of Tudor sovereignty were regarded skeptically and even resisted by some of its most ardent allies. The main problem with Henry VIII's aspirations to godly rule was that he proved a halfhearted reformer, no better a Protestant than a Catholic. Indeed, he not only disappointed many reformers but began persecuting them as well, cracking down hard on unorthodox belief during the last decade of his reign.[60] One of the most renowned victims of the heresy hunts of his last years was Anne Askew. After being cross-examined by the Lord Mayor and the Bishop of London in 1545 and the Privy Council in 1546, she was put to the rack by the Lord Chancellor himself in an apparent attempt to implicate Catherine Parr and her courtly associates in heresy.[61] Henry's last queen was, like Anne Boleyn, an ardent patron of reform, but Parr could not save Askew from martyrdom and had to grovel to save herself from her husband's disfavor.[62] In Askew's own account of her "examinations," she seeks "to exonerate Henry VIII of wrongdoing, . . . preferring to blame his councillors and church officers for her persecution" and thus resorting to the conventional evasion employed by those defying royal authority.[63] Nevertheless, "The Balade whych Anne Askewe made and sange whan she was in Newgate" is shockingly blunt in its apocalyptic vision of monarchy's failure:

> I sawe a ryall trone
> Where Justyce shuld have sytt
> But in her stede was one
> Of modye [angry, wrathful] cruell wytt.[64]

John Bale couples Askew's record of her interrogation with his own heated commentary in the versions he published shortly after Henry's death. He too refrains from blaming the king, but he pours scorn on William Paget's comparison of "Christes presence in the sacrament, to the kynges presence. . . . And as great pleasure (I thynke) he doth the kynge therin, as though he threwe dust in hys face or salte in hys eyes, but that soch flatterynge Gnatoes must do their feates, though they be most blasphemouse."[65] More ardent reformers like Bale had no patience for equations of the real presence with the royal presence and dismissed them with contempt.

Bale's modest hagiography was taken over by John Foxe, whose own vast book of martyrs attained epic proportions. Despite his promotion of godly rule, Foxe was also keenly aware of Tudor shortcomings, and he too sees Henry's last years as dark and discouraging. He takes a particularly jaundiced view of the valedictory "exhortation of King Henry" in which the king promised to put an end to "variety and discord." Foxe caustically contrasts royal words and deeds, saying that "Princes who exhort to concord and charity do well; but princes who seek out the causes of discord, and reform the same do better."[66] Foxe says that Henry would have done better "by taking away the impious law of the Six Articles, the mother of all division and manslaughter," and he even demands "what charity ensued after this exhortation of the king to charity, by the racking and burning of good Anne Askew, with three other poor subjects of the king, within half a year after" before recounting her tribulations (5:537). Divisions cannot be corrected by royal fiat or admonition because true national unity results only from doctrinal rectitude. Indeed, "there is no neutrality, nor mediation of peace, nor exhortation to agreement, that will serve between these two contrary doctrines, but either the pope's errors must give place to God's word, or else the verity of God must give place unto them" (5:536–537). Foxe gives Henry's reforming intentions the benefit of the doubt despite evidence to the contrary, claiming that "if he had continued a few months longer, (all those obits and masses, which appear in his will made before he went to Boulogne, notwithstanding), most certain it is, and to be signified to all posterity, that his full purpose was to have repurged the estate of the church . . . so that he would not have left one mass in all England" (5:692).[67] Yet he concedes elsewhere that during Henry's last years the Mass "flourished, the altars with the sacrament thereof being in their most high veneration, that to man's reason it might seem impossible that the glory and opinion of that sacrament and sacramentals, so highly worshipped and so deeply rooted in the hearts of many, could by any means possible so soon decay and vanish to nought" (8:850). Happily, despite Henry's efforts to preserve traditional religion's sacramental system, "the sacrament of the altar, and the altars themselves, . . . [were] plucked up by the roots" (8:850) almost immediately after his death.

Whatever his beliefs about Henry's intentions, Foxe pointedly declares "the Lord be praised for his most gracious reformation," duly crediting the supreme being rather than royal supremacy or the succession of Edward VI for the fortunate reversal of Henry's lapses in 1547 (8:850). From this loftier providential perspective, it seems significant that, in later editions of the *Acts and Monuments*, Foxe made the iconographic C into the initial of Christ's name, omitting the dedicatory letter to Elizabeth and implicitly subordinating both the Queen and Constantine to the true supreme head of the church.[68] Thus, despite his ardor for godly rule, Foxe reveals what Patrick Collinson describes as the "ideological difficulties, even contradictions" of royal supremacy.[69] Royal supremacy drew much of its strength from older notions of sacred kingship as well as a persistent desire to locate the sacred somewhere. The need to sanctify places, things, institutions, and rulers proved hard to shake even during the earthquakes caused by the Reformation. Nevertheless, Protestant attacks on papist fantasies of a "local presence" combined with recurrent alterations of state shook things hard, and the tremors led to civil war and revolution.

CHAPTER 2

Sacred Space
John Skelton and Westminster's Royal Sepulcher

This worke devysed is
For suche as do amys,
. . . Wyth cry unreverent,
Before the sacrament,
Wythin the holy church bowndis,
That of our fayth the grownd is.
—John Skelton, *Ware the Hauke* (1505?)

FIGURE 10
Henry VII Chapel
Copyright: Dean and Chapter of Westminster

*I*n building Westminster Chapel, Henry VII, the founder of the Tudor regime, created its most enduring and magnificent dynastic monument. Tudor roses, Beaufort portcullises, fleur-de-lys, and other heraldic and regal devices adorn this soaring, fan-vaulted structure, "the last great ecclesiastical work of the Gothic middle ages in England" (figure 10).[1] Rows of saints encircle the chapel, and Christ stands at their center, a book in his hand and his foot placed atop the world, prepared to preside at the Last Judgment.[2] The centerpiece is a marble sarcophagus supporting beautiful bronze effigies of Henry and his queen carved by Pietro Torrigiano (figure 11). Surrounded by an elaborate grille, Henry's tomb is placed directly behind the chapel's high altar. The chapel also contains, in its side altars, imposing tombs for other scions, ranging from Henry's mother, Lady Margaret Beaufort, to his granddaughter, Elizabeth I, the last of her line.

Yet however impressive its dynastic grandeur, Westminster Chapel was intended as a shrine for another, less powerful but holier king. It represents England's last sanctuary for traditional sacred kingship and its intercessory system, designed to give equal prominence to the real and royal presences. Henry VII planned to bury Henry VI in the tomb where his own remains now rest, giving his Lancastrian predecessor pride of place.[3] Henry VI is recalled today, if at all, as the hapless victim of Richard III's villainy in Shakespeare's early history plays, and his vision of Henry Tudor as "England's hope" is his most distinctive contribution to that saga:

> If secret powers
> Suggest but truth to my divining thoughts,
> This pretty lad will prove our country's bliss.
> His looks are full of peaceful majesty,
> His head by nature fram'd to wear a crown,
> His hand to wield a sceptre, and himself
> Likely in time to bless a regal throne.
>
> (*3 Henry VI*, 4.6.68–74)

Shakespeare's sources were early Tudor historians who saw the king's prophetic powers and unworldly innocence as evidence of his sanctity and treated his murder as a form of martyrdom.[4] Indeed, shortly

FIGURE II
Effigies of Henry VII and Elizabeth of York
Copyright: Dean and Chapter of Westminster

after his death in the Tower, Henry VI became the object of a popular cult, and his tomb at Windsor began attracting more pilgrims than Becket's at Canterbury, with many reporting miraculous cures. A mutilated woodcut from the 1490s shows him surrounded by supplicants in dire straits, many with knives and arrows piercing them (figure 12).[5] Henry VII was no less devoted to this cult, and he wished, at first, to be buried next to Henry VI at Windsor. However, John Islip, the Abbot of Westminster, persuaded him to build a magnificent tomb for himself and his predecessor in the abbey by adding a splendid new chapel to Westminster's chancel. The close relationship of monarch and monk can be seen in the illuminated indentures confirming their agreement where Islip is shown, crozier in hand and surrounded by his confrères, kneeling before Henry's throne (figure 13). Henry began construction in 1503, arranging to have his namesake canonized and the remains "translated" to the place of honor in his new royal sepulcher.

In his desire to be linked in death as well as life with Henry VI, Henry VII sought what Francis Bacon calls "celestial honour," motivated by a blend of political calculation and family pride.[6] At the same time, the first Tudor ruler was genuinely devout, and he strongly believed in the sacred power of his holy predecessor's corpse.[7] In traditional Christianity, a saint's burial site was a veritable force field of supernatural energies where, as Peter Brown explains in his study *The Cult of the Saints*, "*praesentia*, the physical presence of the holy" is linked to a sacred "*potentia*."[8] Translation of a saint's remains constituted, in Brown's suggestive phrase, a kind of "rewiring of the spiritual circuitry."[9] This was precisely Henry VII's intention in placing a new tomb for his predecessor near his own. In and of themselves, the latter's saintly remains "leaked" power, affording a balm and blessing to those near them, and placement was crucial. As Patrick Geary explains, "Though miracles could take place anywhere and any time, they tended to be performed in physical proximity to the touchstones of divine power that were the saints' remains. The means by which the faithful approached the saints' relics was essentially the same by which their polytheistic ancestors had approached sites of healing: after preparation by prayer, fasting, and the essential pilgrimage from the normal world to that

FIGURE 12

Miracles of Henry VI

Copyright: Bodleian Library, University of Oxford; MS. Bodl. 277, f. 376v

FIGURE 13

Order of Indentures, Henry VII and Abbot Islip

By permission of the British Library; MS. Harley 1498, f. 59r

of the sacred, the pilgrim would attempt to touch the tomb or at least to come as close to the saint's remains as possible. Often he or she would pass the night near the tomb, [and] . . . the recipient of the miracle is often depicted asleep near the saint's shrine."[10] The remains of Henry VI were expected to continue working as a magnet for pilgrims, and supplicants drawn by hopes for healing and intercession to his shrine would also pray for its founder, Henry VII. To further enhance the shrine's sacred aura, Henry provided additional relics, including "our grete pece of the holie crosse . . . garnished with perles and precious stones; and also the preciouse Relique of oon of the leggs of Saint George, set in silver parcell gilte" (Will, 33). As an additional inducement, the king secured a papal grant of indulgences for pilgrims to Westminster, comparable to those of the Scala Coeli Chapel in Rome, and he blocked subsequent efforts by the pope to retract them.[11]

Henry's model for Westminster Chapel was England's most venerable royal sepulcher, the shrine of Edward the Confessor at the center of Westminster Abbey itself. Proximity to Edward had been a major factor in Henry's selection of his burial site because, as his will indicates, "within the same Monasteire is the commen Sepulture of the Kings of the Reame, and spially bicause that with in the same and among the same Kings, resteth the holie bodie and reliquies of the glorious King and Confessour Saint Edward and diverse others of our noble Progenitours and blood."[12] King Edward had rebuilt the abbey in the eleventh century as his own royal sepulcher and was buried before its high altar; in the Bayeux tapestry, his funeral procession is shown moving toward it as workmen complete the building and God's hand descends to bless it (figure 14). Following his canonization in the twelfth century, his body was moved or "translated" to its own chapel by Henry II and Thomas Becket, and a century later, Henry III erected a magnificent shrine above the tomb. Pilgrims flocked to it, hoping to be cured of their afflictions by Edward's posthumous royal touch, and those seeking even greater proximity to the saint crawled into the niches or "squeezing spaces" in the tomb's foundation, where they often spent the night (figure 15).[13] Many later English monarchs sought their final resting place amid Westminster's royal fellowship of death, and over the centuries, Edward's chapel, ringed

FIGURE 14

Bayeux Tapestry, Burial of Edward the Confessor

By special permission of the City of Bayeux

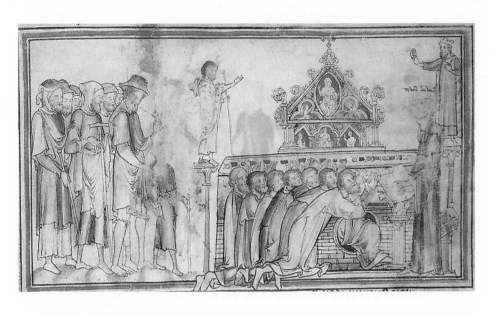

FIGURE 15

Edward's tomb and squeezing spaces

By permission of the Syndics of Cambridge University Library; MS Ed.3.59, f. 20r

with the tombs of five kings and three queens, became a sanctuary for what Frank Barlow calls the "cult of English sacramental kingship."[14] Within its precincts, the royal presence became a sacred presence whose healing powers survived death itself.

In this older, medieval paradigm of sacred kingship, the thaumaturgic royal presence coexisted with and was enhanced by Christ's real presence in the sacrament of the altar. From Edward to Henry VII, English monarchs revered the Eucharist, and its daily sacrifice in the Mass was the main activity of Westminster Abbey.[15] Royal patrons generously endowed its monastery in order to ensure a perpetual offering of commemorative Masses for the repose of their souls. Henry VII's will is almost obsessive in its provisions for vast numbers of Masses, requiring his executors to provide "ymmediatly after our decesse . . . with al diligence and spede" for 10,000 to be said "within our said Monastery, our Citie of London, and other places next adjoinyng to the same, for the remission of our synnes, and the weale of our Soule . . . whereof we wol CXV bee saied in the honour of the Trinitie, MMCV in the honour of the V wounds of our Lord Jhu Crist, MMCV in the honour of the V Joies of our Lady, CCCL in the honor of the IX orders of Aungells, CL in the honour of the Patriarches, CVI in the honour of the XII apostellis, and MMCCC, which maketh up the hool nombre of the said MX masses, in the honour of All Saints" (*Will*, 3). He adds that "for the more redy and sure paiement" for a significant portion of these Masses, "we have delivered in redy money before the hande, to th'Abbot, Priour and Conuent, of our said Monastery of Westminster" a sum that was to be used for no other purpose (10). Prayers of the poor were also thought to be especially effective in reducing the pains of Purgatory, and Henry duly provided funds to be distributed to the "lame, blinde, bedred, and moost nedye folks" but only "to th'entent thei doo praie to almighty God for the remission of our synnes, and salvacion of our Soule" (9). Finally, he endowed a perpetual chantry in which priests would say masses for the repose of his soul on fixed days at the altar before his tomb "contynuelly and perpetuelly, whil the world shall endure" (14).

Henry VII's anxious calculations and elaborate provisions for intercession are based on a belief in Purgatory, the vast postmortem holding pen for the souls of ordinary mortals.[16] Its punishments were said to exceed the worst that the world could inflict, and the fears of the faithful but far from sinless were obviously acute. Reformers objected to abuses associated with Purgatory, especially the sale of indulgences, but the concept of this way station to heaven offered hope for eventual redemption to ordinary sinners. Purgatory also allowed an ongoing connection between the living and the dead, bound together by a "communion of the saints," because the prayers of both the quick and the departed could speed release from suffering. Henry's hope for such aid clearly inspired his devotion to the cult of the saints. His will declares his trust in "the singler mediecion and praiers of al the holie companie of Heven," but it specifies "mine accustumed Avoures, . . . Saint Michaell, Saint John Baptist, Saint Johan Evuangelist, Saint George, Saint Anthony, Saint Edward, Saint Vincent, Saint Anne, Saint Marie Magdalene, and Saint Barbara" (Will, 3). "Avowries" were celestial advocates and protectors for their earthly clients, pleading their cases at the Last Judgment. In what Eamon Duffy describes as an "essentially feudal" relationship, patron saints provided real patronage.[17]

The most urgent pleas in this will are addressed to his heirs and executors, as Henry reminds them "howe necessarie, behoofull, and howe profitable it is to dede folks to bee praied for, entirlye requiring theim" to arrange for various people "to praie for us and the weale of our Soule, soo that oure Soule may fele that as thei loved us in our life, soo thei may remember us after our deceasse; and for the true execucion hereof, we charge their conscience as thei woll aunswere therefor before God" (Will, 10). Henry here invokes the "bond of charity" praised by Thomas Aquinas, which "is valuable not only to the living but also to the dead who have died in a state of love. . . . The dead live on in the memory of the living . . . and so the suffrages of the living can be useful to the dead."[18] As Duffy explains, the dead "were powerless to help themselves" and depended on their survivors to assist them by their prayers and supplications because, "however thorough and elaborate one's provision of Masses, alms, and prayers, for the welfare of one's soul, in the last resort one was at the mercy of the executors."[19]

In the long run, few proved more vulnerable to the actions of his heirs and executors than Henry VII. Within twenty years, his son broke with Rome and launched a Reformation that would destroy the monastic intercessory system he had so generously endowed at Westminster. Henry VI was never canonized, and his remains stayed at Windsor. By the 1530s, Protestant preachers inveighed against the cult of the saints and their relics, shrines and pilgrimages, and the belief in Purgatory, and Henry VIII dissolved the monasteries supporting these beliefs and devotional practices, including Westminster itself.[20] As the Protestant bishop, Hugh Latimer, shrewdly observed, since "The founding of the monasteries argued purgatory to be; so the putting of them down argueth it not to be."[21] Finally, when Edward VI came to the throne, Protestant reformers eliminated the Mass itself, abrogating the most important provision of Henry VII's will. Nevertheless, in the years immediately following his father's death, Henry VIII did his filial duty scrupulously. The funeral he arranged established "a prodigious standard of magnificence" for royal obsequies, and construction of Westminster Chapel continued for more than a decade, until its completion.[22] In the words of one contemporary, Henry VIII proved "an obedient child . . . willing the comfort and relief of the soule of his father, to see the will of his said father and king to be truly performed."[23] This praise came from Edmund Dudley, an unpopular henchman to the old king desperate to win clemency from the new, and though his flattery failed in its purpose, it was still largely accurate. Construction of his parents' marble sarcophagus began in 1512 and was completed about six years later, forming a magnificent centerpiece. In the meantime, two eulogies were commissioned to honor his father and grandmother, written by the priest and poet John Skelton.

Skelton was an excellent choice for the task. His devotion to the Tudor monarchy was ardent and long-standing. Laureate to Henry VII, he had been a tutor to the young prince Henry. Erasmus praised Skelton as "the great light and ornament of English letters" in a letter to Henry VIII endorsing poetry's value to kings, and Skelton shared this lofty sense of his own poetic vocation.[24] He greeted his former pupil's accession enthusiastically with *A Lawde and Prayse Made for Our Sovereigne Lord Kyng* in 1509 and was appointed *orator regius* in 1512, the year he composed the two royal eulogies.[25] That same year, he took up residence in Westminster Abbey, where he remained for the rest of his life, perhaps collecting income as a chaplain.[26] His devotion to the monastery's intercessory system was also lifelong, and his defenses grew more ferocious as attacks by reformers increased. Skelton is probably the author of the Latin epitaphs still inscribed on the tomb.[27] His lengthier eulogies occupied Westminster's sacred precincts long after he was gone, hanging on tablets from the tomb's bronze grating for almost two centuries. Their presence is recorded in several subsequent histories of Westminster, beginning with William Camden's, until their removal "not many Years ago" is reported by Jodocus Crull in 1711.[28] Their surprising durability may have resulted less from his poetry's deathless eloquence than from the vigorous curses directed against any who dared to remove them. In a poetic coda appended to the eulogy for the Queen Mother, Skelton threatens anyone who tears, violates, or steals this "epitome" with a mauling by Cerberus.[29] Skelton's loyalty to Tudor rule and its holiest shrine (*"locus iste sacer"*) comes through powerfully, but, typically, his bland praise of the king and his family is less striking than his ferocity against those threatening their persons or place with desecration.[30]

In Skelton's poetry, curses carry more force than blessings; malediction proves his greatest poetic strength.[31] Skelton was a zealous defender of royal authority and traditional religion, yet he is best known for his scabrous satires, many of them directed against clerical and courtly corruption in general and Cardinal Wolsey in particular. As we shall see, he was later embraced by Protestants as a fellow reformer, and his antiprelatical blasts became part of a poetic tradition continuing from Marprelate to Milton. Indeed, in *Why come ye Nat to Courte?*, Skelton explicitly asks "God of his miseracyon / Send better reformation!"[32] Yet the reformation he desired was profoundly conservative, intended to refurbish rather than challenge the church's and clergy's authority. Long before Protestant reformers began their dissolution of monasteries, Cardinal Wolsey had been busy pillaging ancient ecclesiastical foundations to fund his own ambitious projects. Along with many of his contemporaries, Skelton saw Wolsey as a predatory parvenu, and in popular poems like *Collyn Clout*, he rages against those who rob churches of their treasures and put an end to

> . . . matyns at mydnight,
> Boke and chalys gone quyte
> Plucke away the leedes
> Over theyr heedes,
> And sell away theyr belles
> And all that they have elles.
>
> (406–411)

In Skelton's view, these depredations undermine the entire apparatus of traditional religion, harming the souls of those no longer able to help themselves. "How ye breke the dedes wylles," Skelton exclaims, accusing those who "Turn monasterie into water mylles, [or]/Of an abbey . . . make a graunge" (417–419) of prolonging the purgatorial miseries of the deceased. Skelton was a reformer resolutely committed to defending the inviolability of sacred space, ancient institutions, and the intercessory system.

Skelton's devotion to the Tudor monarchy was no less resolute. *Agaynst the Scottes* was the first English ballad to be printed and circulated, and it trumpets the news of the English victory at Flodden Field in 1513.[33] The Scottish king, James IV, is vilified as a descendant of Cain and "brother unnaturall/Unto our kyng royall," and his abortive rebellion is denounced as heresy:

> He was a recrayed knyght,
> A subtyll sysmatyke,
> Ryght nere and heretyke,
> Of grace out of the state
> And dyed excommunycate.

James's fall from "grace out of the state" has religious as well as political overtones. As Susan Brigden explains, pre-Reformation notions of heresy often had less to do with theological doctrine than broad offenses "against the mores of the community."[34] Skelton's notion of the state of grace—like his idea of heresy—is adamantly authoritarian and conformist. A lapse from these norms brought automatic excommunication, its speed conveyed with stunning force by Skelton's short, sharp rhymes.

A more positive image of community is discernible in a poem celebrating the defeat of *The Douty Duke of Albany* ten years later. The Scots are mocked as a hopeless "rable" that "shall never be hable,/ With us for to compare" (178–179), because the English are unified by their love for their king: "all his subjectes and he/Moost lovyngly agre/ With hole hart and true mynde" (480–482). Indeed, Henry VIII's soldiers "fynde his grace so kynde" (483) that they will sacrifice everything for him,

> Wherewith he dothe them bynde
> At all houres to be redy
> With hym to lyve and dye,
> And to spende their hart blode,
> Their bodyes and their gode
> With hym in all dystresse.
>
> (484–489)

English eagerness to "spende their hart blode" gives their *esprit de corps* an almost sacramental power, as does the advance of this "hoost royall" under "Sainct Cutberdes banner" (61–63). This banner had once been the corporal or altar cloth of St. Cuthbert, founder of Durham Abbey nine centuries earlier. The saint appeared in a dream to the abbey's prior in 1347 and told him to attach the cloth to a spear and carry it into the Battle of Neville's Cross in order to protect the monastery and assist the English force against a Scottish invasion. It worked to secure victory in 1347, it worked again at Flodden Field in 1513, and it worked yet again in 1523 when it helped to rout "the Douty Duke of Albany." According to monastic records, this "holie reliqe & Corporax cloth . . . having a red crosse of read velvett on both sydes over ye same holie Reliqe most artificiallie and cunyngly compiled & framed" was once "carried to any battell as occasion should serve, and . . . (*never*) caryed or shewed at any battell, but by ye especial grace of god almightie, & ye mediacion of holie St. Cuthb: it browghte home ye victorie."[35] Skelton obviously shares the monks' faith in the talismanic power of this Eucharistic relic.

At the same time, Skelton's attitude toward relics, miracles, and even the Eucharist itself is oddly ambiguous. In *Ware the Hawk*, Skelton's own corporal and even the sacrament itself are shockingly abused in verses blending blasphemous travesty with fierce orthodoxy. Evidently written sometime after he became the Rector of Diss in Norfolk around 1505, *Ware the Hawk* describes the invasion of Skelton's church by a neighbor priest who uses the building to train his falcons. Critics are divided about the autobiographical accuracy and tone of the poem; the priest may simply be Skelton's invention and the story an elaborate joke or allegory about church corruption.[36] The speaker's denunciation of his adversary as a tyrant, persecutor, and infidel worse than Nero or Tarquin becomes ridiculous in its bombastic stridency, yet the deeds described are genuinely outrageous. The villainous "preest unreverent" gets down to desecration immediately by using the host in its pyx for target practice (45). After making his hawk fly "streyght to the sacrament" (46), he strips the high altar of its cloth and leaps atop it to shout directions to his birds and "horrible othes/before the face of God" (52–53). The altar is further profaned when the hawk kills a pigeon on it and devours it as "its blode ran downe raw/Upon the auter stone" (59–60). This pollution of the temple culminates with the hawk shitting "Upon my corporas face" (63), and when rebuked, the offender adds blasphemous insult to injury by threatening to repeat the desecration during Mass:

> And that he wysshed withall
> That the dowves donge downe myght fall
> Into my chalys at mas
> When consecratyd was
> The blessyd sacrament.
>
> (182–186)

Skelton's reaction to these sacrilegious insults is completely inscrutable. He proclaims his outrage in stentorian tones and ponderously declares his didactic intentions in the poem's opening lines:

> This worke devysed is
> For such as do amys
> And specyally to controule
> Such as have cure of soule.
>
> (1–4)

He denounces this clerical renegade as "a sysmatyke/or els an here-tike" because his abuse of "the sacrament,/Wythin the holy church bowndis,/That of our fayth the grownd is" (17–18; 12–14) attacks the foundations of the church and its holiest of holies. The other priest is not only obstinately incorrigible, but his dereliction disgraces the priesthood and makes "the churche to be/In smale auctoryte" (139–140). Nevertheless, the speaker's clarion appeals to a higher ecclesiastical court ("*OBSERVATE*," "*CONSIDERATE*," "*VIGILATE*," etc.) evidently fall on deaf ears because the judges have been bribed and so corrupted that:

> The church is thus abusyd,
> Reproched and pollutyd;
> Correctyon hath no place,
> And all for lack of grace.
>
> (160–163)

Despairing of official vindication, Skelton ultimately declines to pursue it, settling instead for the satisfactions of self-aggrandizement and the last laugh. *Ware the Hawk* concludes with a series of impossible riddles in Latin. The first is a description of Skelton as Britain's phoenix, and the last is an invocation of poetic license authorizing poets to defend justice and to attack those too stupid to understand them. Linguistic elitism is his best defense as he deploys a Latin barely understood by his ignorant opponent, "Sir *dominus vobiscum*," to baffle and confound him (286). Skelton has no intention of correcting this fool, aiming only to shame him by a display of arcane erudition. Somewhat incongruously, he concludes by praying that his own poem will be inviolable to his enemies even as he declares his shock at the violation of the sacrament ("*violans tua sacra sacrorum!*") (71). *Ware the Hawk* initially responds to the assault on "the sacrament . . . That of our fayth the grownd is" with the didactic earnestness of the Croxton *Play of the Sacrament*. In the end, it reverts to a Goliardic blend of mockery and pedantry, apparently confident that learned jokes will suffice as a defense of the Eucharist.

Skelton's astonishing humor in the face of sacrilege is in many ways characteristic of both the assured vitality of traditional religion and the mocking detachment of early humanism on the eve of the Reforma-tion.[37] His shit-stained corporal is easily disposed of, figuratively if not literally, by its sarcastic description as a *sacrificium laudis* (64), and his bombastic indignation is qualified and complicated by irony. Here and elsewhere, Skelton delights in desecration even as he denounces it. In his lewd and learned mockery, he has strong affinities with Rabelais, as Richard Halpern has noted.[38] Mikhail Bakhtin's classic study, *Rabelais and His World*, explores the French author's roots in popular culture and the spirit of carnival. In Rabelais, this rambunctious spirit allows pleas-ures both aggressive and illicit as he rubs our noses in the grotesque and obscene aspects of material existence. In the orgies of carnival, the sacred is desublimated into its physical components through what Bakhtin calls "an inverted transubstantiation: the transformation of blood into wine, of the dismembered body into bread, of the passion into a banquet" and, ultimately, of everything into shit.[39] Gargantua's extended inventory of swabs or "ass-wipes" is just one instance of the scatological humor characteristic of such literature; Skelton's shit-stained "corporas face" is another. But, instead of giving scandal and debasing all it touches, this bathetic descent into the mire can paradox-ically sustain, as Bakhtin says, a "renewal of the sacred on the material bodily level."[40] In the words of William Butler Yeats, "Love has pitched his mansion in the place of excrement."[41]

Skelton's coarse but complex humor reveals an unsettling under-side of incarnational religion. In terms deliberately chosen, I suggest that this underside is fundamentally connected to the dirty little se-cret of relics and other sacred objects: many relics, especially those as-sociated with martyrdom, are manifestly nothing more than the stained remnants of what Carolyn Walker Bynum calls the "oozing, disgusting, uncontrollable biological process" that culminates in deg-radation and death.[42] Removed from their gilded reliquaries, they look filthy and disgusting. In appearance alone, Skelton's defiled cor-poral would not look all that different from the miraculous corporal of Bolsena, less as it is depicted in Raphael's sublime version than as shown in an earlier fourteenth-century fresco in Orvieto's cathedral. In a painting by Ugolino di Prete Ilario, the bishop of Orvieto displays the stained corporal to the pope and his awestruck retinue, but, with-out the cruciform pattern of Raphael's depiction, the cloth's more random stain makes it look like the bishop is airing his dirty linen in public (figure 16). The comparison is not merely frivolous or obscene because, from a loftier celestial perspective, even the shroud of Turin can look like dirty linen. These sorry remains are transformed by preservation and faith into tokens of spiritual health and wholeness. More fastidious humanists like Erasmus were increasingly scandalized by this sordid underside of traditional religion, barely glossing over its dirtiest implications. His "Pilgrimage for Religion's Sake" describes the holiest relics in Becket's shrine as "Some linen rags, many of them still showing traces of snivel. With these, they say, the holy man wiped the sweat from his face or neck, the dirt from his nose, or whatever other kinds of filth human bodies have."[43] More ardent reformers than Erasmus were even more disgusted by what Haigh calls "the sacralization of physical things."[44]

Humanists with a strong affection for popular culture, like Skelton and Rabelais, were less repulsed by and more at ease with the grosser aspects of material existence. Pleasure in filth is essential to a poem like Skelton's *The Tunning of Elynour Rummynge*. This jubilant travesty of a witches' Sabbath and communion service describes an ale wife and the customers who give all they have to drink her powerful brew and then "Ryse up, on Gods halfe" (501). Those who are "blessed with a cup . . . founde therein no thornes . . . [and] founde therein no bones" (377–381), unsettling allusions to Christ's bones and crown of thorns, but Elynour does include another secret ingredient "lerned . . . of a Jewe" (208): the dung collected from her hens gives her brew its excellent thickness. Skelton's Elynour flaunts the tricks of her trade much as Chaucer's Pardoner does; his relics range from the bones of "an holy Jewes sheep" to his own shit-stained britches, if Harry Bailey's suspicions are correct.[45] While hardly oblivious to the Pardoner's scabrous cynicism, Chaucer still implies that it does not jeopardize all that is holy; nor does the Pardoner's tale of waste, malice, and death preclude a wholesome moral. The carnival spirit of *Elynour Rummynge* also recalls the liberties taken in the anonymous *Second Shepherds' Play*, where the divine comedy is repeated as slapstick farce when a stolen lamb is disguised as a baby, and Christ, the *agnus dei*, is placed amid the barnyard animals. All these works are the cultural products of a traditional,

FIGURE 16

Ugolino di Prete Ilario, *Miracle of Bolsena*

By permission of the Opera del Duomo di Orvieto

incarnational Christianity, their ironies deriving from an acceptance of the embarrassing proximity of the sacred and the profane.

Skelton was one of England's last great defenders of traditional religion, but his defenses were sophisticated and critical. He was not indifferent to the scandals and controversies surrounding the church in his time, and he wrote a series of blistering attacks on ecclesiastical corruption in the early 1520s, including *Speke Parott*, *Collyn Clout*, and *Why Come Ye Nat to Courte?*. Skelton is also alert to new, unorthodox threats from the Continent, and *Collyn Clout* denounces those who "have a smacke / Of Luthers sacke" (5). However, he initially regards their lapse as merely the latest in a perennial series of heresies stretching back through the Lollards to the fourth-century Arius and Pelagius (540–553). In Skelton's view, wild speculations about "predestynacyon" and "the prescyence / Of divyne assence [essence]" and the "ipostacis [hypostasis] / Of Chriystes manhode" are merely symptoms of entrenched clerical abuses that have provoked the laity "the church to deprave" (513–527). *Collyn Clout*'s real villain is Wolsey, the papal legate and royal chancellor, since his iniquity has driven a wedge "bytwene the clergye / And the temporaltye" (555–556). Prelates for whom "promocyon / . . . is theyr hole devocion" (86–87) have depleted and corrupted the church, scandalized the laity, and provoked the anticlerical hostility that causes heresy's spread. *Speke Parrot* boldly blames the "decaye of monasteries and relygious places" (499) on a single "prelate . . . So bold and so braggyng, and . . . so basely born" (506–507).

Skelton is no less exercised about Wolsey's influence over Henry VIII, and he explicitly equates the royal presence with the real presence, accusing Wolsey of monopolizing both. *Collyn Clout* compares the cardinal's control over access to the king to a priest's denying his parishioners sight of the "sacrynge" (1028) or consecration and thus forbidding them "To loke on God in fourme of brede" (1024) without permission. Skelton charges Wolsey here with simony, the crime in which a clergyman seeks to profit from his access to holy things. In *Why Come Ye Nat to Courte?*, Skelton accuses the cardinal of a more sinister clerical abuse, claiming that Wolsey must have acquired control over the king by "nycromansy" (696) or conjuring, a practice that involves consorting with demons and the dead. As long as they shared the same opponent, Skelton and more radical reformers sometimes made similar criticisms: William Tyndale also accuses Wolsey of necromancy, and John Foxe claims that the cardinal's campaign "to suppress divers abbeys, priories, and monasteries" led to "hatred of the spirituality."[46]

Nevertheless, by the late 1520s, attacks on the cardinal took a more alarming turn by challenging the power of the church and its sacraments. In 1528, two friars from Greenwich, Jerome Barlowe and William Roye, published *Rede Me and Be Not Wrothe*, also known as *The Burial of the Mass*, celebrating the Mass's death by the sword of the gospel. Their tract combines a mock-requiem in the manner of *Phyllyp Sparrow* with an attack on Wolsey so Skeltonic that some readers assumed he was the author.[47] That same year, a young lawyer named Simon Fish published *A Supplication of Beggars*, a devastating critique of the doctrine of Purgatory and its whole monastic support system. Two years earlier Fish had played Wolsey in a masque mocking "misgouernance and euill order" at Gray's Inn in 1526, a satire Skelton might once have endorsed.[48] However, in his 1528 tract, Fish takes on a patron and institution much closer to Skelton's heart. *A Supplication of Beggars* attacks Westminster Abbey as a waste of money, encouraging the king to establish his own hospitals for the poor and arguing that charity toward the living is a better social and spiritual investment than funding greedy, lazy monks and prayers for the dead. He even accuses Abbot Islip of duping Henry VIII's father, among others, claiming that "dyvers of your noble predecessours kinges of this realme" gave generously "to haue a certeyn masses said daily for them whereof they sey neuer one. If the Abbot of Westminster shulde sing euery day as many masses for his founders as his bound to do by his foundacion .M [1,000] monkes were too fewe."[49]

Attacks on Catholicism's intercessory system had to be answered, and church authorities enlisted two of their most eloquent and forceful spokesmen, John Skelton and Thomas More, in a propaganda counterattack. More's *Supplication of Souls* responded to Fish's criticism of Purgatory by having the dead themselves remind the reader of their dependence on their prayers and denounce those "sedyceous persones . . . [who] labour to dystroy them by whome we be much holpen."[50] More saw the reformers' tracts as a two-pronged attack:

"eyther playnly to wryte against the fayth and the sacramentys (wheryn yf they gat them credence . . . they then se well the church must nedys fall therwyth) or els to labour agaynst the church alone / & get the clergye dystroyed / wherupon they parceyue well that the fayth and sacramentes wold not fayle to decay" (7:161). When direct attacks on the sacramental system such as "the blasphemous boke entytled the beryeng of the masse" (7:161) by Barlowe and Roye fail, more cunning heretics like Fish resort to the more popular course of anticlerical mockery. Either way, their "fynall intent and purpose" is to stop "prechyng of the very hole corps and body of the blessed fayth of Cryste / & the mynystryng of the blessed sacramentis of our sauyour Cryste / and of all those in especyall the consecrating of the sacred body the flesh and blood of our sauyour Cryst" (7:154). Skelton had also expressed his distress at heretical attacks "agaynst the the sacramentes" (518) and "agaynst preesthode" (534), but, in *Collyn Clout* and other earlier satires, he blames the prelates for these lapses. Near the end of his life, he changed course, turning his attacks away from church authority and aiming instead at heretics, now clearly recognized as the greater danger. His last poem, *A Replycacion Agaynst Certayne Yong Scolers Abjured of Late*, published in 1528, harshly denounces two Lutheran sympathizers. Nevertheless, Skelton's fury at threats to traditional religion is haunted by a sense of its own futility, and he concludes grimly and accurately that "heresy will never die" (408).

Skelton's *Replycacion* excoriates Thomas Bilney and Thomas Arthur for preaching "howe it was idolatry to offre to ymages of our blessed lady, or to pray and go on pylgrrimages, or to make oblacions to any ymages of sayntes in churches and elswhere" (357). Bilney's and Arthur's unorthodoxy was mild and so too was their punishment—at least on the first offense.[51] Nevertheless, Skelton works himself into a fury at their "popholy and pevysshe presumpcion" and is outraged that "these demy divines, and stoicall studiantes, and friscajoly yonkerkyns . . . fervently reboyled with the infatuate flames of their rechelesse youthe and wytlesse wontonnese" would "preche to people imprudent perilously" (374–375). For Skelton, attacks on the cult of the saints ignore the fundamental hierarchy "of all good Christien order" (226). Different degrees of praise are due to every worthy object. The highest is "*latria*," which "is an honour grete, / Belongyng to the Deitie," whereas *"dulia"* is the honor paid to great men and *"hyperdulia"* the veneration owed the saints and angels. Bilney's and Arthur's "horryble heresy" threatens anarchy because their charge of idolatry means "all thyng ye disorder/thorowe out every border" (282–288; 227–228).

In Skelton's last poem, heresy's threat to hierarchical order ultimately prompts him to embrace a patron he once scorned. The *Replycacion* is dedicated to Wolsey, declaring that his work "shall evermore be, with all obsequious redynesse, humbly submytted unto the ryght descrete reformacyon of the reverende prelates and moche noble doctours of our mother Holy Churche" (373), and it rebukes the young scholars by claiming that their troubles began "whan prelacy you opposed" (106). Skelton's servile sanctimony may be repellent, but it is not hypocritical.[52] Skelton is consistently authoritarian in his religious convictions, and the challenges posed by reformers like Bilney and Arthur revive support for powers once criticized. He now says the "reverende prelates . . . of our mother Holy Churche" are the only ones authorized to undertake the "ryght descrete reformacyon" required. Both Skelton and More had once mocked and criticized church corruption, but when radicals took up their earlier calls for reform, both became fanatical defenders of traditional religion. More too wrote a treatise on Bilney and Arthur, called a *Dialogue Concerning Heresies*, and the publication of Skelton's *Replycacion* and More's *Dialogue* were probably part of a coordinated government campaign.[53] More belabors the same distinctions outlined by Skelton: "callyng the dulya the reuerence or worshyp that man doth to man/. . . The seconde yperdulya that a man doth to a more excellent creature as to aungels or sayntes. The thyrde latria the veneracyon honoure and adoracyon that creatures dothe onely to god." More also concludes that a relapse into heresy and execution are probably inevitable since a crime "so great and so odyous" stems from a malicious pride that can never be uprooted.[54]

For their first offense, Bilney and Arthur were given a punishment to fit the crime, and Skelton's poem gloats over their public humiliation. Since Bilney and Arthur had preached against devotion to Mary and her "pure clennesse virgynall," they were made to march to Paul's Cross in the procession held on the feast of the Immaculate

Conception on December 8, 1527 (32). Assigned a place of dishonor, they carried faggots as a symbol of the fiery fate they had been spared. Skelton's glee is tempered by regret that they got off too easily as well as a suspicion that one felt "small contrycion" and "counted it for no correction" (183; 189):

> Some juged in this case
> Your penaunce toke no place
> Your penaunce was to lyght;
> And thought, if ye had right,
> Ye shulde take further payne
> To resorte agayne
> To places where ye have preched
> And your lollardy lernyng teched. . . .
>
> (197–204)

Bilney should be made, in Skelton's view, to recant everywhere he preached error rather than only once. The poet also feels that a relapse is almost inevitable, regarding both men as:

> For evermore suspecte,
> And banysshed in effect
> From all honest company
> Because ye have eaten a flye,
> To your great vyllony,
> That never more may dye.[55]
>
> (241–246)

Although urging them to "mende your myndes that are mased;/Or els doutlesse ye shalbe blased,/And be brent at a stake" (293–295), he seems to doubt that such a fate can be avoided. The poem's last line holds that, like the fly, "heresy will never die" (408).

Skelton died the next year, in 1529, and these were evidently his last verses. His predictions proved accurate in more ways than one. Though Arthur recanted immediately and was released, the unfortunate Bilney agonized in the Tower for months before admitting error. After his release, he repented his admission and finally resolved to seek martyrdom by preaching without a license in the houses and open fields of Skelton's Norfolk. Bilney was arrested, reexamined, and burned at the stake in 1531, just as the *Replycacyon* predicted. Skelton would undoubtedly have felt vindicated by this outcome, but he would have been appalled by the renown Bilney's death earned him among Protestants. John Foxe records his heroic decision to resume his public preaching and thus "go to Jerusalem" in emulation of Christ's mission, and he includes Hugh Latimer among Bilney's illustrious converts, noting that Latimer was at that time "cross-keeper at Cambridge, bringing it forth upon procession days," an idolatrous practice of the sort Bilney opposed.[56] Bilney's determination to die for his faith gave Latimer and others the courage to follow suit. Years later, during the persecutions of Mary's reign, Latimer's famous last words to his fellow martyr, Nicholas Ridley, would become one of the touchstones of Foxe's monumental work: "Be of good comfort, Master Ridley, and play the man. We shall this day light such a candle, by God's grace, in England, as I trust shall never be put out."[57] Latimer's last words are the positive variation on Skelton's bleak assumption that "heresy wyll never dye."

Shortly after Skelton's death, heresy began to flourish when Henry VIII broke with Rome and embraced the Protestant heretics whom Skelton and More denounced. Heresy not only refused to die but also brazenly used Skelton's satirical style for its own purposes, praising those he scorned and mocking those who persecuted them. The most outrageous example is the anonymous *Image of Ypocrisy*, a poem so Skeltonic that it was attributed to him for centuries afterward despite clear evidence that it not only was written after he died but also refutes all his convictions.[58] The *Image of Ypocrisy* is a "replication" to the *Replycacion*, dealing with the case of Bilney and Arthur from a diametrically opposed perspective. "Father Friska jolly/and *Pater* pecke a lolly" are ridiculed, "A naughty seismatikce/And an heritike" are denounced, and the pretensions of "Doctoure Bullatus/Though *parum literatus*" are mocked.[59] Yet, though some of these phrases are lifted verbatim from *Collyn Clout* (795–796) and *A Replycacion* (401–402), the *Image of Ypocrisy's* villains are Skelton's heroes and vice versa. Thomas More is vilified as the titular "image of hypocrisy" whose "tyranny/. . . causeth cruelly/The simple men to dye/For fayned herisye," and his tracts are denounced as "legendes of lyes/[and] fayned fantasies/. . . Brought out of Vtopia" (436). All sympathy is extended to Bilney and Arthur, and the public humiliation that Skelton celebrated in A Replycacyon is here lamented, as each man stands "In sighte at Paules crosse,/To the vtter losse/Of his good name and fame" (436). The poem concludes on a more hopeful note predicting that, because "God is full of force" (447), the downtrodden will arise and their oppressors will be thrown down.

This reversal set the pattern for Skelton's poetic afterlife in the English Reformation. Later writers adapted Skeltonic parody to blasphemous mockeries of the Mass in order to build support for its suppression. Near the beginning of King Edward's reign, the Lord Protector ordered the House of Lords "to dispute whether bread be in the sacrament after the consecration or not."[60] Recognizing that anticlerical mockery was a more effective weapon against traditional religion than theological dispute, the authorities also permitted publication of dozens of satires like The Endightment agaysnt Mother Messe, in which the host was derided with nicknames like "Round Robin," "Jack-in-the-Box," and "popish idol."[61] John Bale, one of Edward's new bishops, gave Skelton a place of honor in English literary and religious history by praising him for discerning "many evils in the clergy" and attacking "the foolish blathering of the mendicant brothers especially Dominicans," and dozens of "merry tales" attributed to him continued circulating throughout the Reformation.[62] Thus canonized, Skelton became a model for Protestant satirists like Luke Shepherd, praised by Bale as "a very funny poet, not inferior to Skelton in his poems and rhythms."[63] Shepherd wrote a number of the liturgical satires published near the beginning of Edward's reign. John Bon and Mast Person, a dialogue between a bumptious priest and a plain-spoken plowman, includes a woodcut print of a Corpus Christi procession on its title page (figure 17), but the verse below mocks those who think their aching shoulders bear "a great God": "Make of yt what ye wyl, it is a wafar cake/. . . And loke where Idolatrye is, Christ will not be there."[64] Shepherd also wrote Pathose, in which the pope bewails the death of his daughter, the Mass, on whom all his power and profit depended, and his Upcheringe of the Masse is a requiem for "good mestress missa" complete with scattered tags of mongrel Latin in the manner of Phyllype

ℭ John Bon and
Maſt perſon

☞ Alaſſe pooꝛe fooles, ſo ſoꝛe ye be lade
No maruel it is, thoughe your ſhoulders ake
Foꝛ ye beare a great God, which ye your ſelfes made
Make of it what ye wyl, it is a wafar cake
And betwen two Irons pꝛinted it is and bake
And loke where Idolatrye is, Chꝛiſte wyl not be there
Wherfoꝛe ley doꝛwne your burden, an Idole ye do beare
☞ Alaſſe pooꝛe
Fooles.

FIGURE 17

Luke Shepherd, *John Bon and Mast Person*, frontispiece

By permission of the British Library; C.95.a.9

Sparowe.[65] In such works, the "comely corse" of Corpus Christi is made a joke, the "miracle of the mass" is reduced to its material ingredients, and, in the mournful words of a contemporary ballad, "Blessings [are] turned to blasphemies."[66]

For Skelton and other conservative humanists, the Reformation confirmed the law of unintended consequences. Many soon realized that their parodies of church corruption and calls for "better reformation" could no longer be contained by orthodox authority. More and Erasmus watched with horror as their elegant *facetiae* were transformed into blunt weapons used to smash the church and its most venerable institutions. More was so upset that he declared himself ready to burn his own work and his friend's as well as the writings of enemies:

> I saye therfore in these dayes in whyche men by theyr owne defaute mysseconstre and take harm of the very scrypture of god, vntyll menne better amende, yf any man wolde now translate Moria [i.e., *The Praise of Folly*] in to Englyshe, or some workes eyther that I have my selfe wryten ere this all be yt there be none harme therein/folke yet beyng (as they be) geuen to take harme of that that is good./I wolde not onely my derlynges bokes but myne owne also, helpe to burne them both with myne owne handes, rather then folke sholde (though thorow theyr owne faute) take any harm of them.[67]

More's worst fears eventually came true. When Edward VI came to the throne, Protestant authorities ordered placement of Erasmus's *Paraphrases* in every church in order to advance reform among the laity. The proposal prompted Stephen Gardiner to complain to the Lord Protector about the dangers posed by a book in which:

> The Sacrament of the Aulter is so wantonly talked of by him, that as the world is nowe, the reading of him were the whole subvertion. Erasmus in his latter dayes, hath for the Sacrament of the Aultar spoken as reverendley, and said as muche for confirmation of it, as maye be, and cryeth out of them, that would take him otherwayes. But this in thend, when age had tempered

him. In this Paraphrasies, whiche he wrott in his wanton age, the words and termes were able to subverte, if were possible, as Christ saith, thelecte. If the Paraphrasies goo abrode, people shalbe lerned to call the Sacrament of the Aultar holi bread, and a Symbole.[68]

This was, of course, precisely the effect desired by some reformers, particularly those denouncing the host as a mere "wafar cake."

Gardiner's dismay at these developments shows how the unintended consequences of reformation also applied to exponents of royal supremacy. Stephen Gardiner was a conservative bishop, loyal to traditional religion, but, unlike Thomas More, he embraced the principle of royal supremacy under Henry VIII and retained his head and office for the duration of Henry's reign. He also justified accepting royal supremacy in his treatise, *De Vera Obedientia*. Opposed to more radical reform, he fell out of favor under Edward VI and was eventually imprisoned, returning as a bishop only when Mary Tudor came to the throne. Mary's accession brought more lethal reversals to those supporters of royal supremacy who promoted radical reform. Thomas Cranmer was probably the most devoted supporter of Tudor ideas of sacred kingship, but the foundation stone of the church he helped to establish ultimately crushed him; as Diarmaid MacCulloch explains, when Mary became his queen, he became a "rebel against the Crown" and was burned at the stake.[69]

These alterations of state finally had unanticipated, if posthumous, consequences for the supreme advocate of royal supremacy, Henry VIII himself. Henry's own reformation was limited, for while he subjected the church's sacerdotal authority to his own control, he continued to venerate its traditional sacramental system and the Eucharist above all, making the denial of transubstantiation a capital crime. His last will and testament provided for requiem and commemorative masses, requesting that "an altar shall be furnished for the saying of daily masses while the world shall endure" and providing for two chantry chaplains to say "four solemn obits" annually.[70] He also planned a grand funeral monument, though he changed its location to Windsor after his break with Rome. Before then, he had planned to be buried with his father in Westminster in an even grander tomb, and he secured still more papal indulgences for pilgrims to his grave.[71] Nevertheless, Henry's subsequent assault on monasteries, shrines, and relics emboldened Thomas Cromwell to destroy Edward the Confessor's tomb in 1536. This attack on the abbey and sacred kingship's oldest shrine did not prevent Henry from planning an even grander royal sepulcher for himself in Windsor.[72] In a halfhearted gesture toward modesty, his will declares that "for himself he would be content that his body should be buried in any place accustomed for Christian folks, but, for the reputation of the dignity to which he has been called, he directs that it shall be laid in the choir of his college of Windesour, midway between the stalls and the high altar, in a tomb now almost finished."[73] Befitting such lofty "dignity," one of the plans included numerous effigies and more than a hundred statues.[74] He also requested that "there an altar shall be furnished for the saying of daily masses while the world shall endure."[75] Henry's plans were both traditional and grandiose, but his heirs fulfilled none of them.

Ironically, it was royal supremacy, the central tenet of Henry's new version of sacred kingship, that undid his religious settlement and blocked a monument befitting his royal "dignity." After his son and successor, Edward VI, came to the throne, belief in transubstantiation was outlawed. The Chantries Act of 1547 put an end to "phantasying opinions of purgatory and masses satisfactory, to be done for them which be departed," and the second revision of the *Book of Common Prayer* of 1552 removed even the name of "what was commonly called the Masse."[76] Thus, the religious provisions of his will were almost immediately nullified, proving Henry VIII as vulnerable to the actions of his heirs and executors as his father had been. Edward's own will requested the completion of his father's monument, but Mary was hardly eager to honor the heretic who had disowned her. Indeed, for years afterward, rumors circulated that she and Cardinal Pole had even desecrated her father's grave and burned his body.[77] When Elizabeth succeeded her sister, she too refrained from completing her father's monument, and it remained unfinished for more than a century.[78] During the Civil War, parliamentary forces dismantled its stones and sold them, and soldiers led by Robert Hartley smashed the high altar in his father's sepulcher at Westminster.[79] Puritan militants had little regard for monuments to sacred kingship of any sort. Perhaps because the older shrine served a larger ecclesiastical purpose, the father's altar was eventually restored (figure 10), whereas the son's grave remains essentially unmarked. Royal supremacy and divine right repeatedly failed to create a shrine comparable to those erected to traditional sacred kingship, as we shall see. The laureate who honored the royal tomb of Henry VII with his verses might not have imagined that his princely pupil would end up a "sysmatyke." Yet John Skelton would certainly have found such an unquiet grave fitting punishment for that king's violations of "holy church bowndis, / That of our fayth the grownd is."

Rites of Memory
Shakespeare and the Elizabethan Compromise

I have some rights of memory in this kingdom.
—William Shakespeare, *Hamlet* (1601)

FIGURE 18
Tomb of Elizabeth with Henry mourning; *Hakluytus Posthumus*
(detail of figure 24)
By permission of the Folger Shakespeare Library

$\mathcal{M}$ary Tudor came to the throne in 1553 determined to reverse the Protestant reformations of her predecessors. One of her first steps was the restoration of Westminster Abbey and its most venerable shrine to sacred kingship. Whatever she may have done to the grave of Henry VIII, she was eager to repair the damage done to the tomb of Edward the Confessor during her father's reign, so she ordered John Feckenham, the new abbot of Westminster's revived Benedictine community, to rebury the royal saint and to rebuild the monument. Edward's reburial was conducted with a solemn gravity duly recorded by the diarist, Henry Machyn, who writes that on the "xx day of Marche was taken up at Westmynster agayn with a hondered lyghtes kyng Edward the confessor in the same plasse wher ys shryne was, and ytt shalle be sett up agayne as fast as my lord abbott can have ytt don, for yt was a godly syte to have seen yt, how reverently he was cared from the plasse that he was taken up whe he was led when that the abbay was spowlyd and robyd; and so he was cared, and goodly syngyng and senssyng as has bene sene, and masse song."[1] Feckenham subsequently completed the restoration of the tomb that still stands (figure 19), perhaps the only enduring achievement of Mary's brief reign.

At the time, Abbot Feckenham saw the restored shrine more hopefully, as a harbinger of a lasting counter-Reformation. In a speech asking Parliament to extend the law of sanctuary in 1557, he describes Edward's corpse as *"insignia rerum"* or signs of things, a term for relics, indicating their potency as a sign and conduit of God's grace; Feckenham adds that "we have here the most precious relics in this realm, next unto the Divine relics of faith, the most Holy Sacrament and Sacramental. I mean the body of that most holy King, St. Edward, remaineth there among us, which body, the favour of Almighty God so preserved during the time of our late schism, that though the heretics had power upon that wherein the body was enclosed, yet on that sacred body they had no power; but I have found it, and since my coming I have restored it to its ancient sepulture" among "the best Kings of this realm."[2] In defending the privilege of sanctuary, Feckenham reaffirms the sacred bond between the real and royal presence established by its founder's burial within the abbey's inner sanctum. Heretics had tried to shatter this connection by abolishing the Mass, dis-

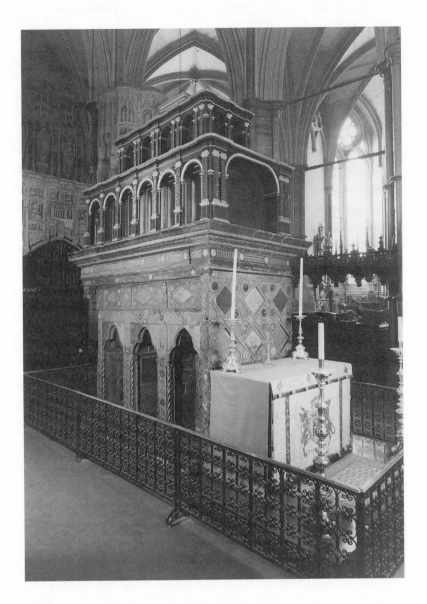

FIGURE 19
Edward the Confessor's shrine
Copyright: Dean and Chapter of Westminster

mantling shrines and altars, and dissolving Westminster's monastery. Now, with the restoration of the abbey and its royal patronage, the new abbot is certain that both Edward's "sacred body" and the body and blood of Christ have been securely restored to their rightful place at the center of the church. For a brief interval, the older, medieval version of sacred kingship and its monastic intercessory system reclaimed their holiest space at the center of Westminster Abbey.

All this changed when Elizabeth Tudor came to the throne. The harmonious relationship of monarch, monk, and Mass was once again shattered, and the traditional model of sacred kingship was replaced by the more assertive Protestant version in which the church was subordinated to the monarchy. The new queen displayed far less respect for Westminster and its solemnities than her stepsister had. When Abbot Feckenham and his confrères greeted Elizabeth's first passage to Parliament with tapers, incense, and holy water, she dismissed them, saying, "Away with those torches, we see very well." Inside the abbey church, she gave precedence to her own chapel choristers, who sang the litany in English, and a Marian exile delivered a sermon urging the abolition of monasteries.[3] Elizabeth's attitude toward the Mass seemed even more shocking to many Catholics. For Mary Tudor, "the celebration of the mass was . . . the centre of her spiritual life," and she supposedly died right after making the responses to the elevation of the host.[4] By contrast, as a good Protestant, Elizabeth saw the host's elevation, once the sacred high point of the service, as a form of Catholic idolatry and superstition, and she ordered the bishop who would preside at her coronation not to raise it, immediately asserting her royal supremacy.[5] The confusing records of her coronation make it hard to know what happened next; she may have replaced the bishop with her chaplain or she may have abstained from receiving communion or attending the Mass. In these skimpy accounts, the religious service is reduced to an obscure sideshow. By contrast, her civic progress the day before had been both more visible and better publicized, making what was formerly a mere prelude into the main event.[6] Shortly afterward, her government authorized publication of The Quenes Maiesties Passage, a detailed account of the "wonderfull spectacle, of a noble hearted princess toward her most loving people, and the peoples excading comfort in beholding so worthy a soveraign."[7] By shifting attention from religious ritual to civic ceremony and courtly pageantry, the tract accelerated "the migration of the holy" launched by her father's reformation, overshadowing controversies over the real presence with veneration for the royal presence. The "wonderfull spectacle, of a noble hearted princess" carried before her adoring people became another icon of Tudor sacred kingship. In the heraldic drawings of her coronation progress (figure 20), the queen is carried in a canopied litter like the host—or Christ himself (figure 3)—in a Corpus Christi procession. These ceremonial parallels had been long-standing features of traditional sacred kingship. In Paris, the same canopy had been used for both Corpus Christi and royal processions throughout the Middle Ages.[8] Later in Elizabeth's reign, the suppression of the Corpus Christi feast and procession eliminated the ecclesiastical competition.[9] The queen had the ceremonial stage to herself, and she made the most of it with processions that became perennial rituals of a cult of Elizabeth.

Elizabeth's cult would become the most successful Protestant version of sacred kingship in the English Reformation. Its success was attributable to several factors. The first was the queen's quick grasp of her role as "a noble hearted princess," manifest in her brilliant performance at the start of her reign. Another was the solemnity of ordinary court protocol combined with the grandeur of the annual pageants, processions, and tournaments staged in her honor. As noted earlier, Sir Thomas Smith describes a deference that transforms the presence chamber into a kind of tabernacle, and her courtiers' performances in the Accession Day tilts grew more extravagant each year.[10] No less important to Elizabeth's success was a religious settlement unyielding on royal supremacy but open to compromise and obfuscation on doctrinal and liturgical matters. Elizabeth was thus able to nurture religious consensus among most of her subjects as she carefully managed the transition from Catholic to Protestant conformity. This combination of authoritarianism and ambiguity provoked dissent and even resistance, as did the more preposterous pretensions of the cult of Elizabeth. As her reign neared its end and fears about the succession grew, the strains on her cult increased, erupting in an attempted coup in 1601. Yet Elizabeth and her advisers

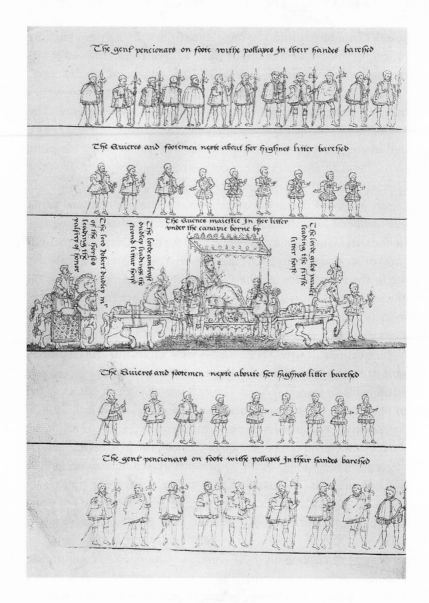

FIGURE 20

Elizabeth's coronation progress

By permission of the College of Arms; MS. M.6, f. 41v

were both adroit and lucky in responding to these conflicts, and they managed this last crisis and the succession itself very effectively. Finally, as we shall see, the cult of Elizabeth continued to flourish long after her death, sustaining devotion to "Queen Elizabeth of blessed memory" for decades afterward. Shakespeare's *Hamlet* was first performed during this final crisis of Elizabeth's reign, and it reflects many of the political anxieties of an unsettled succession as well as the religious ambiguities of the Elizabethan era. As noted earlier, the play also suggests the deep uncertainty surrounding ideas of sacred kingship in the English Reformation. The "divinity [that] doth hedge a king" (4.5.123) is hardly unassailable, and, unless a king "build churches," Hamlet doubts "a great man's memory may outlive his life half a year (3.2.129–131). Henry VII built such a church at Westminster Chapel, but that was a shrine to an older intercessory version of sacred kingship, now obsolete. *Hamlet* repeatedly raises doubts about the adequacy of commemoration, Protestantism's replacement for intercession for the dead. Nevertheless, as we shall see, the legacy of both the play and the monarch in whose reign it was first performed ultimately confirms the resilience and strength of what *Hamlet* calls the "rights of memory" (5.2.394).

Elizabeth's religious attitude was ambiguous from the beginning of her reign. Catholics were alarmed by her apparent disregard for the Mass and the Eucharist, and several foreign dignitaries were so scandalized that they boycotted the coronation, seeing signs of a return to the bad old days of Edward's reign. The Venetian emissary who reported the incident with the bishop described a Twelfth Night court masque consisting "[of] crows in the habits of Cardinals, of Asses habited as Bishops, and of wolves representing Abbots."[11] Another said that attacks on Catholic churches and processions by mobs went unpunished and that "squibs and lampoons, or ballads . . . are sold publicly, of so horrible and abominable a description that I wonder their authors do not perish by the act of God."[12] Yet here and elsewhere, Elizabeth sent deliberately mixed and confusing signals. Even while giving Protestant liturgical directions, she retained a Catholic bishop for her coronation and subsequently made this a point of her legitimacy, assuring the French ambassador that "she had been crowned and anointed according to the ceremonies of the Catholic church, and by

Catholic bishops, without, however, attending the mass."[13] She also went out of her way to assure other Catholic ambassadors that "she differed very little from us as she believed *that God was in the sacrament of the Eucharist,* and only dissented from two or three things in the Mass."[14] Her assurances of orthodoxy were somewhat encouraging, but another correspondent sounds more wistful than confident: "This Queen, referring no doubt to the beginning of her reign, told me that she had to conceal her real feelings to prevail with her subjects in matters of religion, but that God knew her heart, which was true to His service. She said other things to give me to understand that she was right in spirit, but not so clearly as I could have wished."[15] This lack of clarity became a hallmark of Elizabeth's religious settlement and was, in many ways, the secret of her success as a ruler.[16]

Mixed and confusing signals were a deliberate strategy, first proposed in an anonymous memorandum called the "Device for the Alteration of Religion" circulated at the beginning of Elizabeth's reign. Her accession in 1558 marked the third alteration of state in little more than a decade, and this memo, drawn up shortly afterward, seeks to address and forestall whatever "dangers may ensue upon the alteration" pending.[17] A shrewd assessment of conflicting interests leads to a balanced treatment of Elizabeth's foreign and domestic adversaries, and she is advised to make peace with France, ignore the pope, and consolidate her control over justices of the peace and the local militia. Major changes in religious doctrine and practice should be postponed until Parliament is summoned, and only minimal alterations, such as communion in both kinds, permitted in the interim. In its caution, the "Device" anticipates and recommends many of the evasions and ambiguities of Elizabeth's religious settlement. Marian bishops and clergy will oppose any change because they "see their own ruin" (196), the author says, but their unpopularity will force them to "conform themselves to the new alteration" (199). On the other hand, reformers who want more radical changes "shall be discontented, and call the alteration *a cloaked papistry* or *a mingle-mangle*" (197), but they will have no other source of support. Radical discontent should be ignored since "better it were that they did suffer than Her Highness or commonwealth should shake, or be in danger"

(200). Realizing, as Dekker does, "What an Earth-quake is the Alteration of State," the "Device" advises against any changes that would shake the state or throne and encourages muddled compromises in order to assure stability.

The Elizabethan religious settlement developed accordingly, defined from the start by murky ambiguities unsettling to more ardent reformers. Changes made in *The Book of Common Prayer* published at the beginning of her reign were seen by some as a step backward from progressive reform. The first vernacular prayer book of the English Reformation had been published at the beginning of Edward's reign in 1549, and even conservatives like Stephen Gardiner could find satisfaction in its vestigial Catholicism. It retained phrases emphasizing the incarnational and sacrificial aspects of the communion service, referring to "the bodye of our Lord Jesus Christ which was geven for the[e]."[18] Within three years, Cranmer had moved toward a less material view of the sacrament as commemoration in which spiritual reception is crucial; his new version of the prayer book speaks of "remembrance" and feeding "in thy heart by faith."[19] Moreover, the 1552 version also includes the so-called "Black Rubric," a commentary explicitly denying "any reall and essencial presence" in the sacrament.[20] Nevertheless, nostalgia for the Mass persisted despite these radical changes. Many Tudor subjects remained "habitual Catholics," reluctant to forego old ways of worship even while refraining from the risks of recusancy.[21] Alexandra Walsham shows that, while zealots on both sides denounced these "church papists" as superficial temporizers, the Elizabethan church was happy to nurture what its greatest theologian, Richard Hooker, calls "the feeble smoke of conformity."[22] Elizabeth's religious settlement blunted previous liturgical reforms by introducing yet another revision. The 1559 *Book of Common Prayer* removes the "Black Rubric" from its communion service and combines references to "the body of our Lord Jesus Christ which was given for thee" and to the "perpetual memory" of that sacrifice in a rite blending both sacrificial and commemorative elements.[23]

This 1559 prayer book was a classic Elizabethan compromise, and an even odder one was adopted the next year: the revival of the requiem. A growing belief in predestination, the subordination of human works to faith alone, and the abolition of Purgatory and indulgences made traditional Catholic funeral practices such as the requiem, the annual obit, and other intercessory rites and prayers unnecessary. Elizabeth's bishops, meeting in convocation in 1563, reaffirmed the Protestant position and denounced "sacrifices of Masses . . . for the quick and the dead" as "blasphemous fables, and dangerous deceits," and the requiem continued to be left out of the vernacular funeral service in *The Book of Common Prayer*.[24] Nevertheless, as Eamon Duffy points out, "Funeral practice was, inevitably, one of the areas where feeling remained most conservative" because mourners still wanted to retain contact and do something for their dead loved ones.[25] In an apparent concession to such feelings, Elizabeth in 1560 authorized publication of a Latin prayer book, the *Liber Precum Publicarum*, which included a requiem communion service or *"Celebratio coenae Domini, in funebribus, si amici & vicini defuncti communicare velint"* [the celebration of the Lord's Supper at funerals, if the friends and neighbors of the dead wish to communicate].[26] The Queen's letters patent acknowledge the inconsistency of this provision by simply declaring that "we have commanded to be appended certain special things fit to be repeated at the funerals and obsequies of Christians, the aforesaid Statute of the rite of public prayer . . . promulgated in the first year of our reign, to the contrary notwithstanding."[27]

Such liturgical double bookkeeping may have made the Elizabethan settlement more of a confusing *"mingle-mangle"* than a stately *via media*, but it succeeded in preserving stability by placating a conservative majority. More radical Protestants denounced its inconsistencies in precisely the terms the "Device" had predicted. One of the newly returned Marian exiles, John Jewel, writes to an associate that "doctrine is every where most pure; but as to ceremonies and maskings, there is a little too much foolery."[28] He and others were particularly upset by the candlesticks and crucifix in the royal chapel: "That little silver cross, of ill-omened origin, still maintains its place in the queen's chapel. Wretched me! This thing will soon be drawn into a precedent."[29] The Latin prayer book had been justified by its use in collegiate chapels, but students at Cambridge balked at having *"the Pope's Dreggs"* forced on them, and the requiem service and prayers for benefactors were finally dropped from a new version of the *Liber Precum* in 1571.[30] For the most part, however, church authorities brushed such criticisms aside. The next year, a Puritan manifesto denounced the English *Book of Common Prayer* as "an unperfecte booke, culled & picked out of that popishe dunghil, the Masse booke full of all abhominations."[31] The prayer book itself had answered such attacks from its first edition by justifying traditional ceremonies as a means of securing "decent order."[32] Opposition by "private judgment" was condemned in the Thirty-nine Articles as a threat to "the common order of the Church, . . . the authority of the magistrate, and . . . the consciences of the weak brethren."[33]

Royal supremacy remained a basic premise of "common order of the church," and the cult of Elizabeth became a crucial component in enforcing submission to "the authority of the magistrate." John Whitgift, Archbishop of Canterbury for Elizabeth's last two decades, proved the most effective enforcer of this order and authority. Whitgift was the scourge of his church's Puritan critics, crushing those responsible for the Marprelate pamphlets, and he also promoted increasingly lofty theories of divine right rule.[34] Obedience had always been a key principle of Tudor notions of sacred kingship, and it became the categorical imperative of perennial Elizabethan homilies.[35] Shortly after he became the Archbishop of Canterbury in 1583, Whitgift delivered a sermon making obedience the supreme commandment. He condemns "mockers" and "despisers of government," warning that "papists, anabaptists, and our wayward and conceited persons"are "naturally prone to speak ill of two kinds of persons: viz. Of bishops and magistrates," and he exhorts his auditors *"to be subject unto principalities and powers,* [and] *to obey magistrates"* because "All power is of God."[36] Whitgift chose his occasion carefully, delivering his sermon at Paul's Cross on November 17, 1583, "the anniversary day of Q. Elizabeth's coming to the crown."[37] By this midpoint of her reign, the queen's Accession Day had become the holiest feast day of a cult well on its way to becoming a "state religion."[38] The event was celebrated annually by bell ringing, court pageantry, and sermons whose claims for the monarchy grew more extravagant each year; in one of the last, the preacher claimed that England's monarchs are "absolute without limitation [and] accountable only to God for their

Actions."[39] Court ceremony was no less grandiose. Tilts and tournaments were staged to honor "a holiday which passed all the pope's holidays," and her courtiers strove to outdo one another in devotional pageants that became increasingly liturgical.[40] In 1575, her champion, Sir Henry Lee, presented himself as a hermit at prayer at her shrine, and at his retirement tilt in 1590, he erected a pavilion in the tiltyard "like vnto a Church, within it were many Lampes burning. Also, on the one side ther stood an Altar couered with cloth of gold and thereupon two waxe candles burning in rich candlesticks."[41] For some, the cult of Elizabeth encouraged the same reverence toward the royal presence once accorded to the real presence.

The pomp and solemnity of Elizabeth's court also prompted the same skepticism and defiance that had greeted earlier Tudor pretensions to sacred kingship. In one of his courtly devices, Sir Philip Sidney mocks the obsequious flatteries of Sir Henry Lee by presenting his uncle, the Earl of Leicester, in *The Lady of May*, as a "huge *catholicam*" praying to the queen with rosary in hand.[42] Others found the papist trappings of her cult no less offensive than the *"cloaked papistry"* of her religious settlement, and some denounced such practices as rank idolatry. A chaplain to another Puritan nobleman was arrested for claiming that *"To have a sermon on the queens day, and to give God thanks for her majesty was to make her a god,"* and he and his patron were interrogated and held until they both recanted.[43] That such criticisms continued anyway is clear from an Accession Day sermon in 1601 that stridently defends the day's *"ioifull exercises, and Courtly Triumphs"* against *"sclanderous Accusations"* that its *"church service, and those exercises and disports . . . are materially foolish, meere parasiticall, and spiced with flattery, which reduce men backe again to the fearfull abomination of heathenish Idolatrie."*[44]

The final years of Elizabeth's reign placed the most severe strain on these courtly tributes because fears of her imminent death were compounded by the lack of an heir and dread of an unsettled succession. Her cult suffered its gravest crisis in 1601, when Robert Devereux, the Earl of Essex, attempted a coup against her rule. Essex had been one of her personal favorites and a star in the tiltyard, determined to surpass all his rivals in professions of devotion to the Queen, but his divided loyalties and military ambitions wrecked his relationship with her.[45] For more than a decade, Essex had been secretly corresponding with James VI regarding the succession, promising to support the Scottish king as the legitimate heir to the English throne. By 1598, their relationship had become so well known that "the French ambassador could refer to the earl as the King's trusted intermediary at the English court."[46] The next year, he was given command of a huge army, but he failed to suppress revolt in Ireland, and, after returning against orders, he was placed under house arrest for nearly a year. Facing financial ruin after his release, he attempted an abortive coup on February 8, 1601. His aims were never entirely clear, but he wrote to James in advance, assuring the Scottish king that he "shall be declared and acknowledged the certain and undoubted successor to this Crown and shall command the services and lives of as many of us as undertake this great work."[47] When the earl's revolt failed, he was arrested and tried for treason. At his trial he was accused of declaring to his followers that the "Queen was now an old woman . . . and was no less crooked . . . in mind than she was in body," a shocking affront to the doctrine of the queen's two bodies as well as the cult of Elizabeth.[48] Essex could hardly be pardoned for such offenses, and he was executed for high treason on February 25, 1601.

Hamlet first appeared amid this crisis between 1599 and 1601, and its portents of "some strange eruption to our state" (1.1.72) and allusions to "the late innovation" (2.2.331) undoubtedly reflect topical fears of an unsettled succession and the risks of a coup d'état. Stuart Kurland makes a convincing case for the relevance of the Essex revolt and the succession crisis, and Steven Mullaney relates the play's notorious misogyny to "the gap or internal fissure that was, in the 1590s, increasingly apparent between the queen's two bodies."[49] At the same time, Hamlet also evokes more long-range anxieties about "the cease of majesty" (3.3.15). Elizabeth's entire reign was pervaded by such anxieties. Indeed, it had been one long succession crisis, as Patrick Collinson has shown, because from the start, she refused to marry, had no heir, and was threatened by perennial conspiracies.[50] This prolonged crisis was linked to a religious settlement that, in Collinson's words, "settled nothing."[51] The Elizabethan settlement had remained an ambiguous compromise from its inception, haunted, in the words of Diarmaid MacCulloch, by a "ghost . . . of an older world of Catholic authority and devotional practice."[52]

Hamlet also comprehends the deeper theological ambiguities of the Elizabethan compromise. Stephen Greenblatt has recently discussed the central importance of Catholic beliefs in Purgatory and the real presence for the work, showing how contradictory vestiges of these doctrines "intensify the play's uncanny power."[53] Certainly *Hamlet* is haunted by its own ghost from an older religious world, one claiming to return from a suppressed Catholic Purgatory where his "foul crimes . . . / Are burnt and purg'd away" (1.5.12–13) and demanding perverse, and perhaps diabolical, acts of intercession.[54] Later on, the consolation of a requiem for Ophelia is briefly invoked and then withdrawn, leaving mourners with a sense of "maimed rites" (5.1.212).[55] The chief mourners seem as distressed by the funeral arrangements as they are by the death of their loved ones: Hamlet is nearly mad with melancholy at the unseemly brevity of his mother's mourning; Laertes is furious at the ignominious obscurity of his father's "hugger-mugger" interment (4.5.84) and enraged at the priest for denying his sister "sage requiem" (5.1.230). As I have argued elsewhere, this is a play obsessed with getting a decent burial, which nobody seems able to do.[56] By the end, intercession for the dead degenerates into revenge and the ritual slaughter of the last act, aptly described as a "black mass."[57] Commemoration may be a more feasible alternative and "Remember me" a clearer imperative, but the strength of memory is doubtful throughout the play. Hamlet has reason to doubt that "a great man's memory may outlive his life half a year" (3.2.129–130). In various ways, the play traces the troubled transition from intercession to commemoration described by Ralph Houlbrooke, who claims that Protestants remained divided and uncertain about both functions: "English reformers, after pulling down the structure of inherited observances, failed (partly because of their own divisions) to create a generally accepted way of death thoroughly imbued with their own spirit."[58] *Hamlet* can easily be seen as a textbook demonstration of the theological irresolution and liturgical failure of the Elizabethan religious settlement.

Finally, Shakespeare's play raises profound questions about the basic premises of Reformation sacred kingship. Hamlet suggests that a "great man's memory" might last longer, "But by'r lady a must build churches then, or else shall a suffer not thinking, on with the hobby-horse, whose epitaph is 'for O, for O, the hobby-horse is forgot'" (3.2.130–133). Without a church and its traditional intercessory system, it is not clear that the royal memory will long survive "the cease of majesty." The first Tudor built Westminster Chapel, one of the greatest churches of Shakespeare's time and a splendid shrine for traditional sacred kingship. The last was buried there, but, as we shall see, her grave, like her father's, was an unquiet one. Can "a great man's"—or great woman's—memory survive without a church and its traditional intercessory practices? Hamlet suspects not, and in some ways his own funeral, the play's fourth and last, seems to confirm his own suspicions. "The rite of war" ordered by Fortinbras seems at least vaguely menacing, even if his arrival is not staged as an invasion.[59] The man ordering this rite seems more intent on asserting his own "rights of memory in this kingdom" (5.2.394) than honoring Hamlet's.

Nevertheless, as we shall see, both the last act and the entire play powerfully vindicate Hamlet's own "rights of memory." They also suggest, through a typical Shakespearean pun, that the "rites of memory" developed by the Elizabethan compromise were more effective than many assume. Finally, Hamlet sustains the numinous aura of the "divinity [that] doth hedge a king" (4.5.123) despite the cynical calculation of the king claiming it. The dramatic ironies of such claims are deeply unsettling, making it nearly impossible to assess their validity. They encourage and even demand the "negative capability" that John Keats describes as Shakespeare's greatest accomplishment, leaving us suspended between belief and doubt, mystification and disenchantment.[60] Norman Rabkin describes this state of mind as "complementarity," and shows how it enables us "at almost any point in the play to read its world as godless or divine."[61] Shakespeare thus affirms some of the mysterious force of sacred kingship not through propagation of its claims but through an ambiguous equivocation.[62]

Nowhere is this dramatization of the ambiguous power of sacred kingship more intense than in Hamlet's closet scene, which William Kerrigan aptly describes as the "greatest scene in Hamlet, the greatest of Shakespeare's plays."[63] Here the prospect of a miraculous royal survival in which the legitimate king returns "in his habit as he lived" (3.4.137) briefly sustains a kind of reunion of the king's two bodies. Hamlet is stunned by this apparition, and he hints at its extraordinary possibilities when he exclaims, "His form and cause conjoined, / preaching to stones/Would make them capable" (3.4.125–127). In a world where so much is "out of joint," such a conjunction might be "a consummation/Devoutly to be wished" (3.1.63–64), but the meaning of this *hendiadys*, one of the play's recurrent rhetorical devices that is itself a form of conjunction, is not immediately clear.[64] Form can be taken as a synonym for the king's pitiful appearance, while the *cause* of his return is presumably that "foul and most unnatural murder" (1.5.25) revealed only to Hamlet at their earlier encounter. In the first scenes, everyone else sees the ghost, but Hamlet alone hears the cause, and he refuses to disclose it. Now the reverse holds true as he tells Gertrude that the king was murdered, but she cannot see the ghostly form. Recognition of both form and cause could resolve these discrepancies and make the hidden truth manifest to others besides Hamlet, perhaps sparing him of the need to act alone. At the same time, the abstract, almost scholastic quality of both nouns suggests a more philosophic, even cosmic significance.[65] Rosemond Tuve's analysis of the links between *image* and *cause* in Renaissance poetics is useful because it suggests the large intellectual significance of the latter word, which she defines as an "untranslatable Elizabethan term" bound up with occult meanings, the "Aristotelian 'final cause,' " and ultimately, Renaissance philosophy's "definition of the real."[66] The reality that Hamlet hopes might be revealed by this conjunction occupies a comparably higher ontological and spiritual plane.

Hamlet's reference to stones made capable certainly gives his hopes greater theological significance. He alludes to the gospel of Luke 19:37–40, where Christ is greeted by "the whole multitude of the disciples," who spread their garments on the road and rejoice "with a loude voice, for all the great workes yt [that] thei had sene, Saying, Blessed *be* the King that cometh in the Name of the Lorde"; told by the Pharisees to silence his disciples, Christ replies, "I tel you, that if these shulde holde their peace, the stones wuld crye."[67] By invoking this passage, Hamlet indirectly identifies his father's ghost with the incarnate Christ at a moment of messianic triumph and wants him to be recognized as a "King who comes in the name of the Lord." He may also be grasping at the consolation offered by various Hebrew prophets. At the nadir of the Babylonian captivity, Habakkuk assures the chosen people that the wicked will be punished without need for human assistance because "the stone shal crye out of the wall, and the beame out of the timber shal answer it" (Habbakuk 2.9–11). If the ghost could move even stones to cry out against all that is rotten in Denmark, his son might be spared the need to act. For Hamlet, this supernatural visitation might provide a miraculous solution to his miseries.

At the same time that he yearns for a regal apotheosis, Hamlet also wants a kind of sacramental miracle, suggested by that intriguing term, *conjoined*. That word's usual connotation is the sacrament of marriage, reinforced by references to Gertrude as the "imperial jointress of this warlike state" (1.2.9) whom Claudius finds "so conjunctive to my life and soul" (4.7.14). But here and elsewhere matrimonial implications acquire a mystical political significance when applied to a king. James I described his relationship to England accordingly in his first speech to Parliament, declaring that "God by his almighty Providence hath preordained . . . that union which is made in my blood. . . . What God hath conjoined then let no man separate. I am the husband and the whole Island is my lawful wife."[68] James is invoking the doctrine of the king's two bodies, and Edmund Plowden, the Tudor jurist who gave this doctrine its definitive formulation, uses the same term: "For when the Body politic of King of this Realm is conjoined to the Body natural, and one Body is made of them both, the Degree of the Body natural and of the Things possessed in that Capacity is thereby altered, and the Effects thereof are changed by its Union with the Body and do not retain their former Degree, but partake of the effects of the Body politic. And the Reason thereof is, because the Body Natural and the Body Politic are consolidate into one, and the Body politic wipes away every Imperfection of the other with which it is consolidated."[69] Plowden describes a sacramental alteration of state akin to transubstantiation, and Hamlet clearly desires a comparable conjunction. As noted earlier, many reformed theologians use the same term to define the Eucharist.[70] Calvin and others insisted that such a conjunction permitted a spiritual but efficacious reception even while denying a local presence. Richard Hooker agrees, allowing that while Christ's "actuall *position*" cannot be "restrained and tied to a certain place," his presence in the sacrament "by *waie of conjunction* is in some sort presence"; indeed, the Eucharist "is by vertue of that conjunction made the bodie of the Sonne of God . . . [and] this giveth it a *presence of force and efficacie* throughout all generations of men."[71]

In the closet scene, Hamlet desperately longs for a sacramental miracle along these lines, a supernatural conjunction of the king's two bodies that, in the words of Plowden, "wipes away every Imperfection" through what Hooker calls a mystical *"presence of force and efficacie."* Unfortunately, no such miracle occurs. The ghost proves evanescent, confusingly sinister, and only partially visible. While it almost becomes a real presence for Hamlet, Gertrude sees nothing but "vacancy" and "incorporal air" (3.4.117–118). For her, the ghost of the legitimate king is no more substantial than Claudius is for Hamlet, a king who "is a thing . . . of nothing" (4.2.27–29) and, despite the promise of his vision, form and cause are not firmly conjoined: "The body is with the King, but the King is not with the body" (4.2.26–27). In some ways, the closet scene is cruelly anticlimactic, tantalizing Hamlet with visions of a supernatural *rex ex machina* who then disappears, never to be seen again. The apparition leaves Hamlet unhinged and, despite the promise of conjunction, has an oddly divisive and debilitating effect.[72] Hamlet fears that the ghost will "convert/My stern effects. Then what I have to do/Will want true colour—tears perchance for blood" (3.4.128–130). Until its appearance, Hamlet's "stern effects" had never been more forceful, his words "like daggers" entering Gertrude's ears (3.4.95) and reducing her to abject penitence, but now he fears that her suspicions of his sanity will divert her from her "trespass" to his "madness" (3.4.148). The division between them widens throughout the rest of the scene as Hamlet reverts to the tortuous double talk that is his specialty. He tells his mother first to confess and repent, and then, if she cannot, to be a hypocrite ("Assume a virtue if you have it not" [162]); his ultimate double message commands her not to do what "I bid you do" (183) but instead let Claudius "Make you to ravel all this matter out" (188). Like Claudius, Hamlet remains "to double business bound" (3.3.41), and the best he can hope for by way of conjunction is the meeting of "two crafts" in "one line" (3.4.212).

The theatrical impact of the ghost's last appearance is profoundly ambiguous. Hamlet wants a royal Eucharistic miracle in which his ghostly father becomes a real presence. He gets something more indeterminate. Gertrude does not see or hear it, but we do, according to the stage directions, for the ghost both enters and speaks. For both Hamlet and the audience, form and cause are conjoined, however fleetingly. Shakespeare places us in the same position that Dürer assigns his viewers in the miracle of St. Gregory. In that picture, those sharing a space with the central figure remain oblivious to the supernatural action transpiring before his—and our—eyes (figure 4). Yet, while Dürer's illustration assures us that we can believe what Gregory sees, since God and his angels are shown witnessing Christ's presence on the altar, the ghost's reality in Shakespeare's closet scene is far more dubious. Critical opinion is divided. Robert Watson argues that the ghost is an illusion, and, entitling his chapter on *Hamlet* "Giving Up the Ghost," he concludes that the play urges us to do just that because "Calvinist theology created a blank wall between the living and the dead."[73] Marjorie Garber gives her chapter the same title, but she concludes that enacting that phrase is not so easy, citing Jacques Lacan to explain the uncanny hold of a "presence without present of a present which, coming back only *haunts.* The ghost, *le re-venant*, the survivor, appears only by means of figure or fiction, but its appearance is not nothing, nor is it a mere semblance."[74] The ghost is indeed "not nothing," for it assumes a palpable and unnerving form. Some sort of conjunction still occurs for Hamlet and the audience, permitting and imposing the kind of relationship described by Beza, which has such "true and solid subjects and objects in wholly natural things, as father and son."[75]

The ghost never returns, but Hamlet takes its place and acquires some of its uncanny powers in the last act, permitting a kind of communion of the living and the dead. In a notorious syntactic impossibility, Hamlet twice declares that "I am dead" (338; 343). Tantalizing all who "look pale and tremble at this chance, / That are but mutes or audience to this act" with intimations of what "I could tell you" (339–342), he reprises his father's earlier role of a ghost come from the grave who "could a tale unfold" (1.5.15) while declining to do so. Hamlet also repeats his father's categorical imperative, "Remember me" (1.5.91). When Horatio tries to join him in death, Hamlet implores his friend to "Absent thee from felicity awhile,/And in this harsh world draw thy breath in pain/To tell my story" (5.2.352–354). His dying appeal to "Report me and my cause aright/To the unsatisfied" (344–345) suggests he too wants his own "form and cause conjoined." A report that could get Hamlet and his motives "aright" would constitute an awesome conjunction of form and cause. It might even attain the force of what Michael Neill calls "metamorphic narration," a "persistent motif in the play"; as Neill notes, the closet scene and the last scene hold out the prospect of an "untellable tale— one so astonishing and compelling that, could it only be told it would leave its audience utterly changed."[76] Although Hamlet is pained by "all that remains untold as though his life were an unfinished story still struggling for expression," the play itself has told that story and thus stands as a "living monument" to Hamlet; its conclusion provides, as Neill says, considerable "consolatory power."[77] This is certainly true, but before considering its effects, we must turn to the forces arrayed against this memorial.

Poor Horatio has been assigned a difficult, if not impossible, task. No eulogy or funeral rite could ever match Hamlet's own "dying voice" (308), and his promised recitation of "carnal, bloody, and unnatural acts" (335) could never achieve the intensity of all that we have seen.[78] In any case, his attempt to honor Hamlet's memory is quickly disrupted by the arrival of Fortinbras. The Prince of Norway, whose father was slain by old Hamlet in single combat thirty years earlier, has been intent from the start on recovering "by strong hand/ And terms compulsative those foresaid lands/So by his father lost" (1.1.101–103). Deflected from invading Denmark by his uncle's agreement with Claudius, he now returns victorious from battle in Poland, only to find his opponents dead. The "warlike noise" (5.2.302) of his approach interrupts Hamlet's request of Horatio to "tell my story" (5.2.301) and also disrupts the benediction begun by Horatio: "Good night sweet prince,/And flights of angels sing thee to thy rest.—/ Why does the drum come hither" (5.2.312–314). Such an approach suggests that Norway's original belligerence toward Denmark has not abated, as do the orders for Hamlet's somewhat incongruous military funeral:

> Let four captains
> Bear Hamlet like a soldier to the stage,
> For he was likely, had he been put on,
> To have proved most royally; and for his passage,
> The soldiers' music and the rites of war
> Speak loudly for him.
>
> (5.2.349–354)

The likeliest occasion to put Hamlet to such a proof would have been a rematch over the contested lands, an aim Fortinbras may never have relinquished. Hamlet has given his "dying voice" (5.2.308) to Fortinbras, and Horatio is eager to speak for his dead friend "whose voice will draw on more" (5.2.346). However, before he can do so, Fortinbras asserts his own authority, indifferent to any conferred by his dead rival: "For me, with sorrow I embrace my fortune. / I have some rights of memory in this kingdom, / Which now to claim my vantage doth invite me" (5.2.342–345). Fortinbras is neither as coarse nor as murderous as Claudius, but his brisk self-assertion still recalls one who can "with wisest sorrow think on him / Together with remembrance of ourselves" (1.2.6–7).[79] Whatever Horatio has to say, Fortinbras is now the man in charge, taking control in Denmark on the basis of his own ancestral claims.

Hamlet ends by ceding a throne with no heir to a foreign ruler whose parent was killed by one of its previous occupants, anticipating a comparable resolution of England's own contemporary succession crisis.[80] Within a few years, James VI of Scotland would succeed the childless queen who executed his mother. Elizabeth also gave James her "dying voice," but he kept insisting on his own ancestral rights as the "next and sole Heire of the Blood royall of this realme."[81] Whether or not he foresaw each of these developments in detail, Shakespeare certainly understood the tumultuous impact of such alterations of state and the division of loyalties they demand; Rosencrantz and Guildenstern are ground up between "the pass and fell incensed points / Of mighty opposites" (5.2.61–62), and Horatio might be in danger of the same fate.[82]

The death of Elizabeth placed many of her powerful subjects in a comparable predicament. Thomas Dekker's *Wonderful Year* makes the moment of transition sound particularly nerve-wracking: "Vpon Thursday it was treason to cry God saue king *Iames* king of *England* and vppon Friday hye treason not to cry so. In the morning no voice hearde but murmures and lamentation, at noone, nothing but shoutes of gladnes and triumphe."[83] For some, the dilemma proved fatal. Robert Devereux, the Earl of Essex, sided prematurely with James VI. The failure of the earl's revolt threw James into a panic, but Robert Cecil, the late earl's rival, quickly took up the secret correspondence and managed to allay the king's anxieties.[84] Cecil proved no less adept at managing the succession itself, summoning the Privy Council after Elizabeth's death and reading the proclamation declaring James I King of England. He made certain that James was informed of Lord Cobham's "ordinary axiom both since the death of Essex and before. . . . That it was not possible for any man to be a loyal subject to his gracious mistress, that respected King James in any degree, either present or future."[85] Cecil then accused Sir Walter Ralegh and Lords Grey and Cobham of conspiring to block James's accession. Cecil was a virtuoso at managing divided loyalties, but even he had awkward moments. *Hamlet* begins and ends with state funerals, and, as Shakespeare shows, these are often delicate affairs, demanding a precarious balance of "delight and dole" (1.5.13). Cecil had to tell his new ruler that funeral protocol and the doctrine of the king's two bodies required the late monarch to be interred before the successor arrived; Elizabeth's reign lasted as long as her mortal body remained unburied. In explaining these arrangements to James, he and the other privy councilors declared that "we are a little troubled when we consider how it will stand together in one letter that we should both profess our infinite longing for you and yet in the same propound some courses to retard your coming hither."[86] James agreed to hang back until Elizabeth was interred, proceeding only as far as York, but he still demanded that Cecil deliver enough regalia to permit a properly majestic entry into "the second city of our kingdom."[87]

King James himself strove for a decorous blend of "delight and dole," vowing to abstain from any "ceremony of our own joy . . . as long as her body is above ground," and promising to have "all things observed which may testify the honour we bear to her memory."[88] Once she was buried, however, he moved as aggressively as Fortinbras to assert his own "rights of memory in this kingdom." The cynical view of the "rights of memory" as a "rite of war" waged by survivors against those they succeed and motivated largely by "remembrance of ourselves" was certainly confirmed by the ambiguous tribute he paid to his predecessor. Elizabeth was originally interred at her own request, as Julia Walker has shown, near her grandfather, Henry VII, and her stepbrother, Edward VI. The last Tudor monarch chose to be buried at the center of Westminster Chapel, the shrine constructed by the first. King James, however, had other designs on this space, and he pursued them with a shocking disregard for hers. He dug up Elizabeth's casket from its original gravesite and placed her in a side chapel with her Catholic stepsister, Mary.[89] He then erected a monument to Elizabeth with marble effigy and canopy (figure 21), completed in 1606, but he subsequently built a more expensive, attractive, and loftier memorial for Mary Stuart directly across the nave. In 1612, his mother's remains were "translated" from Peterborough, where Elizabeth had had her buried after her execution, to Westminster, "where the kings and queens of this realm are usually interred."[90] Walker convincingly argues that James aimed to marginalize his predecessor by relocating her in a side chapel with her childless stepsister and making their burial site into an architectural dead end.[91] In his most brazen move, James claimed Elizabeth's original gravesite, behind Henry VII in the middle of Westminster Chapel, for his own. Aligning himself with the patriarch of the Tudor dynasty, he aimed to establish his central place as the head of a reinvigorated and more fruitful royal line.[92] James intended, as Jennifer Woodward explains, to transform Westminster Chapel into "a royal necropolis for the Stuart dynasty," and it gradually acquired "an impressive collection of Stuart heirs," including Prince Henry, Princess Elizabeth of Bohemia, and the children of Charles I as well as the remains of Charles II and his offspring.[93] James planned an especially grand monument for himself at the center, but it was never built (figure 22).[94] Indeed, James's ambitious designs went awry well before his demise, thwarted in part by the tomb he built for Elizabeth. That memorial ultimately affirmed the surprising autonomy and longevity of her "rights of memory in this kingdom."

FIGURE 21

Tomb of Elizabeth I

Copyright: Dean and Chapter of Westminster

FIGURE 22

Inigo Jones, design for James's tomb

By permission of the Provost and Fellows of Worcester College, Oxford

James's reign was initially greeted with great enthusiasm because he was Protestant, male, and married with three healthy children, and, in the words of one contemporary, "the people were generally weary of an old woman's government."[95] Over the course of his reign, however, his popularity diminished and nostalgia for the days of "good Queen Bess" increased. By his last years, discontent with his rule sparked a so-called "Blessed Revolution" when renewed tensions with Spain fueled a saber-rattling ardor for the glories of the Armada defeat, and James found himself stalked by a number of Elizabethan ghosts.[96] Tracts like *Robert Earl of Essex His Ghost Sent from Elizium* and *Sir Walter Rawleighs Ghost, or Englands Forewarner* were published in 1624 to sound the call to arms against Spain. Portraits of Elizabeth as an Amazonian St. George or a celestial spirit (figure 23) circulated, fostering fond memories of her reign's chivalric glories.[97] An especially striking image of Elizabeth's tomb appears in a book published during James's last year on the throne, Samuel Purchas's *Purchas his Pilgrimes* (figure 24). James and Charles are shown on the left of the frontispiece, the heir apparent confidently straddling the realm. On the right, there is an astonishingly Hamlet-like portrait of James's older son, the late Prince Henry, shown meditating upon a skull and mourning at the monument of his true kindred spirit. Revered as the Stuart paragon of chivalric heroism and Protestant zeal, Henry had been regarded by many opponents of James's foreign policy as a worthier heir to Elizabeth than either his father or his brother, and his death left many deeply bereaved.[98] The appearance of all these ghosts *"sent from Elizium,"* an Elysian realm renamed in honor of his predecessor, cast a shadow over the end of his reign. James's sleep was disturbed by nightmares of George Buchanan, his old tutor and a defender of popular resistance, "who seemed to check him severely as he used to do," and cannons fired at Gray's Inn during the Christmas revels in 1622–23 so frightened him that he awoke shouting "Treason! Treason!" putting "the city . . . in an uproar."[99] These revenants from James's past clearly retained considerable power.

Elizabeth's monument itself took on an odd prominence in the events of the Blessed Revolution. In 1621, a petition against the abuses of James's reign was placed "into the hand of Queen Elizabeth's statue in Westminster by an unknown person."[100] Addressed to "the

PER TAL VARIAR SON QVI.

Lo here her Type, who was of late, the Propp of Belgia, Stay of Fraunce:
Stayner Foule Faithe Shield, and Queene of SAGE, Of Armes, and Learning, FAITE, and Chaunce
In briefe; of woman, nere was seene so greate a Prince, so good a Queene

ELIZABETHA REGINA·

FIGURE 23

Francis Delamar after Nicholas Hilliard, Elizabeth as celestial spirit

By permission of the Folger Shakespeare Library

FIGURE 24

Hakluytus Posthumus or Purchas his Pilgrimage, title page

By permission of the Folger Shakespeare Library

blessed Saint Elizabeth of famous memory" and signed by the late queen's "perpetual and faithful beadsmen, and daily orators, the poor distressed Commons of England," it asks for her help in seeking celestial relief from courtly corruption.[101] The verse proposes to "make the name of great Eliza/Equal the name and glory of Maria" by building a monument that "shall make proud Rome/On pilgrimage to come, and at thy shrine/To offer gifts as to a thing divine." Those who composed and placed the "Petition of Long Afflicted England" on Elizabeth's tomb self-consciously evoked older intercessory practices long associated with Westminster's royal sepulcher, but they were also mocking Romish superstition; presumably, few petitioners spent the night squeezed into the base of her tomb. The older medieval system of sacred kingship had been shattered by the Reformation's assault on monastic foundations and intercessory prayers, the cult of the saints and pilgrimages, shrines, and even sacred space itself. A few Catholic stalwarts kept hoping for its revival; on hearing of Mary Stuart's new monument, a Scottish seminarian wrote from Bologna that "I hear her bones, lately translated to the burial place of the Kings of England at Westminster, are resplendent with miracles."[102] James certainly disappointed such hopes, for he had no interest in cultivating his mother's legend or supporting her religion; once again, he was more intent on asserting his own "rights of memory in this kingdom" rather than hers.[103]

Elizabeth's tomb never became a site of pilgrimage or miracles, but it remained an object of veneration, perpetuating her cult beyond the grave in a less spectacular fashion. According to Thomas Fuller, a seventeenth-century church historian, engravings of her "fair tomb in Westminster" (figure 25) spread throughout the realm, "the lively draught whereof is pictured in most London and many country churches, every parish being proud of the shadow of her tomb, and no wonder, when each loyal subject erected a mournful monument for her in his heart."[104] Something like a reversal of the process described by Walter Benjamin occurs here, as the mechanical reproduction of "the shadow of her tomb" preserves and disseminates its aura rather than dissipating it.[105] The cult of Elizabeth continued to flourish despite and ultimately because of her grave's dislocation. These pictures of Elizabeth's "fair tomb in Westminster" extend "the

FIGURE 25

Elizabeth's monument; Henry Holland, *Heruuologia*, D4r

By permission of the Folger Shakespeare Library

migration of the holy" by displacing older notions of sacred space and real presence from an actual site while preserving the feelings they arouse through the circulation of images and other mementos; sacred space is thus internalized. Indeed, memorial objects of this sort permit a sustained if tenuous connection between the living and the dead, allowing commemoration to acquire some of the power of intercession and reinforcing "the rights of memory."

A similar phenomenon occurs in Shakespeare's plays as a result of their eventual detachment from the Elizabethan and Jacobean stage. As Stephen Greenblatt explains, these scripts have achieved a "marginal and impure autonomy" by becoming literature, allowing their readers more intense "absorption"; accordingly, "Shakespeare's imagination yields forth its sublime power not to a spectator but to one who, like Keats, sits down to reread *King Lear*."[106] The image of Hamlet has maintained its strong hold on our imaginations long after his last act, and he overwhelms all his rivals, including those striving for the last word. Fortinbras makes his claim at the play's end, but who leaves the theater thinking of him? Moreover, Hamlet replaces and surpasses his father's ghost, making the paternal imperative, "Remember me," wholly unnecessary. Indeed, this figure has so dominated modern memory that he has acquired a kind of palpable historical power. The great Romantic critic, William Hazlitt, eloquently describes the extraordinary impact of what is finally a fiction: "Hamlet is a name; his speeches and sayings but the idle coinage of a poet's brain. What then, are they not real? They are as real as our own thoughts. Their reality is in the reader's mind. It is *we* who are Hamlet. The play has a prophetic truth, which is above that of history."[107] Such a truth sounds like religious transcendence, but Hazlitt describes a "reality" firmly anchored in "our own thoughts." He offers a reception theory of a real presence resulting not from transubstantiation but from a meeting of minds over time. Such merely human conjunctions may be evanescent and tenuous, but they can still sustain relationships between the actual and the imaginary, as well as the living and the dead. In this sense, the play's last act allows something like the conjunction described by Richard Hooker, one sustaining "a *presence of force and efficacie* through all generations." *Hamlet* thus confirms the power of both the rites and "rights of memory."

CHAPTER 4

Idolizing Kings
John Milton and Stuart Rule

The People, exorbitant and excessive in all thir motions,
are prone ofttimes not to a religious onely, but to a civil kinde
of Idolatry in idolizing thir Kings.
—John Milton, *Eikonoklastes* (1649)

FIGURE 26
Eikon Basilike, sig. A4v, B1r
By permission of the Folger Shakespeare Library

The first Stuart monarch was initially greeted, as we have seen, with great enthusiasm and relief. According to one contemporary, "the contentment of the people is unspeakable, seeing all things proceed so quietly, whereas they expected in the interim their houses should have been spoiled and sacked."[1] Another reported that "the people both in citie and counties fynding the iust feare of 40 yeres, for want of a known successor, dissolved in a minute, did so reioyce, as few wished the gracious Quene alive again: but as the world is [they too] were inclined to alteracion of government."[2] Once safely past, alterations of state could prove immensely popular. The prospect "of a known successor" was, in fact, one of James's greatest attractions. That he was married, the father of three healthy children, and Protestant assured his subjects that future alterations could be governed by the reliable principle of hereditary succession. Looking back on the previous century, Sir Francis Bacon sees the Tudor dynasty as a series of bizarre aberrations, spawning "the strangest variety that in like number of successions of any hereditary monarchy hath ever been known. The reign of a child; the offer of a usurpation, . . . the reign of a lady married to a foreign Prince; and the reign of a lady solitary and unmarried." In contrast to the "barren princes" sired by Henry VIII, James I was properly progenitive; Bacon accordingly expected the Stuart line to endure forever.[3] James himself promoted this image of patriarchal and dynastic durability in his speeches and treatises and, as we have seen, his rearrangement of Westminster Chapel was prompted by the same aim.

Hereditary succession was, in James's view, the inviolable principle of divine right and the incarnation of sacred kingship. In *The Trew Law of Free Monarchies*, he insists that "the duty and allegiance which the people sweareth to their prince is not only bound to themselves but likewise to their lawful heirs and posterity, the lineal succession of crowns being begun among the people of God and happily continued in divers Christian commonwealths."[4] He regarded it as the basis of his own claim to the English throne, repeatedly insisting that his status as the "next and sole Heire of the Blood royall of this realme" derived from his "own lawful, unstained, and unblemished" descent from the Tudor dynasty.[5] James attributed to consanguinity a mystical, even sacramental power that conferred absolute legitimacy on his succession and unified the realm in his person. In a speech to his first Parliament, he declared that "God by his almighty Providence hath preordained . . . that union which is made in my blood. . . . What God hath conjoined then let no man separate. I am the husband and the whole Island is my lawful wife."[6] He thus linked hereditary right to divine right, assuring that "the state of monarchy is the supremest thing upon earth; for kings are not only God's lieutenants upon earth, and sit upon God's throne, but even by God himself they are called Gods."[7] Other authorities in his government endorsed these arguments, including England's Chief Justice, Sir Edward Coke, who writes that "the king's matie, in his lawfull, juste and lineall title to the crowne of Englaunde, comes not by succession onelye, or by election, but from god onelye . . . by reason of his lineall discente"; such claims made divine right an "inherent birthright" that overrode both statute and common law.[8] Consanguinity's legal and political preeminence is affirmed in Sir Thomas Craig's *Right of Succession to the Kingdom of England* (1603), which says that "Rights of Blood . . . are not subject to any Civil bond."[9] After the Restoration, Stuart apologists would take these claims to even grander heights, maintaining that the crown always descended through "the sacred channel of birth-right and proximity of blood" and adding that "this political capacity being of that sublimity, . . . is no wayes subject to any human imbecilities of infamy, crime, or the like, [because] it draweth all imperfections and incapacities whatsoever from that natural body, where-with it is consolidate, & (as it were) consubstantiate."[10] This equation of the body and blood of the monarch with Christ's body and blood in the Eucharist makes hereditary succession explicitly sacramental, a form of political consubstantiation.

The sermons and pageantry of the Stuart court took up these themes with a new fervor, conflating the real and royal presence in a comparable manner.[11] In 1620, the Bishop of London, aptly named John King, launched a drive to restore St. Paul's Cathedral as "the chamber of the British Empire" with a sermon declaring the church's resemblance to "the bodie of the King, a building not made with hands, but shaped of flesh and bloud" and inviting James to "afford his own bodily presence, and set himself to the worke [and] . . . marke the pillars and pinnacles, and make it his princely care."[12] In Inigo Jones's plan for its reconstruction, the cathedral's west portal would have a portico topped with statues of English kings, and the space before it was to be cleared to serve as a site for the "triumphal conclusion" of a royal civic progress (figure 27).[13] Around the same time, Jones rebuilt the Whitehall Banqueting House, making it into a shrine of Stuart sovereignty. Modeled on Solomon's temple, it was subsequently adorned with paintings by Rubens depicting James's apotheosis (figure 28). Here too, the royal presence comes to resemble the real presence in paintings suffused with the belligerent melodrama of the Counter-Reformation. In similar paintings commissioned by the Hapsburgs, Rubens shows Eucharistic Truth trampling Luther and Calvin along with Rebellion and Falsehood as she points to the words of the consecration, *Hoc est Corpus Meum* (figure 29).[14] Rubens's painting of James's triumph as *Rex Pacificus* over the forces of War and Discord (figure 30) depicts a comparable triumph in Whitehall.

The new Whitehall became the venue for increasingly solemn courtly rituals, including healing ceremonies, celebrations of the feast of the Order of the Garter, entertainment of foreign embassies, and court masques by Ben Jonson and others.[15] In his "Dedication of the King's New Cellar to Bacchus," Jonson assigns its wines a sacramental as well as hospitable function, and Whitehall festivities acquire the unifying power of the Eucharist as Jonson invites the god to bless the "causes and the Guests too" whenever James holds court:

> Be it he hold Communion
> In great Saint *Georges* union;
> Or gratulates the passage
> Of some wel-wrought Embassage:
> Whereby he may knit sure up
> The wished peace of *Europe*:
> Or else a health advances,
> To put his Court in dances.[16]

Indeed, as Stephen Orgel has suggested, court masques "included strong elements of ritual and communion, often explicitly religious," and under the Stuarts, their ritual aspirations grew more extravagantly

FIGURE 27

Inigo Jones, design for reconstruction of St. Paul's Cathedral

By permission of the British Library; 55.1.8

FIGURE 28
Peter Paul Rubens, *Apotheosis of King James*, Whitehall

Crown Copyright: Historic Royal Palaces; Reproduced by permission of Historic Royal Palaces
under licence from the Controller of Her Majesty's Stationery Office

FIGURE 29

Peter Paul Rubens, *Triumph of Eucharistic Truth*

Copyright: Museo del Nacional del Prado, Madrid

FIGURE 30

Peter Paul Rubens, James as *Rex Pacificus*, Whitehall

Crown Copyright: Historic Royal Palaces; Reproduced by permission of Historic Royal Palaces
under licence from the Controller of Her Majesty's Stationery Office

solemn—and poignantly deluded.[17] In one of his last performances before the Civil War, Charles I appeared in William Davenant's *Salmacida Spolia* (1640) as Philogenes, the "Lover of his People" whose occult healing powers dissipate the forces of Fury and Discord and restore England's "halcyon days." Its finale shows a tableau reminiscent of Raphael's *Disputa* (figure 5), its massive architectural monuments capped by cloud-filled vistas (figure 31) as "a heaven opened full of deities; which celestial prospect, with the Chorus below filled all the whole scene with apparitions and harmony."[18] In the royal masque, the king would become the focal point, much as the host does in Raphael's painting.

Charles Stuart's ceremonial enthusiasm was even greater than his father's, and it was reinforced by an earnest self-righteousness and piety. He assured his Archbishop of Canterbury near the beginning of his reign that "we have observed that the Church and State are so nearly united and knit together that though they may seem but two Bodies, yet indeed in some relation they may be accounted but as one. . . . This nearness makes the Church call in the help of the State to succour and support her . . . and . . . the State call on for the service of the Church both to reach that duty which her members know not, and to exhort them to, and encourage them in that duty they know."[19] He remained committed to this close partnership of church and state throughout his reign, for, in the view of his admirers, "he was not satisfied in being religious as a particular Christian but would be so as a king . . . by giving ornaments and assistances to the external exercise . . . that so, carnal minds, if they were not brought to an obedience, might yet to a reverence."[20] Charles's desire to assist "carnal minds" renders his sense of the duties of sacred kingship explicitly incarnational. In contrast to James I, his son was particularly enthusiastic about the royal touch and performed it with great fervor.[21] For Charles, the feast of the Order of the Garter and its patron, St. George, was the highest of holy days and the supreme manifestation of his vision of sacred kingship: in its solemnities, "the interdependence of Church and state was perfectly summarized . . . and presided over by Charles, both king and priest."[22] The king's devotion to what Jonson calls "Communion/In great Saint *Georges* union" is evident in the prominence of its insignia and ceremonies in so many of his

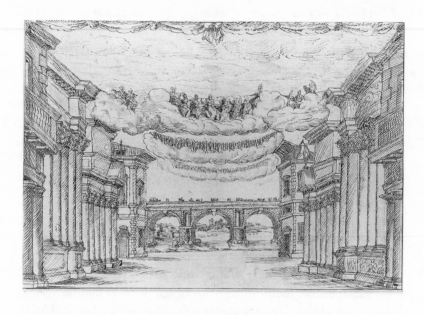

FIGURE 31
Inigo Jones, designs for *Salmacida Spolia*, final scene
Devonshire Collection, Chatsworth. Reproduced by permission of the Duke of Devonshire
and the Chatsworth Settlement Trustees. Photograph: Photographic Survey,
Courtauld Institute of Art

paintings.[23] Indeed, he made the medal of St. George his most solemn final bequest to his son at his execution.[24]

Charles appointed an Archbishop of Canterbury who shared his enthusiasm for religious ceremony and the sanctity of *jure divino* sovereignty. Determined to revive the "beauty of holiness," William Laud set out to rebuild decayed churches and to elevate and enclose altars with communion railings. His concern with religious decorum led him to stress the affinity of sovereignty and the sacred, preaching that the church was "God's own house and presence chamber" and "the presence chamber on earth of the king of heaven and earth."[25] Other preachers also emphasized the connection between celestial and courtly protocol, insisting that, even as "the Chaire of estate loses not its relation and due respect, though the King be not alwaies there," the altar must be venerated as God's throne even when no service is being conducted.[26] But Laud's fixation on "God's more especial presence" in the church and its sacraments moved beyond a concern with decorum to deeper sacramental beliefs.[27] When Laud proclaims that "the altar is the greatest place of God's residence upon earth, greater than the pulpit; for there 'tis *hoc est corpus meum*," he revives powerful ideas of a real and local presence.[28] Indeed, many Caroline court sermons recall the raptures of Eucharistic miracles and their visions of "the comely corse." Fulke Robarts, for example, preaches "that the neerer a man approacheth to that table, whereupon he *Seeth with his eyes* the sacred body & blood of his Lord and Saviour *Jesus Christ* layd forth for him, to feede upon, to everlasting life: the more should he find himselfe ravished with devotion."[29]

Laud's campaign to restore an aura of sanctity to the English church horrified most reformers, as did his harsh persecution of nonconformity, and his efforts to deprive the laity of control over the clergy gravely offended many powerful laymen. His enemies eventually retaliated with force. After more than a decade of Personal Rule by Charles without Parliament, Puritan indignation finally erupted in the Long Parliament of 1640. One of their first acts was to impeach the king's counselors, Lord Strafford and Archbishop Laud, for treason, accusing both of conspiring in a nefarious "popish plot" to subvert English law and religion.[30] The Root and Branch Petition formulated the grounds for their hostility, attacking Laud for turning "the Communion-table altar-wise . . . [while] terming the altar to be the mercy-seat, or the place of God Almighty in the church, which is a plain device to usher in the Mass"; the petition also denounced Laud's "christening and consecrating of churches and chapels" and of "fonts, tables, pulpits, chalices, churchyards, and many other things" as an attempt at "putting holiness in them."[31] Having been muffled for more than a decade, Calvinist objections to carnal fantasies of a "local presence" resounded with full-throated ferocity, and Laud was imprisoned in the Tower in 1640 and executed in 1645.

In the wake of Laud's fall, John Milton stepped forth as one of the archbishop's most eloquent opponents. In 1641, he began publishing volumes of political tracts denouncing the bishops' authority and promoting reform. In 1642, he complained of having been "Church-outed by the Prelats" (CPW 1:823) while declaring that his own poetic talent was "the inspired guift of God," comparable in power to "the office of a pulpit" (CPW 1:816). In 1644, Milton imagined his own parliamentary address in Areopagitica, and, following the lines of the Root and Branch Petition, he appeals for "the reforming of Reformation it self" (CPW 2:553). Near its conclusion, he turns his attention to the Assembly of Divines then meeting at Westminster to devise a new religious settlement and warns them against the mistakes of old priests and new presbyters who would impose sectarian conformity. Their venue in the old abbey might tempt them to try to confine religion to a fixed location, but, he writes, they should not "devote our selves again to set places, and assemblies, and outward callings of men; planting our faith one while in the old Convocation House, and another while in the Chappell at Westminster; when all the faith and religion that shall be there canoniz'd, is not sufficient . . . to edifie the meanest Christian, who desires to walk in the Spirit, and not in the letter of human trust, for all the number of voices that can be there made" (566–567). Milton derides Westminster Chapel as a haunted house of traditional religion where ghosts from its graves threaten to join forces with the living enemies of an ongoing Reformation. They do not frighten Milton, who says that "though Harry the 7. himself there, with all his liege tombs about him, should lend them voices from the dead, to swell their number" (567), no genuine Christian should heed their sound. In Milton's exhortation, the forces of reaction must not be strengthened by the influence of dead kings.

Milton's attack is an act of bold iconoclasm, mocking both Westminster's sacred space and the mystique of monarchy. It parallels the attacks mounted by other Puritans who had advanced from petitioning against the "consecrating of churches and chapels" in 1640 to physical assaults in 1643. Popish books and images like Charing Cross were burned and toppled, and Westminster Chapel itself was attacked, its stained glass shattered and the altar before Henry VII's tomb demolished by Sir Robert Harley.[32] Three years later, in 1646, Parliament ordered the demolition and sale of the stones for Henry VIII's tomb at Windsor to cover war costs.[33] Royalists denounced such acts as sacrilege, but some considered the destruction of Tudor monuments fit punishment for Henry VIII's dissolution of monasteries and destruction of shrines.[34] In his *History and Fate of Sacrilege*, Henry Spelman blames his own family's prolonged disputes over former monastic properties on "meddling with consecrated places," and he attributes the Tudors' dynastic extinction and loss of the crown to "the Ocean of Iniquity and Sacrilege" that engulfed the reign of Henry VIII.[35] The title page of Sir William Dugdale's *Monasticon Anglicanum* (1655–73) contrasts a devout medieval monarch (who may resemble Charles I) kneeling before a high altar with the willful Henry VIII, who declares *"Sic volo"* ("Thus I will") as he points to a monastic ruin (figure 32); Charles I had ordered Dugdale, the Garter King-of-Arms, to compile the records of these suppressed foundations and their imperiled monuments in order to preserve them.[36] The book's solid architectural frontispiece stands as an emblem of its value. A collection like Dugdale's becomes an equivalent of sacred space itself, its splendid illustrations, like the pictures of Elizabeth's tomb, acquiring something of the aura of the original site.

As the war neared its end, charges of sacrilege grew more strident on both sides. England's Civil War was one of Europe's last religious wars, and passions aroused by its climactic battles became increasingly apocalyptic. As John Morrill explains, "many officers and soldiers were convinced that God was responsible for their victory in the first civil war; that it was, in a sense, a trial by battle in which both sides put themselves under the judgement of God. For such men, the

FIGURE 32

Sir William Dugdale, *Monasticon Anglicanum*, frontispiece

By permission of the Folger Shakespeare Library

king's decision to begin a new war was no less than sacrilege—an attempt to challenge God's decision. It left the way clear to his trial and execution. He had delegitimized himself and his office: he was a 'Man of Blood,' one who had so offended God that he had to be destroyed."[37] Denunciations of the king led to demands for his death in sermons such as the one delivered by Thomas Brook in the House of Commons citing Numbers 35:33: "Ye shall not pollute the Land wherein ye are; for blood it defileth the Land, and the Land cannot be cleansed of the blood that is shed therein, but by the blood of him that shed it."[38] Regicide was seen as the only way to purge the realm.

After the king's execution in 1649, these same charges were turned against the regicides with a vengeance. *They* were now denounced as men of blood, and their assault on the Lord's anointed was decried as the worst sacrilege of all, comparable to the Crucifixion itself. The ultimate iconoclastic assault on monarchy had ironically transformed the dead king into an even more powerful icon. Charles's absence rendered him a more compelling presence in death than he had ever been in life. This paradoxical effect was confirmed by the success of the best-selling *Eikon Basilike*, in which the king is presented as the "father and patron" of the church determined to defend it against "the sacrilegious eyes of many cruel and rapacious reformers."[39] Indeed, as its supreme governor, he thinks that "both offices, regal and sacerdotal, might well become the same person," but, as a prince and priest deprived of both his sovereignty and his chaplains, "I am sorry to find myself reduced to the necessity of being both or enjoying neither" (144). Faced with execution, the king resolves to emulate Christ and exchange the heavy "crowns of this world . . . for the substance of that heavenly kingdom with Himself" (177); "If I must suffer a violent death with my Saviour," he declares, "it is but mortality crowned with Martyrdom" (254). The identification with Christ permits Charles to indulge in a triumph of passive aggression as he declares his gratitude for "that charity which is the noblest revenge upon, and victory over, my destroyers. By which, I thank God, I can both forgive them and pray for them, that God would not impute my blood to them further than to convince them what need they have of Christ's blood to wash their souls from the guilt of shedding mine" (176). Charles is depicted here and elsewhere as a Christlike "Man of

Sorrows" whose ostentatious pathos recalls late medieval images of the Savior, and the fixation on blood and wounds recalls some of the techniques of "vulneral sacramentalism."[40] An enameled locket with his portrait backed by a bloodstained remnant of his garments provides a vivid example of such an image in its recollection of the sacred heart of Jesus (figure 33).

Other royalist publications were even more bloody and bellicose in their calls for revenge. In one, civil war and regicide have drowned the realm in a "Red Sea" of blood, and such horrors will not soon abate because, though "som have thought it good,/To quench my raging *flames* with guiltless *Bloud/. . .* that fire which was made/With bloud at first, can be with bloud allay'd."[41] The verses in another collection alternate between vulneral sacramentalism and bloodthirsty pugnacity: one poet declares his *"Faith* boy'd up" by the king's "sacred blood," whereas the Earl of Montrose threatens to write the King's *"Epitaph* with the *Bloud* and *Wounds"* of his enemies in a poem allegedly penned "with the point of his sword."[42] Several tracts combine motifs of sacramental and sacrificial kingship, attributing miraculous powers to royal blood. *The Cry of the Royal Blood Against the English Parricides* denounces the soldiers who sold the king's "hairs, mud colored with his blood, and bloody chips of the block on which the royal neck had lain when it was about to be cut," but his remains were still venerated as precious relics.[43] *A Miracle of Miracles: wrought by the blood of King Charles the First . . . upon a Mayd at Detford* describes the cure of a mortally ill blind girl with a "Handkercher . . . which had been dipped in the Kings blood on the day that he was beheaded."[44] Nevertheless, grief and misery prevail as the authors "consider what a precious Jewell we lost" in a realm ruled by those who "can kill the kings friends; but here are none that can cure the Kings Evill."[45] Similarly, *The Cry of the Royal Blood* describes a church bereft of its supreme governor, its true priests, and even its sacraments, yearning for the healing touch of the king of kings: "With these sores, these ulcers, the sick Anglican Church labors in a wretched fashion and feels its entrails eaten up, and moans, as it calls upon the help of the greatest doctor for the remedy of the greatest evil."[46] Still other works exult in exhibitionist pathos, *The Princely Pellican* assuring that the "way to cure wounds, is not to *close* but discover them."[47] Surrounded by regalia and perched atop a

FIGURE 33
Locket with portrait of Charles I
Copyright: The Trustees of the National Museums of Scotland

pedestal, the pelican, a traditional symbol of Christ, plunges its beak into its breast to nurture its fledglings with its own blood and declares, "*Queis pario, pereo*" ("I perish that you flourish") (figure 34). Both the emblem and the ensuing text, which includes "sundry choice OBSER-VATIONS, Extracted from His MAJESTIES *Divine Meditations,*" aim to reveal the king's benign "Royall intendments" toward his subject by rendering his "breast . . . transparant."[48]

None of these other works was as effective in arousing sympathy for Charles as the *Eikon Basilike*. As Lois Potter has shown, readers of the King's Book were convinced that it, "like his blood, had come from his heart."[49] Such convictions made the book a memorial more enduring and vibrant than any shrine; in the words of one admirer, Charles's work is not only "the Repertory of all his Actions . . . [and] the quintessence of knowing zeal" but also the "greatest *monument of Piety* of any *Kings* since the Creation."[50] Even John Milton, its most articulate detractor, had to concede its extraordinary value and vitality for defeated royalists, describing "this Book as the best advocat and interpreter of his own actions, and . . . the chief strength and nerves of thir cause" (*CPW* 3:340). In an uncanny and alarming manner, the *Eikon Basilike*'s success shows how Milton's own reverence toward books returns to haunt him. In one of *Areopagitica*'s most stirring and beloved passages, he writes that books "are not absolutely dead things, but doe contain a potencie of life in them," and he compares censorship to homicide because it threatens to destroy the "precious life-blood of a master-spirit, embalmed and treasured up on purpose to a life beyond life" (*CPW* 2:492–493).[51] Few books in Milton's lifetime were as successful as the *Eikon Basilike* in preserving the "life-blood" of a royal "master-spirit" to a purpose much larger than his life.

Milton's aptly named *Eikonoklastes* was commissioned as a response to the *Eikon Basilike*, justifying the execution of Charles I while attempting to counter the propagandistic success of the King's Book. Milton attacks the *Eikon Basilike* as an idolatrous exercise, noting that "the People, exorbitant and excessive in all thir motions, are prone ofttimes not to a religious onely, but to a civil kinde of Idolatry in idolizing thir Kings" (*CPW* 3:343). Even the king's former enemies are "ready to fall flatt and give adoration to the Image and Memory of this Man" (*CPW* 3:344). Milton condemns such adulation as the

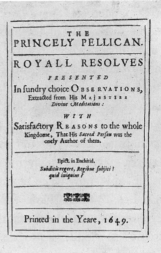

FIGURE 34

The Princely Pellican, frontispiece and title page

By permission of the Folger Shakespeare Library

result of mere "Stage-work" (530) and insists that "quaint Emblems and devices begg'd from the old Pageantry of some Twelf-nights entertainment at *Whitehall*, will doe but ill to make a Saint or Martyr" (343). He also chides King Charles for drawing inspiration from William Shakespeare, "the Closet Companion of these his solitudes" (361). Yet most readers were dazzled by the histrionics of the King's Book.[52] Indeed, its "Stage-work" recalls and surpasses Shakespeare's, in some ways. One of the book's most powerful features is its emblematic frontispiece; in some editions, it was combined with tendentious explanation (figure 35). This combination of image and gloss, whether implicit or explicit, resembles the conjunction so ardently desired by Hamlet. Shakespeare's prince is convinced that the mere sight of the murdered king's "form and cause conjoined,/ Preaching to stones, would make them capable." In the wake of Charles's execution, many royalists shared similar hopes, convinced that all "must now weep blood; these stones by teares doe call/For vengeance."[53] King Charles's last word was "remember," repeating the injunction of Hamlet's father, and many suspected his intentions were no less vindictive. Royalists denied this, the Bishop of London claiming that the king meant "that if I could gain access to the prince his son and heir, I should bear him this last command of his dying father: that when he is restored to his kingdom and power, he should pardon you, the authors of the king's death."[54] Milton is certainly skeptical of such claims, and he is certain that the *Eikon Basilike* means to stir up "the people to bring him that honour, that affection, and by consequence, that revenge to his dead Corps, which hee himself living could never gain to his Person" while "intimating, That what hee could not compass by Warr, he should atchieve by his Meditations" (342). He describes the oblique strategy fitfully embraced by Hamlet, who also renounces war's straightforward belligerence for a more devious and meditative revenge, but the results in Shakespeare's play are more tragically ambiguous. The *Eikon Basilike* may not be great literature, but its passive aggression proves more crudely effective: form and cause are successfully conjoined, arousing desires for revenge in a much larger audience.[55]

Milton's *Eikonoklastes* and his other republican tracts aim to dismantle such compelling Shakespearean "Stage-work" by exposing the

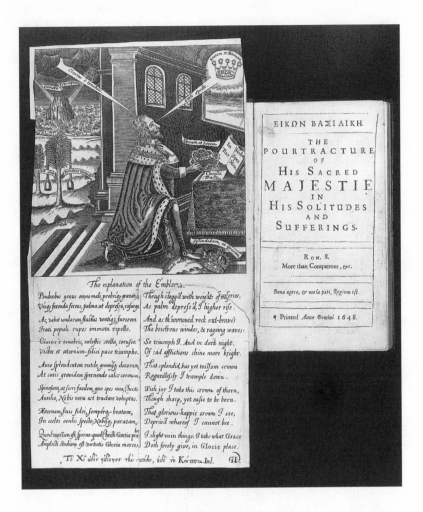

FIGURE 35

Eikon Basilike: "The Explanation of the Embleme," frontispiece and title page

By permission of the Folger Shakespeare Library

Eikon Basilike's ghostwritten fraudulence, plagiarism, and histrionics while revealing its belligerent ulterior motives. By disjoining the book's theatrical form from its vindictive cause, Milton attempts a radical deconstruction of the props of sacramental kingship. The task proves difficult because even some of the king's fiercest adversaries were vulnerable to sovereignty's idolatrous allure in the wake of his execution. In the *Tenure of Kings and Magistrates* (1650), Milton attributes the pity aroused by the king's misfortunes not to any "true, and Christian commiseration, but either levitie and shallowness of minde, or else a carnal admiring of worldly pomp and greatness, from whence they see him fall'n" (*CPW* 3:193), and he is particularly hard on the craven remorse of the Presbyterians. He attacks the hypocrisy of those who once bore "armes against thir king, devested him, disannointed him, nay, curs'd him all over in thir Pulpits and thir Pamphlets" but now condemn the execution (191). The wretched excess of their curses is matched by their horror at the consequences. After reducing him to the status of an "ordinary man" by "doom of Law . . . in the sight of God and his people" and cursing him "to perdition worse then any *Ahab* or *Antiochus*" (234), they now "acquitt . . . absolve . . . , [and] unconfound him, though uncoverted, unrepentant, unsensible of all thir pretious Saints and Martyrs whose blood they have so oft laid upon his head: and now againe with a new sovran anointment, can wash it all off, as if it were as vile, and no more to be reckon'd for then the blood of so many Dogs in a time of Pestilence" (235–236). Milton mocks the Presbyterians for resorting to the same sanguinary rhetoric and overblown hagiography in both their demands and their laments for the king's death, which are so saturated with blood and unction and primitive priestcraft that he finds them disgusting. The sacramental pretensions of their anointing and disanointing confirm Milton's conviction that "New *Presbyter* is but old *Priest* writ large."[56]

In justifying regicide, Milton rigorously distinguishes between the person and the office, king and kingdom, sovereignty and justice. In each of his political treatises, he is determined to shatter the false conjunctions wrought by the image of the king enshrined in the *Eikon Basilike*. In the *Eikonoklastes*, Milton explicitly sets out to separate royal cause from royalist forms, condemning those belated adherents who "never lov'd him, [and] never honour'd either him or his cause, but as they took him to set a face upon their own malignant designes" (3:345). He also maintains that the king's individual cause has no connection to a higher cause, opposing "the single person of a Man . . . against his own Majesty and Kingship" (525) and the king's "self-will'd conscience" to the "Kingdoms good" (418). In *The Tenure of Kings and Magistrates*, "the King is a name of dignity and office, not of person" (3:233) and "Justice is the onely true sovran and supreme Majesty upon earth" (237). He adds that "law and reason abstracted as much as might be from personal errors and frailties" must be "set above the Magistrate" (200). Most important, Milton maintains that the regicides are backed by a higher power, since "if God and a good cause give them Victory, the prosecution whereof for the most part, inevitably draws after it the alteration of Lawes, change of Government, [and] downfal of princes with thir families" (192). For Milton, the Commonwealth's victory is an alteration of state far more profound and legitimate than any brought about by the death or deposition of kings. Attempts at godly rule that remain fixated on monarchy are hamstrung by contradictions, as the hypocrisy of Presbyterians indicates: after striving to divest and disanoint their royal opponent, they then try to cleanse his sins "with a new sovran anointment" of martyr's blood. Milton is confident that the Commonwealth's "good cause" can never be conjoined with such corrupt and decadent forms.

That confidence was soon disappointed. Though Milton and several others welcomed the execution of Charles I and the establishment of a republic, most of his contemporaries were not ready for such radical alterations of state and were eager for a return to royalty.[57] The political and religious divisions besetting the Commonwealth proved unmanageable, prompting the establishment of a Protectorate with "somewhat of a monarchical power in it."[58] As Roy Sherwood suggests, when Oliver Cromwell became Lord Protector in 1653, he became "king in all but name."[59] Although he repeatedly declined the crown, he held court in an increasingly grand manner, and his second investiture in 1657 took place in Westminster Abbey on St. Edward's coronation throne; in Clarendon's account, it "had nothing wanting to a perfect formal coronation but a crown and an archbishop."[60] The first defect was supplied at Cromwell's funeral, when his effigy was displayed in solemn state, bedecked with crown and scepter, and he was buried amid Westminster's royal fellowship of death in what one contemporary called "Seventh *Henry's*, or *Cromwell's* Chapel."[61] This designation did not last long; neither did the burial arrangements. Cromwell's older but less able son, Richard, briefly succeeded him in 1658, affirming principles of primogeniture and hereditary rule, but his claims were soon trumped by those of Charles II, restored to the throne in 1660. Shortly afterward, the Protector's body was disinterred, mutilated, and expelled from Westminster's sacred precincts. Cromwell's burial and its sequel show sacred kingship could entangle some of its opponents in its traditions. The English monarchy's fiercest enemy took its holiest shrine as his final resting place, even briefly claiming it as his own, but, in other ways, the shrine first claimed and then brutally disowned him.

John Milton never succumbed to monarchy's allure. In the interval between Cromwell's death and the Restoration, he denounced the Protectorate and made a last desperate pitch for republican rule.[62] In *A Ready and Easy Way to Establish a Free Commonwealth*, Milton's revulsion against monarchies where "a king must be ador'd like a Demigod" (7:425) is undiminished, and he asks how a supposedly Christian king

> can assume such extraordinarie honour and worship to himself, while the kingdom of Christ, our common King and Lord, is hid to this world, and such *gentilish* imitation forbid in express words by himself to all his disciples. All Protestants hold that Christ in his Church hath left no vicegerent of his power; but himself without deputie, is the only head thereof, governing it from heaven. . . .
>
> (7:429)

Nevertheless, Milton seems resigned to defeat. Although he includes a defense of *"the good Old Cause"* (462), he ends with a sorrowfully familiar jeremiad, crying out "with the Prophet, *O earth, earth, earth*: to tell the verie soil it self, what her perverse inhabitants are deaf to" (462–463). He still hopes that there are some Englishmen "whom God may raise of these stones to become children of reviving libertie," but he worries that most will seek "a captain back for *Egypt*" and embrace their servitude (463). As his hopes fade, Milton prays for God's intervention, but he doubts that his own preaching will make stones capable. Despite its hopeful title, *The Ready and Easy Way* foresees no facile conjunction of political form and godly cause.

Any hopes Milton entertained for republican rule were soon defeated by the restoration of Charles II. Milton was denounced as a "blind beetle that durst affront the Royal Eagle," his books were burned, and orders were issued for his arrest.[63] He was apprehended and imprisoned late in 1660 but was spared execution and freed after friends paid his fine and convinced his enemies that his blindness was punishment enough. According to one early biographer, he still lived "in perpetual terror of being assassinated, though he had escaped the talons of the law," and for a time he remained "so dejected that he would lie awake whole nights."[64] Amid these misfortunes, he composed *Paradise Lost*, publishing the first edition in 1667; *Paradise Regained* and *Samson Agonistes* appeared in print a few years afterward, in 1671, and a second edition of *Paradise Lost* was published shortly before his death in 1674. In *The Reason of Church Government*, Milton had declared himself willing to set aside his epic literary ambitions in order "to imbark in a troubl'd sea of noises and hoars disputes" (*CPW* 1:821). Now in defeat, more than twenty years later, he returned to the epic tasks once reluctantly relinquished, turning from prose polemic to sacred verse.

As Mary Ann Radzinowicz notes, readers have disagreed about the significance of this adjustment to defeat for many years, some, like Samuel Coleridge, seeing Milton's late poetry as a renunciation of politics while others, like William Blake, read it as a form of "politics encrypted."[65] Radizinowicz concludes that neither interpretation is adequate because Milton's political perspective in the poem is both detached and engaged. He consistently denounces rulers who impose "empire tyrannous" (12:32) on a primal state of "fair equality" (12:26), and he includes a jibe at monarchs that some contemporaries found alarmingly topical. *Paradise Lost* first appeared at a time of ominous national disasters including the great fire of London, an outbreak of the plague, and a sequence of military defeats. Amid all these other calamities, a solar eclipse in 1666 struck many as one more sign that the end of the world was at hand. In his discussion of this context, Nicholas von Maltzahn says that all these events revived the millennial apprehensions of the Civil War and inspired "a chorus of publications . . . urging repentance and spiritual self-renewal both individual and national."[66] Alarmed by these volatile exhortations, church authorities felt it necessary to warn against paying too much attention to "Planetary Aspects, or great Conjunctions," urging instead, "Fear not the Signs of Heaven, but the Sins on Earth."[67] *Paradise Lost* audaciously encompasses both, and it includes among its heavenly portents "the dim Eclipse [which] disastrous twilight sheds/On half the Nations, and with fear of change/Perplexes monarchs" (1:597–599). One episcopal censor read this as a barely veiled threat to Stuart rule by an inveterate enemy and tried to block publication.[68] In writing a poem determined to "justify the ways of God to men" (1:26), Milton must have found it tempting to stoke fantasies of providential intervention, especially at a time when celestial conjunctions portended alterations of state. Nevertheless, the signs and wonders of *Paradise Lost* are generally muted and enigmatic, and the poem refrains from inflaming apocalyptic hopes and fears. Politics are neither renounced nor transcended but remain indefinitely unsettled. Struggle is continuous and victory delayed until, in the words of Michael's final prophecies in *Paradise Lost*, "the day/Appear of respiration to the just,/And vengeance to the wicked" (12:538–540), that is, Judgment Day. All other climactic resolutions are consistently postponed.

Having surveyed in his last two books the whole of world history, Milton rejects attempts by worldly authorities of church and state to claim access to God's truth in the here and now. He denounces the successors to the first apostles who seek to turn "the sacred mysteries of Heav'n/To thir own vile advantages" (12:509–510). Such fraudulent disciples embrace "Secular power, though feigning still to act/By spiritual" (517–518) and strive to reduce "from that pretense,/Spiritual Laws by carnal power" (520–521). He also denounces secular authorities who claim to rule by divine right. After the flood, Adam's descendants enjoy a brief golden age until Nimrod usurps "Dominion, undeserv'd/Over his brethren" (12:25–29). Nimrod succeeds in enslaving his fellows by arrogating supernatural authority, "from

Heav'n claiming second Sovranty" (69). Milton remains adamantly opposed to the pretensions of sacred kingship, and he shows how this vicious cycle of tyrannous presumption and degenerate abasement prompts God to abandon his wretched creatures:

> Thus will this latter, as the former World,
> Still tend from bad to worse, till God at last
> Wearied with their iniquities, withdraw
> His presence from among them, and avert
> His holy Eyes; resolving from thenceforth
> To leave them to thir own polluted ways.
>
> (12:105–110)

God's withdrawal of his presence from the world may be the Fall's most painful consequence in *Paradise Lost*, almost driving Adam to despair. Michael's final visitation is crucial to Milton's justification of "the ways of God to man" (1:26) because it clarifies—as much as possible—the mystery of our relationship with God. The archangel teaches Adam to accept an absence that is not absolute while adjusting to a divine presence that is not all there and not "real" in conventional theological terms. At first, Adam laments his expulsion from paradise because

> . . . departing hence,
> As from his face I shall be hid, depriv'd
> His blessed count'nance; here I could frequent,
> With worship, place by place where he voutsaf'd
> Presence divine, and to my Sons relate;
> On this Mount he appear'd, under this Tree
> Stood visible. . . .
>
> (11:315–321)

Adam had once hoped to build "many grateful Altars . . . in memory, / Or monument to Ages" (11:323–326).[69] Moreover, his fall from Eden's heights reduces his political and patriarchal authority, literally leveling the original hierarchy. Michael says that Paradise might have been

Perhaps thy Capital Seat, from whence had spread
All generations, and had hither come
From all the ends of th'Earth, to celebrate
And reverence thee thir great Progenitor.
But this preëminence thou hast lost, brought down
To Dwell on even ground now with thy Sons.

(343–348)

At the same time, Michael is quick to assure Adam that the divine "Omnipresence fills/Land, Sea, and Air" (336–337); and, though harder for man to discern, God remains ubiquitous:

. . . in Valley and in Plain
God is as here, and will be found alike
Present, and of his presence many a sign
Still following thee. . . .

(349–352)

Adam must "surmise not then/His presence to these narrow bounds confin'd/Of Paradise or *Eden*" (341–342). In the visions that ensue, Michael shows Adam Paradise destroyed by the flood in order "To teach that God attributes to place/No sanctity, if none be thither brought" (11:836–837).

Paradise Lost thus affirms one of the Reformation's fundamental premises: there is no sacred space. The final books repeatedly reinforce this lesson, displacing Adam from both Paradise itself and the attachments formed there.[70] A new, less direct relationship to God becomes the basis of Adam's faith, which finds its first expression in the prayers offered at the beginning of Book XI. Inspired by God's "Prevenient grace" (11.3), Adam and Eve pray; their appeal is presented by the Son, who now serves as humanity's "great Intercessor . . ./Before the Father's Throne" (19–20), and the Father immediately accepts this appeal, proclaiming "all thy request was my Decree" (47). Adam cannot see or hear this transaction, and, though faith in God's grace comes relatively easy for him, confidence in the value of human prayer is hard; as he tells Eve in his explanation of his uncertainty:

Eve, easily may Faith admit, that
The good which we enjoy, from Heav'n descends;
But that from us aught should ascend to Heav'n
So prevalent as to concern the mind
Of God high-blest, or to incline his will,
Hard to belief may seem. . . .

(141–146)

Nevertheless, the experience of prayer and submission combined with God's grace enables him to regain his faith in their connection as "persuasion in me grew/That I was heard with favor" (152–153). Stanley Fish astutely observes that Adam's evolving credo is the same one Milton advances in the *Christian Doctrine* where, citing Hebrews 11:1, he says that faith is "the substance of things hoped for where by 'substance' is understood as a certain persuasion of things hoped for, as if they were not only existing, but actually present."[71] In his epistle to the Hebrews 11:1, Paul says that "faith is the substance of things hoped for, the evidence of things not seen." This was a favorite text of an earlier reformer, Peter Martyr, who used *virtue* as a synonym for *substance* in Eucharistic disputation in order to avoid all carnal connotations and to indicate a quality more active than inert.[72] Like Milton, Martyr also says, "it is proper to faith to grasp things absent as though present."[73] Faith draws its grace and strength from a God-given attitude or conviction rather than a thing or substance. That Adam has achieved this faith is clear from his last exchange with Michael: "Henceforth I learn, that to obey is best,/And love with fear the only God, to walk/As in his presence" (12:561–563). For Milton, human experience of God's real presence must be conditional rather than absolute.

In *Paradise Lost*, the divine presence is no more immediate in heaven than on earth. The poem takes its readers to a celestial height where the Son can approach as "great Intercessor . . ./Before the Father's Throne" (19–20), but even here our point of view is oblique. The chronology and stage directions of this heavenly assembly are notoriously disorienting.[74] Earlier, when proclaiming the Son's "great Vice-gerent Reign" (5:609), the Father addressed the angelic host "as from a flaming Mount, whose top/Brightness had made invisible" (598–599); in heaven as on earth, "as" and "as if" shift God's location to the realm of the analogous and conditional. As William Myers says of this scene, "Actor and action are programatically displaced. . . . God cannot be used to underwrite presence in the poem any more than he can be relied upon to constitute its centre. In the poem, in discourse, he can never be *there*."[75] Neither Father nor Son needs to be all there because their harmonious reciprocity makes full presence unnecessary. Mutual glorification is the source of their greatest strength: "First, Highest, Holiest, Best, thou always seek'st/To glorify thy Son, I always thee,/As is most just" (723–726). Myers explains that in *Paradise Lost*, the Son "effaces himself before a reality greater than himself," while "the will of the Father [is] expressed by, and therefore concealed within, the sign of the Son."[76]

In 1671, Milton published *Paradise Regained*, and this odd sequel to his great epic brings the Son down to earth. In doing so, it paradoxically displaces this enigmatic divine presence even more. The poet dramatizes human salvation by turning not to the incarnation or Crucifixion, the usual high points of the gospel narrative, but to the more cryptic and austere forty-day fast in the desert, where paradise is regained by "one man's firm obedience fully tried" (1:4). In *Paradise Lost*, when Michael prophesies the rematch of the Son and Satan on earth, he warns Adam not to expect heroic combat or sacrificial pathos: "Dream not of thir fight/As of a Duel, or the local wounds/Of head or heel" (12:386–388); "local wounds" were the mainstay of older renditions of Christ's real presence on earth, ostentatiously displayed in the artwork of vulneral sacramentalism. Michael and Milton renounce all efforts to locate the source of our salvation. In *Paradise Regained*, each of Satan's three temptations also tries to place Jesus somewhere, confining him first to a real presence, then to a royal presence, and finally to a full, unmediated divine presence. The Son resists those attempts rigorously and ingeniously and thus defeats his adversary.

In their first encounter, Satan appears disguised as an old rustic and asks the Son to turn stones to bread. The Son refuses, saying that "Man lives not by Bread only, but each Word/Proceeding from the mouth of God" (349–350). Faith makes such nourishment sufficient, and the Son rebukes Satan for his transparent bad faith, "Knowing who I am, as I know who thou art" (355–356). Thus exposed, Satan concedes that his temptation of mankind was initially prompted by malicious envy and a desire "to gain/Companions of my misery and woe" (396–397). Misery loves company, and companions, as the word's etymology indicates, are those who break and share bread together. The companionship Satan seeks is a debased travesty of communion, much as the miracle he demands is a coarsely material form of transubstantiation. When Jesus resists implication in these crude deformations, Satan asks only "To see thee and approach thee, whom I know/Declar'd the Son of God" (384–385) as a real presence. Satan's perverse sacramental and sacerdotal aspirations become clear when he brazenly compares himself to "the Hypocrite or Atheous Priest" whom God permits to "minister/About his Altar, handling holy things" (487–489) and asks that the Son "disdain not such access to me" (492). Intent on reducing "holy things" to tangible objects, Satan vainly presumes that he can approach and handle the Son's divinity. Later, back in hell, the fiend even boasts to the other devils that he "tasted him" (2:131), a word originally meaning to test by touch as well as tongue, but both connotations reinforce the first assault's impertinent Eucharistic undertones. Here and elsewhere, Satan never grasps his own distance from the Son. Fully aware of his adversary's sinister aims, the Son remains remotely indifferent, responding by saying "I bid not or forbid" (1:495). Nevertheless, he is confident that Satan's evil automatically excommunicates him from true communion or companionship because "Lost bliss [is], to thee no more communicable" (419) and "lying is thy sustenance, thy food" (429).

In his second temptation, Satan offers the Son worldly power in order to reduce Jesus to a royal presence. He first proffers vast wealth, since "Great acts require great means of enterprise" (2:412). When riches are rejected, Satan promises "fame and glory, glory the reward/That sole excites to high attempts the flame/Of most erected Spirits" (3:25–27). This too is scorned as the vain praise of "a herd confus'd" (3:49), since for the Son, only divine "approbation" matters (61). Satan then reminds him that "to a Kingdom thou art born, or-dain'd/To sit upon thy Father *David's* Throne" (152–153), while invoking "Zeal of thy Father's house, [and] Duty to free/Thy Country from her Heathen servitude" (175–176). They tour "The Monarchies of th'Earth . . ./to inform/Thee . . . in regal Arts,/And regal Mysteries; that thou mayst know/How best their opposition to withstand" (246–250), and their journey ends in "*Rome*, Queen of the Earth" (4:45), where Satan urges the Son to topple the corrupt Tiberius and to liberate the chosen people, fulfilling a dynastic destiny amid the "Monarchies of th'Earth."

The Son refuses to take on this role and to emancipate those "Deservedly made vassal" (133) or "by themselves enslaved" (144). This is not his messianic mission because his kingdom is not of this world. Its nature, time, and place remain mysterious, apprehended only through similes:

> Know therefore when my season comes to sit
> On *David's* Throne, it shall be like a tree
> Spreading and overshadowing all the Earth,
> Or as a stone that shall to pieces dash
> All Monarchies besides throughout the world,
> And of my Kingdom there shall be no end:
> Means there shall be to this, but what the means,
> Is not for thee to know, nor me to tell.
>
> (146–153)

Such a threat might make "All Monarchies" tremble, but the Son's refusal to reveal his means to victory baffles and thwarts his adversary because Satan cannot comprehend any of the Son's similes.

Satan's recurrent misunderstanding of divine analogies is ultimately the source of his defeat. Analogies are the crucial challenge for Reformation theology. As Joseph McLelland explains in his study of Peter Martyr's sacramental theories, "Revelation leads to faith, not sight, to analogy, not identity: it poses the problem of the meaning of earthly signs."[77] Many critics of *Paradise Regained* have noted that Satan's struggle with the Son hinges on interpreting correspondences and what Ashraf Rushdy calls "a divine skill in hermeneutics."[78] One of the fiend's biggest mistakes involves his confused interpretation of the alignment of the stars marking the Son's arrival on earth. These constellations,

In their conjunction met, give me to spell,
Sorrows, and labors, opposition, hate,
Attends thee, scorns, reproaches, injuries,
Violence, and stripes, and lastly cruel death.
A Kingdom they portend thee, but what Kingdom,
Real or Allegoric I discern not
Nor when, eternal sure, as without end,
Without beginning; for no date prefixt
Directs me in the Starry Rubric set.

(4:385–393)

Satan is baffled by these mixed signals from on high. He cannot comprehend how a regal, messianic identity can be reconciled with "scorns, reproaches, injuries,/. . . and lastly cruel death." Similarly, he cannot understand the nature of Christ's kingdom, which must be either "Real or Allegoric," committed, presumably, to worldly *realpolitik* or nebulous utopian ideals. His crude binary recalls the error Beza attributes to those who fail to understand the nature of Christ's presence in the Eucharist, mistaking it for either "transubstantiation or trope." For Beza, the sacrament is neither a "real" presence nor an allegorical symbol. Rather, it is a conjunction of divine grace and earthly sign that permits the faithful a relationship with Christ. Similarly, Peter Martyr sees the sacraments as a means of establishing "relations between disparates" despite the enormous gap between them: "But we ought to know that things by nature called disjunctive are yet by the institution of God so conjoined that both names and properties communicate with the other. For what could be more distant than the divine nature and the human?"[79] In *Paradise Regained*, Satan is no better at understanding his relationship to the Son than he is at interpreting sacramental analogies, planetary conjunctions, or the meaning of the kingdom of God. For him, the "Son of God is to me yet in doubt" (501) because that term

bears no single sense;
The Son of God I also am, or was,
And if I was, I am; relation stands;
All men are Sons of God; yet thee I thought
In some respect far higher so declar'd.

(517–521)

Although he dimly recognizes their difference in status, he still tries to force a "single sense" on "Sons of God" and their relationship. *Paradise Regained* shows its readers how to avoid this mistake, for, as Jeffrey Morris points out, even as we recognize "a sort of kinship between Christ and us, we must also be aware of our differences."[80] For those who can understand God better than Satan, "Relation stands" without eradicating distance or difference.

The pressure to define and fix his relationship to the Son becomes most intense in Satan's last temptation. Determined to put Jesus in his place, "having caught him up," Satan flies "through the Air sublime/Over the Wilderness and o'er the Plain" until they reach Jerusalem and its Temple, and "There on the highest Pinnacle he set/The Son of God" (541–550). Satan wants to force a theophany by coercing the miracle prophesied in Scripture: "Now show thy Progeny; if not to stand,/Cast thyself down; safely if Son of God" (4:554–555). Satan thus tries to make Jesus reveal himself in his full, divine presence. The Son parries brilliantly and enigmatically by quoting Scripture himself: "Also it is written,/Tempt not the Lord thy God, he said and stood./But Satan smitten with amazement fell" (4:560–562). The Son's final answer to Satan is characteristically evasive and inscrutable. By refusing to indicate whether he asserts his faith in the Father or himself as "the Lord thy God," he precipitates Satan's fall without having to assert himself. As in *Paradise Lost*, where "he all his father full expressed" (6:720), here too he blends and effaces his own identity with his Father's, and victory over the fiend is jointly theirs.

After defeating Satan, Jesus ascends into heaven, but our vision of his celestial apotheosis is blurred by perpetual motion:

> True Image of the Father, whether thron'd
> In the bosom of bliss, and light of light
> Conceiving, or remote from heaven, enshrin'd
> In fleshly Tabernacle, and human form,
> Wand'ring the wilderness, whatever place,
> Habit, or state, or motion, still expressing
> The Son of God, with Godlike force endu'd. . . .
>
> (4:596–602)

The Son undergoes constant alterations of "place,/Habit, or state" as he moves from heavenly throne to his "fleshly tabernacle" in the wilderness, all the while "still expressing/The Son of God." The "True Image of the Father" continually eludes our gaze, never congealing into a fixed iconostasis or clear conjunction of form and cause.[81] Instead, at the poem's end, "hee unobserv'd/Home to his Mother's house private return'd" (638–639). Obscurity shrouds his "deeds/Above Heroic, though in secret done" from beginning to end (1:14–15).

Paradise may be regained, but God's presence remains elusive. The Son of God comes to earth only to withdraw first to the desert and then to his mother's house. The apostles' reaction to the first withdrawal recapitulates Adam's chagrin at the loss of Paradise—as well as parliamentary dismay at the defeat of the Good Old Cause. "Now missing him thir joy so lately found," the Son's followers succumb to doubt (2:9–11), lamenting "from what high hope to what relapse/Unlook'd for are we fall'n!" (30–31). They are cast down because, at first, they misunderstood the Son's mission in the same way that Satan did. Having initially set their hopes on political emancipation, they believed that "deliverance is at hand" (35), but their "joy is turn'd/Into perplexity and new amaze" (37–38). They then prayed to the "God of *Israel*" asking Him to "send thy Messiah forth, the time is come;/Behold the Kings of th'Earth how they oppress/Thy chosen" (42–45). However, the apostles can move beyond Satan's mistake, and they recover a deeper faith in God's Providence in the course of their prayer, resolving to wait; "Thus they out of their plaints new hope resume" (58). The apostles thereby attain the essential component of Miltonic faith: "a persuasion of things hoped for, as if they were not only existing, but actually present." Faith and hope, patience and obedience provide the only basis in Milton's epics for a sound relationship with God. He rejects desires for a more palpable real or royal presence and apocalyptic deliverance as Satanic snares and delusions. Milton's persistent critique of these delusions represents his most resolute form of resistance to oppression by "Kings' of th'Earth." The Son's "deeds/Above Heroic, though in secret done" regain a paradise surpassing the original "seat of earthly bliss" (4:612), and they sustain an alteration of state beyond "All Monarchies besides throughout the world" (4:149).

CHAPTER 5

Sacramental to Sentimental
Andrew Marvell and the Restoration

This is the only *Banneret*
That ever Love created yet:
Who though, by the Malignant Starrs,
Forced to live in Storms and Warrs;
Yet dying leaves a Perfume here,
And Musick within every Ear:
And he in Story only rules,
In a Field *Sable* a Lover *Gules*.

—Andrew Marvell, "The Unfortunate Lover" (1649)

FIGURE 36
Robert White, *The Wreck of the* Royal Sovereign
(detail of figure 41)
By permission of the British Library; 193.e.10, pt. 2

*J*ohn Milton died in 1674, a few years after the publication of *Paradise Regained* and shortly after the second edition of *Paradise Lost*. Despite his best efforts in poetry and prose, civil idolatry seemed to be making a comeback. Early the next year, a statue of Charles I was erected at Charing Cross, and Edmund Waller, Milton's longtime rival, wrote a poem in praise of this equestrian image:

> That the First Charles does here in triumph ride,
> See his son reign where he a martyr died,
> And people pay that reverence as they pass
> (Which then he wanted!) to the sacred brass
> Is not the effect of gratitude alone
> To which we owe the statue and the stone;
> But Heaven this lasting monument has wrought,
> That mortals may eternally be taught
> Rebellion, though successful, is but vain,
> And kings so killed rise conquerors again.
> This truth the royal image does proclaim,
> Loud as the trumpet of surviving fame.[1]

In Waller's pious description, this "royal image" (11) was not the product of artifice or propaganda. It derived, instead, from spontaneous popular "gratitude" (5) for the Restoration and, even more dramatically, from divine intervention. "Heaven this lasting monument has wrought" (7) in order to teach mere mortals that "Rebellion, though successful, is but vain" (9). A mere statue thus becomes "sacred brass" (4), and a king's graven image compels the same "reverence" (3) as the *Eikon Basilike* did twenty-five years earlier. Waller's rhapsodic idolatry would have appalled Milton as much as the claim that "kings so killed rise conquerors again" (12).

Plans for an even greater memorial to the martyr king were made that same year. Charles was to be reburied in a solemn state funeral in St. George's Chapel at Windsor Castle, and Parliament commissioned a monument by Christopher Wren for his tomb; Wren's model was the same Bramante tempietto that Inigo Jones had used in his plan for James I's sepulcher (figure 37; cf. 22).[2] Grinling Gibbons and Caius Gabriel Cibber submitted plans for statuary designed to

FIGURE 37
Sir Christopher Wren, design for Charles's Tomb
By permission of the Warden and Fellows of All Souls College, Oxford

confirm revolt's futility by showing the apotheosis of Charles, triumphing over Rebellion and Heresy (figures 38 and 39). The poses of each group recall Rubens's painting of James I defeating War and Discord (figure 30) as well as the one depicting Truth trampling Rebellion and Falsehood and Luther and Calvin (figure 29).[3] Charles's tomb was to be one of England's greatest shrines to sacred kingship. Waller was equally enthusiastic about this memorial, and he said that Charles's sepulcher would surpass the splendors of Westminster Chapel because, "Though Henry VII was a great Prince . . . this King was a great Martyr for the Church and Laws."[4] The established church had been eager to strengthen a partnership of church and crown from the start of the Restoration. Preaching in 1661, Dr. Robert South proclaimed that "the Church of England glories in nothing more than she is the truest friend of kings and kingly government, of any other church in the world."[5] Those promoting the cult of Charles as martyr were eager to revive Archbishop Laud's campaign for ceremonial decorum and religious conformity, and a new shrine for the dead king would have helped to advance their agenda.[6]

Efforts by church and crown to impose their authority in the Restoration still met with many obstacles. Clerical control was thwarted because, according to one contemporary, "the liberty of the late times gave men so much light, and diffused it so universally amongst the people, that they . . . are become so good judges of what they hear that the clergy ought to be very wary before they go about to impose upon their understandings, which are grown less jumble than they were in former times."[7] Charles II also found his own absolutist impulses blocked. Although he "thought government was a much safer and easier thing where authority was believed infallible, and the faith and submission of the people was implicit," his Catholic sympathies antagonized both clerical allies and dissident adversaries, and his toleration policies undermined the partnership of Anglican church and state.[8] His brother's conversion to Catholicism in 1673 provoked almost hysterical alarm since James, Duke of York, was heir to the throne. Andrew Marvell gave voice to widespread apprehensions in his *Account of the Growth of Popery, and Arbitrary Government in England* in 1677, writing that "There has now for divers years a design been carried on to change

FIGURE 38

Grinling Gibbons, design for monument to Charles I

By permission of the Warden and Fellows of All Souls College, Oxford

FIGURE 39
Caius Gabriel Cibber, design for monument to Charles I
By permission of the Warden and Fellows of All Souls College, Oxford

the lawful Government of England into an absolute Tyranny, and to convert the established Protestant Religion into downright Popery."[9] Allegations of a "horrible popish plot" to assassinate Charles II in 1678 helped split Parliament into Tories and Whigs, and amid these emerging partisan divisions, bills were introduced to exclude James from succession to the throne.[10]

The Exclusion Crisis of 1678–81 radically challenged Stuart ideas of sacred kingship. For Stuart monarchs, hereditary succession had been an article of faith, fundamental to their idea of divine right. From the beginning of his reign, James I had earnestly promulgated this principle because it placed "kingdoms ever at God's disposition, . . . [it] lying no more in the king's nor people's hands to dispossess the righteous heir."[11] The Restoration itself was predicated on an assumption of automatic hereditary succession and the denial of an interregnum. Royal proclamations of 1660 date the reign of Charles II from his father's death in 1649 and give thanks for his "Restauration to the actuall possession of his undoubted hereditary Soveraigne and Regall Authority."[12] When James II attained the throne, he also insisted on the providential validity of hereditary succession: "For where the crown is hereditary (as it is in these kingdoms, thanks be to God) His Almighty power alone can dispose of it."[13] In fact, his belief in the sanctity of hereditary right was a major factor in his dangerous attraction to Catholicism. James II was convinced that the Catholic church was the only one with "a constant succession from the time of the apostles to the present. . . . It was this consideration which principally led me to embrace the communion of the Roman church."[14] For a time, indefeasible or inalienable hereditary succession, the bedrock principle of Stuart divine right, held firm. In parliamentary debate, efforts to exclude James from the throne were opposed as dangerous and futile, one member arguing that "Acts of Parliament have not kept the succession out of the right line but brought in blood and sword . . . show me one man excluded . . . that had right of descent but has come in again."[15] In Waller's words, "kings so killed rise conquerors again." The stigma of regicide and rebellion tainted the Whig opposition, and its leaders were executed in 1683 for allegedly conspiring to assassinate James and Charles. James survived the Exclusion Crisis and was crowned king, succeeding his brother in 1685. Nevertheless, his victory was brief since, in 1688, he lost his kingdom and his crown in the Glorious Revolution, the most drastic alteration of state since his father's execution almost forty years earlier.

The Glorious Revolution posed a far graver challenge to hereditary sovereignty than the Exclusion Crisis. The birth of a son and heir to James II in 1688 threatened to prolong the Catholic claim to the English crown, and those once reluctant to oppose their hereditary monarch, Tories as well as Whigs, now united against him. Both groups immediately questioned the new heir's legitimacy, and some invited William of Orange, Dutch prince and Protestant consort to James's daughter, Mary, to invade England. James fled into exile, and the accession of William and Mary was broadly acclaimed on all sides. A small Tory minority, known as "nonjurors" for their refusal to swear allegiance to the new regime, could not accept this affront to hereditary right, but most others struggled to find ways to rationalize the widely desired coup d'état. Some Whigs argued that James had broken the contract between sovereign and subject and then abdicated, leaving the throne vacant and thus voiding his claims. By contrast, Tory moderates had trouble with both the contractual theory and abdication, since vacancy implied another interregnum. As Mark Kishlansky explains, "the whole premise of hereditary succession was that the throne was never vacant: it passed instantaneously from holder to heir: 'The King is dead, long live the King!' If the throne was vacant, and if Parliament could fill it, then the nation had passed to elective monarchy."[16] Various parliamentary proclamations sought to finesse this dilemma by replacing "abdicated" with "deserted" or even "demised." Other proponents sought to shift the argument to a higher plane, contending that the Protestant succession was only preserved by an act of God.

The providential argument soon became the preferred defense of the Glorious Revolution, and invocations of a celestial conjunction were a frequent rhetorical recourse. In a sermon preached at Whitehall in 1690, the Whig preacher, Gilbert Burnet, assured William and Mary that their accession was the result of a happy combination of natural, political, and cosmic forces: "There are other more solemn Occasions, in which some second causes are raised above their own pitch, and are animated beyond the ordinary rate. . . . This has never appeared with more eminent Characters than in the Revolutions of States and Empires, in which both the course of Natural Agents, the Winds and Seasons, and the tempers of men's minds, seem to have been managed by such a direction, that not only every thing, but every circumstance has co-operated to carry on Great Designs in such a Conjunction, that those who observe them with due attention, are forced on many occasions to cry out 'This is the finder of God! This is the Lord's doing!' "[17] A similar claim was later made by a prominent Tory churchman, Francis Atterbury, who maintained that "since the Age of Miracles ceas'd as it did, when the Testimony of the Gospel was fully Seal'd, the chief way, in which God hath been pleas'd to give Extraordinary Indications of his Power and Providence, hath been by such Signs of the times, such Wonders of Government."[18] Earlier in the Restoration, amid the calamities of 1666, royalists had discouraged speculation about "Planetary Aspects, or great Conjunctions," but, in the wake of the Glorious Revolution, even Tories looked to the heavens for celestial support.[19]

Nonjurors, die-hard defenders of hereditary right, mocked these expedients. When William Sherlock invoked Providence in a sermon before the House of Commons in 1692 and claimed that "those who believed the Doctrine of Non-Resistance and Passive Obedience to be a good Doctrine before may think so still, and be never the less Friends to the present Government," another member reacted with scorn:

> Your observing Readers laugh at your confidence, in saying, that the late *Revolution hath made no Alterations in the Principles of Government and Obedience*: And to use your own words, *Some* think your Providential Right a *Tottering Foundation for the Monarchy that cannot long support it*, and every jot as *tottering* as that of the *Power of the People*, which you explode; because the People, if they get the Supream Power of the King, they will plead Providence for it, whether they have actually a *Superior* Power over him or no.[20]

Providential arguments were still favored anyway because they allowed acceptance of the new regime while making the Glorious Revolution look less radical. Such defenses also upheld a deeply ingrained religious conception of politics. Kingship remained sacred and alterations of state sacramental, marking divine right by a conjunction of signs and wonders. Gilbert Straka rightly describes these arguments for celestial intervention in political events as "the final phase of divine right theory in England," which "appealed to an older but still potent piety."[21] Nevertheless, as J. P. Kenyon says, for all their potency and appeal, arguments from Providence were still "irretrievably damaged" by their obvious sophistry.[22]

The inconsistencies of providential arguments gradually undermined incarnational notions of sacred kingship. By subordinating hereditary rights to a higher principle, they prepared the way for a more pragmatic and less mystical conception of politics founded on calculations of expedience and the common good. In *A Brief Justification of the Prince of Orange's Descent Into England, and of the Kingdoms Late Recourse to Arms*, published in 1689, Robert Ferguson advances the Whig argument that the succession is "not to be governed by proximity of blood, but by weighing what is most expedient for the benefit of the community," and he concludes that "reason of state obligeth to lodge it where it may be most for the publick good."[23] Reasons of state now justified alterations of state. Algernon Sidney had been condemned for comparable sentiments at his trial in 1683, but, as Jonathan Scott notes, ideas once deemed dangerously radical and even treasonous became patriotic truisms in the wake of the Glorious Revolution.[24] Similarly, John Miller concludes that "in retrospect many saw the Revolution as vindicating the principle that kings existed for the good of the people."[25] So broadly acceptable had the priority of the public good become that even the last Stuart monarch firmly embraced it. When Queen Anne, Mary's sister and the daughter of James II, came to the throne in 1702, many hard-core Tories hoped for a revival of Stuart absolutism and older notions of divine right. Anne's enthusiasm for the royal touch may have encouraged these traditional allies, but she ultimately disappointed them by rejecting arguments for indefeasible hereditary succession and high church efforts to crush dissent.[26] She subsequently urged the Tories to put aside their partisan agenda for the sake of the common good, saying that "I hope there will be no concentration among you but who shall most promote the public welfare."[27]

Queen Anne's reign marks a watershed for what Mark Kishlansky calls "a monarchy transformed." At the beginning of the eighteenth century, the British monarchy was more securely established than it had ever been, but the grounds of its authority had shifted from a sacred to a more secular basis, or, in the words of J. A. I. Champion, "from theology to ethics."[28] This shift actually placed kingship on a firmer ideological footing because, as Kishlansky explains, while "the potential theoretical power of the monarch had been greatly diminished, its real practical power [was] greatly enhanced."[29] Paradoxically, regard for royalty was in some ways increased by a new recognition of human weaknesses. In describing Anne's popularity, Kishlansky says that "despite all of her obvious deficiencies—or perhaps because of them—Queen Anne was a monarch beloved. She desired nothing so much as to be a mother, and if she couldn't achieve this with her children then she would with her subjects. Her pitted face and bulging, watery eyes that limited her vision, her ailments and constant pain, all made her seem a monarch of the people."[30] By the end of the eighteenth century, during the reign of George III, even greater sympathy for royal infirmities was required and often given. Linda Colley says that the king's "severe bouts of illness, his encroaching age and his bevy of dissolute sons seem not so much to have detracted from the reputation of monarchy, as to have increased public protectiveness towards the king himself. By being manifestly vulnerable, he became more not less appealing."[31] Colley claims that the madness of George III provided a "more personal foundation for monarchy, giving the very old notion of the king's two bodies a new and more secular twist" by focusing on the frailties of the physical body rather than the exalted powers of the mystical one.[32] Thus, by the end of the eighteenth century, much of the imagery and terminology of kingship had migrated from the sacramental to the sentimental and the sympathetic. As John Barrell explains, a monarch like Louis XVI or George III became the subject of "sad stories," seen not as "a public hero or martyr exalted above the reach of the grief and sympathy of his former subjects and present admirers, but as a private individual whose chief concerns as he contemplated his end were such as those who thought themselves as ordinary people would expect to feel."[33] Royalty's appeal partly derived from a sense of human pathos rather than divine awe.

During this same period, the image of Charles I also ceased to inspire divine awe and became more pathetic, but in his case pathos rendered his cause increasingly irrelevant and reduced the charisma of sacred kingship. In the Restoration, plans were made for his body's reburial in a sacred space meant to surpass Westminster Chapel, but that memorial was never erected. After the Glorious Revolution, both his rights and rites of memory continued, but they became more fraught when entangled in conflicts over legitimate succession. The anniversary of his execution was still solemnly observed, but some mocked the ceremonial devotions of William and Mary as rank hypocrisy. In her analysis of Charles's posthumous cult, Laura Knoppers cites an anonymous poem posted on the door of Whitehall's chapel in 1696, where William and Mary attended a church service in his honor. It derides those who "Fast and Pray,/For the Horrid Murder of the day,/And at the same time drive ye Son away," since "Sins, whilst unrepented, cannot be forgiven."[34] From this critical perspective, Charles haunts the realm much as Hamlet's father did, chiding those who deprived James of his throne and now occupy it. William is forced to recognize, as Claudius does, that one cannot "be pardoned and retain the offence" (*Hamlet* 3.3.56), and supporters of the new regime are accused of "strange Contradictions."[35] Such contradictions beset English ideas of sacred kingship throughout the Reformation, and recurrent alterations of state usually forced most to rationalize or ignore them.

These contradictions only increased in the eighteenth century, further undermining Stuart ideas of divine right. When the eleven-year-old Duke of Gloucester, heir apparent and last surviving child of Princess Anne, died in 1700, moderate Tories agreed to a Protestant Act of Settlement even if it meant denying the crown to her stepbrother, the legitimate Stuart heir.[36] The problems with this settlement were temporarily muted by the accession of Anne in 1702, for she ensured a felicitous combination of Protestant and Stuart legitimacy for the duration of her reign. However, when she died without an heir in 1714, the crown went to George I of Hanover because the son born to James II in 1688 refused to renounce Catholicism.[37] James Francis Edward Stuart became the "Old Pretender" to the throne, and he and his son continued to challenge the rule of the Hanovers.

There were Jacobite uprisings on their behalf in 1715, 1719, and 1745, but repeated defeat rendered their cause ever more inconsequential.[38]

The decline of the Jacobite cause reduced Charles I to the protagonist of lugubrious "sad stories" such as William Havard's *King Charles the First, An Historical Tragedy written in Imitation of Shakespeare* (1737). Havard's supposedly *"Historical"* drama took the poetic liberty of assembling several otherwise absent family members for a last exchange with the condemned king, including the queen and Prince James, because he wanted a "pleasing Distress at their Parting."[39] The play's frontispiece (figure 40) depicts this poignant gathering, its caption demanding "At this sad SCENE who can from tears REFRAIN?" Except for Cromwell, few in this play can. James must struggle to "stop these Tears of Sorrow" so that he can clearly see and "Copy my Royal Father in his Death," but Charles himself declares "Heart, thou art Marble, not to break at this."[40] Laura Knoppers describes a comparably sorrowful evocation of the martyr king in a Jacobite engraving of 1745. It shows Charles Edward Stuart, "the Young Pretender," in defeat, and the verses below offer only the consolation of abject melancholy: "glorious in Thought! But now my Hopes are gone;/ Each Friend grows shy—& I'm at last undone." In the bottom corner of the picture is a small, fragmentary image of Charles I, but, as Knoppers explains, this diminutive *eikon basilike* has been marginalized, obscured, and "almost hidden from view": "No longer an image of the divine expressed in the physical world, the image of Charles becomes merely narrative, even sentimental."[41] The king's transition from a sacred icon to sentimental story constituted a subtle but insidious alteration of state more subversive than regicide.

Few poets anticipate these corrosive changes from sacramental to sentimental views of kingship as astutely as Andrew Marvell. Marvell's politics changed dramatically during the course of the Civil War and Restoration, and he gained a sophisticated understanding of the decline of sacred kingship. In Blair Worden's succinct account, the crucial turning point occurred in 1650, a year after the king's execution. "To simplify, he was a Royalist before that year, and a Cromwellian and then a Whig after it," Worden says, adding an important qualification in order to explain the poet's characteristic complexities: "Marvell, as always, resists such simplification."[42] As a royalist, Mar-

At this sad SCENE who can from TEARS refrain?

FIGURE 40

William Havard, *Tragedy of Charles I*, frontispiece

By permission of the British Library; 643.g.12 (H.)

vell praises the cavalier warriors, Richard Lovelace and Francis Villiers, and damns the republican turncoat, Tom May, and anyone else who would exult in "great *Charles* his death."[43] As a Whig, he proved a skilled satirical poet, acquiring so much renown in that vein that all sorts of lampoons were attributed to him in early collections of Whig verses.[44] Satire was an increasingly potent political weapon in the Restoration, and, as George deF. Lord says in his introduction to *Poems on Affairs of State*, it contributed to "a fundamentally secular attitude toward monarchical government."[45] Some of the satires attributed to Marvell take direct aim at the pretensions of sacred kingship: a rejoinder to Edmund Waller's homage to the equestrian statue at Charing Cross caustically suggests "That a Monarch of Gingerbread would doe as well" (48). Yet other satires, such as *The Last Instructions to a Painter*, are more muted and deferential, sounding almost royalist in their description of Charles II as the "Sun of our world" (956). Marvell's Cromwellian panegyrics are even more ambiguous, especially *An Horatian Ode upon Cromwell's Return from Ireland*. In praising Cromwell, he allows that "Much to the Man is due" (28) but still registers shock at the "bleeding Head" (69) resulting from regicide and admiration for the royal adversary's dignity in death. Kingship's "ancient rights" are acknowledged in the *Horatian Ode* (38) as well as in *Tom May's Death* (69), but in the former they "hold or break/As men are strong or weak" (39–40), implying Cromwell's strength and Charles's weakness. In the *Horatian Ode*, the monarch is diminished by larger forces, and his death and Cromwell's ascendancy assure a "happy fate" (72) for the Republic. Moreover, while the conduct of "the *Royal Actor*" (53) upon the "*Tragick Scaffold*" (54) is impressively exalted, his performance in "that memorable Scene" (58) is largely theatrical, as are the pity and terror aroused by it. At the end of his reign, Charles's sovereignty can be described with a phrase Marvell uses in another poem composed during the same period, *The Unfortunate Lover*: "he in Story only rules" (63). In each of these poems, the characters' afflictions arouse considerable sympathy, but such sentiments can prove as damaging to the mystique of sacred kingship as the jeers of satirical mockery because both reduce the king to human scale. In the *Horatian Ode*, Marvell comes to see through the illusions of sacred kingship with the sharpened insight of an apostate, yet his attitude toward it remains so complex because it combines radical skepticism toward royalist myths with recognition of their poignant appeal and utility.

The contrast with John Milton is telling. Marvell sought to enter government service as an assistant to Milton in 1653, and he replaced the older poet as Latin Secretary to the Protectorate in 1657. After the Restoration, he defended Milton against his enemies and wrote a renowned prefatory poem to the second edition of *Paradise Lost*. Nevertheless, looking back on the Civil War more than twenty years later, Marvell advances a more detached view of "the good old cause" than his old ally, and he takes a more moderate position on monarchy:

> Whether it were a War of Religion, or of Liberty, is not worth the labour to enquire. Which-soever was at the top, the other was at the bottom; but upon considering all, I think the cause too good to have been fought for. Men ought to have trusted God; they ought and might have trusted the King with the whole matter. The *Arms of the Church are Prayers and Tears*, the Arms of the Subjects are Patience and Petitions. The King himself being of so accurate and piercing a judgment, would soon have felt where it stuck. For men may spare their pains where Nature is at work, and the world will not go the faster for our driving. Even as his present Majesties happy Restoration did it self, so all things else happen in their best and proper time, without any need of our officiousness.[46]

To simplify again, Marvell was more of a Whig than a Republican, one prepared to accept a constitutional and limited monarchy. He became a staunch opponent of Stuart absolutism, but even his strongest attack, *An Account of the Growth of Popery and Arbitrary Government* (1677), strikes a note of balanced and sly restraint: "So that the Kings of England are in nothing inferiour to other Princes, save in being more abridged from injuring their own subjects . . . there is nothing that comes nearer in Government to the Divine Perfection, than where the Monarch, as with us, injoys a capacity of doing all the good imaginable to mankind, under a disability to all that is evil."[47] Similarly, in *The Rehearsal Transpros'd, The Second Part*, while acknowledging that the "Power of the Magistrate does most certainly issue from the Divine Authority," he addresses "the modester Question . . . [of] how far it is advisable for a Prince to exert and push the rigour of that Power which no man can deny him" (232–233). As Annabel Patterson points out, these smoothly deferential concessions to royal prerogative and divine right are offset by unyielding assertions of the subject's rights and liberties.[48]

Marvell undermines the props and pretensions of sacred kingship in two ways. Sometimes he resorts to a sharp polemical style whose jibes recall Milton's antiprelatical tracts. *The Rehearsal Transpros'd* (1672), which came out two years before Milton's death, reflects their shared scorn for clerical trimming and ambition. Marvell's work is a scathing rejoinder to a treatise written by Samuel Parker. An ardent Puritan in his youth, Parker switched sides after the Restoration, taking orders in 1664 and writing tracts in defense of church hierarchy, religious conformity, and the royal prerogative. He was rewarded for his polemical efforts with various ecclesiastical offices, eventually becoming Bishop of Oxford. Parker attacked toleration and liberty of conscience throughout his career, but it was his unctuous preface to Bishop John Bramhall's *Vindication of Himself and the Episcopal Clergy from the Presbyterian Charge of Popery* (1672) that provoked Marvell's stinging counterattack. *The Rehearsal Transpros'd* not only reviles Parker's reactionary principles but also skewers his obsequious careerism and bad taste, contending that "it is the highest *Indecorum* for a Divine to write in such a stile as this [part Play-book and part-Romance] concerning a Reverend Bishop," and adding that "these improbable Elogies too are of the greatest disservice to their own design, and do in effect diminish alwayes the Person whom they pretend to magnifie" (12). Marvell's contempt for Parker's ecclesiastical "Ostentation and Pageantry" (97) recalls Milton's derision for the *Eikon Basilike*'s "Stage-work" in *Eikonoklastes* (*CPW* 3:530). Warren Chernaik says that "Marvell's satires are all essentially iconoclastic, directed at illegitimate assumptions of heroism, dignity, and grandeur, the impressive but specious 'Pageantry' and "Chimaeras' with which men deceive others and themselves."[49]

Marvell's best satires nevertheless rely more on the deflationary ridicule of the mock-heroic rather than iconoclasm's frontal assaults. His *The Last Instructions to a Painter* presents a far more devastating (and reliably attributable) rebuke to Waller's royalist effusions than *"The Statue at* CHARING CROSS." The former is one of a series of satires inspired by Waller's *Instructions to a Painter,* a poem celebrating the Duke of York's triumph over the Dutch fleet at Lowestoft in 1665. Waller's description of the English victory at sea revisits the ancient competition of poetry and painting or *"pictura poesis,"* advanced in antiquity by Horace and revived in the Renaissance by Sir Philip Sidney, among others.[50] In the late Renaissance, the theory inspired a popular advice-to-a-painter genre, aimed at combining the best of both arts through vivid pictorial description. Waller's immediate model was a poem written a decade earlier by Gian Franco Busenello to celebrate a Venetian victory over the Turks and translated into English in 1658.

Waller's *Instructions to a Painter* are increasingly patronizing toward his artistic counterpart because he finds mere pictorial technique inadequate to his epic task. Eventually, he asserts the superiority of his own talents because only the poet can truly illuminate the murk of battle and celebrate the bravery shown there:

> Painter, excuse me, if I have a while
> Forgot thy art and used another style,
> For, though you draw armed heroes as they sit,
> The task in battle does the Muses fit.
> They, in the dark confusion of a fight,
> Discover all, instruct us how to write,
> And light and honor to brave actions yield,
> Hid in the smoke and tumult of the field.
>
> (287–294)

In his concluding direct address to the king, Waller also presents himself as the only one who can do justice to the royal image because a poetic portrait can probe beyond superficial appearances. Just as the poet brings light and honor to the *chiaroscuro* of battle, so too he creates a more authentic *eikon basilike,* beyond the capacity of a mere painter:

> Those which inhabit the celestial bower,
> Painters express with emblems of their power . . .
> But your great providence no colors here

> Can represent, nor pencil draw that care
> Which keeps you waking to secure our peace,
> The nation's glory, and our trade's increase.
>
> (313–320)

By combining vivid image and grandiloquent text, Waller's verse incorporates and surpasses emblematic illustration, attaining a more complete conjunction of form and cause.

Waller's *Instructions* thus aspires to the higher standard that Annabel Patterson describes, in which *"ut pictura poesis* became associated with an ideal of perfection, whether physical or moral, which it was the duty of both arts to express."[51] This transcendent perspective permits him to discern the patriotic purpose behind the battle's carnage, as the "smoke and tumult of the field" (294) clears to reveal a spectacular theatrical scene. His lofty overview transforms war's brutal mayhem into a ritual sacrifice upon an altar.

> Happy! To whom this glorious death arrives,
> More to be valued than a thousand lives!
> On such a theatre as this to die,
> For such a cause, and such a witness by!
> Who would not thus a sacrifice be made,
> To have his blood on such an altar laid.
>
> (149–154)

Waller's version of *"ut pictura poesis"* thus promotes another Horatian ideal: *"dulce et decorum est, pro patria mori."*[52] Here and elsewhere, he strives for a visionary conjunction of patriotic cause and dramatic, ceremonial form, held together by loyalty to king and country. Unfortunately for Waller, his aspirations were soon mocked by ignominious defeat and a chorus of satirical jeers.

The British won the battle of Lowestoft but failed to pursue their victory and rapidly lost a protracted war, leaving England undefended. The humiliating upshot was an invasion in 1667 in which Dutch ships sailed up the Thames and Medway and burned the English fleet. In the wake of these calamities, Waller's premature panegyric looked increasingly ridiculous. Several travesties, including *The Last Instruc-*

tions to a Painter, were composed, mocking the poet's epic pretensions and the government's incompetence and corruption. Patterson
attributes the *Second and Third Advices* as well as the *Last* to Marvell
and suggests that they helped to create "a new satirical strategy" that
emulated the painterly technique of Waller's poem in order to de-
molish it.[53] *The Last Instructions to a Painter* is especially complex because it includes a moving passage of heroic pictorial description, far
surpassing anything written by Waller. In Marvell's view, political division and drift had left England vulnerable to the Dutch invasion of
1667, and his poem begins by recounting the sordid struggles of court
and parliamentary factions in mock-heroic style. The actual battle is
marked almost entirely by "Confusion, folly, treach'ry, fear, neglect"
(610), but one figure stands out as a unique example of courage in this
otherwise inglorious rout. As the fleet burns and sinks, one brave captain, Archibald Douglas, goes down with his ship, and Marvell describes his last moments, etching a noble image sharply defined by
the fire surrounding him:

> His shape exact, which the bright flames infold,
> Like the Sun's Statue stands of burnish'd Gold
> . . . And, as on Angels Heads their Glories shine,
> His burning Locks adorn his Face Divine.
> But, when in his immortal Mind he felt
> His alt'ring Form, and soder'd Limbs to melt;
> Down on the Deck he laid himself, and dy'd,
> With his dear Sword reposing by his Side.
> And, on the flaming Plank, so rests his Head,
> As one that's warm'd himself and gone to Bed.
>
> (679–690)

The death of Douglas is genuinely stirring, and Marvell praises him
twice, here and again in a separate poem, "The Loyall Scot." Douglas's radiant image is both picturesque and poignant, and his calm
composure in death resembles the dignity attributed to King Charles
in *An Horatian Ode*. They share a tendency toward recumbence, for
there too, the king "bow'd his comely Head, / Down as upon a Bed"
(63–64), and this resemblance renders both figures oddly passive as

well as doomed. Moreover, their beautifully emblematic stasis is exceptional and largely irrelevant to the larger forces surging through both poems. The "restless *Cromwel*" of *An Horatian Ode* (9) is a figure in constant movement, while the erratic antics of various characters in *The Last Instructions* make them elusive and hard to paint "in Coulours that will hold" (79). Marvell adapts his technical advice accordingly: "So thou and I, dear *Painter*, represent / In quick *Effigy*, others Faults, and feign / By making them ridiculous to restrain" (390–392).

This "quick *Effigy*" constitutes Marvell's new satirical style. Rather than smashing the icons and emblems of the powerful, he displaces them with effigy and caricature. In *The Last Instructions*, he disrupts the smooth conjunctions of Renaissance pictorialism by rendering them preposterous. Even when he entertains the prospect of a more edifying image, a subtle disjunction prevails: neither the "immortal Mind" (685) nor the "alt'ring Form" (686) of Captain Douglas can be linked to some larger historic cause. As Donald Friedman says, both *The Horatian Ode* and *The Last Instructions* suggest an "inevitable separation of the greater 'things' that in the figures of Douglas and Charles were 'contained.' "[54] Marvell's skepticism mocks the glib presumption of Waller's transcendent aspirations. Waller begins his *Instructions to a Painter* with a peremptory celestial cue that recalls the stage directions of a stately masque: "Make Heaven concerned, and an unusual star / Declare the importance of the approaching war" (7–8). Heaven shows no concern for the calamities of *The Last Instructions*, and the coarse spectacles seen in that poem, including a skimmington ride, resemble the rude disorders of an antimasque (375–389). Elsewhere, in *The Rehearsal Transpros'd*, Marvell explicitly rejects the facile celestial conjunction that Waller attempts, warning ambitious royalists against "hooking things up to Heaven in this manner; for though you look for some advantage from it, you may chance to raise them above your reach, and if you do not fasten and rivet them very well when you have them here, they will come down again with such a swinge, that if you stand not out of the way, they may bear you down further then you thought of" (255). Marvell was thus one of the first to challenge providential rationalizations of divine right, the last resort of sacred kingship.

Marvell's subtle skepticism toward sacred kingship and its symbols can be traced back to another poem written shortly after Charles's execution, less familiar than *The Horatian Ode*. *The Unfortunate Lover* describes an allegorical shipwreck whose sole survivor clings to a rock in a storm-tossed sea. Impaled by the cruel arrows of "tyrant Love" amid all his other adversities, the protagonist seems, at first glance, to be nothing more than a generic miserable young lover. Peter Davidson, however, convincingly suggests that the poem's "unfortunate and abject Heir" (30) is meant to be one of Charles's surviving sons, and Davidson reads it as a romantic but complex recapitulation of "propaganda images circulating on the continent amongst the exiled royalists."[55] These images included pictures of the princes in the manner of the frontispiece of the *Eikon Basilike*; just such a portrait of James is described by Sir Richard Fanshaw, a royalist exile, in which the Duke of York "is represented as one in peril on a stormy sea, the captain thrown overboard, the ship broken up, thrust upon a rock, but clinging to an anchor, the trident of the ruler of the sea."[56] A similar picture appears as a frontispiece to a later history of the Civil War, showing a ship foundering in a terrible storm as the crew throws their crowned captain overboard. On shore, many onlookers gape in horror while some quarrel among themselves, and lightning strikes the church that stands as a lighthouse (figure 41).[57]

The images in Marvell's poem certainly resemble these harrowing scenes, and "the unfortunate lover" can readily be seen as a stand-in for one of the Stuart princes. At the same time, Marvell treats his protagonist and plot with characteristic ambivalence, undermining any propaganda value the poem might have. *The Unfortunate Lover's* drama unfolds with many of the emblematic trappings of the *Eikon Basilike*, but, in contrast to that work's vision of composure in adversity and a heavenly crown shining from a realm beyond its storms, the scene in Marvell's poem is more desperate and dismal. More shockingly, it is also less consequential. The cosmic insignificance and transience of this sad struggle is made clear from the beginning, when the turbulent passions of "infant Love" quickly expire:

> But soon these Flames do lose their light,
> Like Meteors of a Summers night:

Printed for A. Mearne, T. Dring, B. Tooke, T. Sawbridge, & C. Mearne

FIGURE 41

Robert White, *The Wreck of the* Royal Sovereign

By permission of the British Library; 193.e.10, pt. 2

> Nor can they to that Region climb
> To make impression upon Time.
>
> (5–8)

In the *Horatian Ode*, Cromwell blasts *"Caesars* head" (23) and ruins "the great Work of Time" (34). The contrast with his fiery celestial force makes the unfortunate lover and the blaze he ignites look rather puny. The unfortunate lover himself is swept overboard when a "master-Wave" (13) drives his ship upon the rocks and splits it, with Cromwellian force, "In a *Cesarean section*" (16). He is then "cast away" before he was even "brought forth" (12). The abortive end of this "unfortunate and abject Heir" (30) is in some ways as paltry as it is pitiful, rendering its victim oddly irrelevant.

The odd inconsequence of all this anguish is increased by Marvell's detached perspective and tone. In depicting his hero's tragic sufferings and demise, Marvell creates apocalyptic special effects as stunning—and stagy—as Waller's. The shipwreck occurs "While round the ratling Thunder hurl'd / As at the Fun'ral of the World" (23–24). Yet, as his emphasis on the "masque of quarrelling Elements" (26) indicates, Marvell's staging of this spectacle is just as self-consciously theatrical as his depiction of the *"Royal Actor"* in the *Horatian Ode*. He also evokes a "spectacle of Blood" (42) as lurid as any of those found in other publications decrying the king's execution. But Marvell contemplates bloodshed and ogles the victim's nudity with the bemused detachment of a voyeuristic connoisseur rather than the outrage of a zealous partisan:

> See how he nak'd and fierce does stand,
> Cuffing the Thunder with one hand;
> While with the other he does lock,
> And grapple, with the stubborn Rock:
> From which he with each Wave rebounds,
> Torn into Flames, and ragg'd with Wounds.
> And all he saies, a Lover drest
> In his own Blood does relish best.
>
> (49–56)

The poem is suffused with the same sanguinary pathos pervading all those laments for King Charles, but instead of becoming a Christ-like man of sorrows, the unfortunate lover is seen as a sexual object whose nudity arouses "relish" rather than grief-stricken reverence. As in Havard's *Historical Tragedy*, the effect desired is a "pleasing Distress," and royalty's predicament now offers the sweet savor of sentimental tenderness. In *The Unfortunate Lover*, the pleasure is enhanced by a dash of erotic pleasure in another's sufferings.

The final glimpse of this "unfortunate and abject heir" is strangely picturesque, diminishing his importance even further. The scene arouses little pity and terror. On the contrary, the death of this character "Forced to live in Storms and Warrs" is delectably sweet to those who witness it. Moreover, the emblematic qualities of his blood are reduced from a sacramental to a heraldic and ornamental significance:

> Yet dying leaves a Perfume here,
> And Musick within every Ear.
> And he in Story only rules,
> In a Field *Sable* a lover *Gules*.
>
> (61–64)

The poem's final line uses heraldic terminology, *gules* being the technical term for a slash of red against the black background of "a Field *Sable*." The same combination occurs in *Hamlet*, where, as Elsie Duncan-Jones points out, the "rugged Pyrrhus" has his "black complexion smeared/With heraldry more dismal. Head to foot/Now he is total gules" (2.2.448–453).[58] The Greek warrior attains a kind of emblematic clarity in which appearance and intention are perfectly matched. Hamlet desperately yearns for such powerful conjunctions of form and cause throughout the play, as we have seen, and the player's speech momentarily provides one, but the effect is ephemeral. As long as the speech lasts, Hamlet is enraptured, but as soon as it ends, he dismisses it as "a fiction" and "a dream of passion" (546). Similarly, Marvell's unfortunate lover achieves emblematic perfection as his bloody body glimpsed amid the dark storm transforms him into "the only *Banneret*/That ever Love created yet" (57–58). But his perfection is also purely fictional, since "he in Story only rules" (63). In each instance, the conjunction so strongly desired and briefly glimpsed proves evanescent and unsustainable—and largely illusory.

Beware of "hooking things up to Heaven," Marvell warns in *The Rehearsal Transpros'd*, casting doubt on the celestial conjunctions repeatedly invoked to justify divine right rule. The dry skepticism and detached pathos of his political verse ultimately proved more corrosive to the pretensions of sacred kingship than regicide. Civil idolatry did not end with the bang of the ax on the block in 1649. Instead, it faded more gradually after the Restoration, amid whimpers stirred by sentimental tales and titters aroused by satires. After the seismic upheavals of the Civil War and Glorious Revolution, English kings and queens continued to rule and flourish for the next two centuries. Their authority was more firmly secured on solid, practical grounds, but their links to heaven became more tenuous. Alterations of state were no longer seen as cosmic events, and rulers seen from a sentimental or satirical perspective were considered more human than divine. In the eighteenth and nineteenth centuries, sacred kingship was no longer a tenable belief.

By the end of the eighteenth century, the human frailties of the English monarchy were increasingly conspicuous. The madness of George III was alarming enough, but his prodigal son's misconduct was even more outrageous. Personal vanity, bloated obesity, and sexual misadventures made the Prince of Wales the butt of satires throughout his regency (1811–1821), and his political ineptitude deprived him of the sympathy extended to his father. Brilliant caricatures such as James Gillray's "Voluptuary under the Horrors of Digestion" (1792) or George Cruikshank's "Prince of Whales" (1812) lampooned his insatiable appetites and reckless excesses.[59] One of Cruikshank's pictures vividly illustrates a new, more secular and comic perspective on royal mortality, while affording a droll comparison of George and his predecessors. Entitled "Meditations Amongst the Tombs," it depicts an event that occurred early in the regency. On April 1, 1813, the Prince of Wales, his personal physician, Sir Henry Halford, and a few others undertook a visit to the tomb of Henry VIII at Windsor after builders broke a hole in the vault. According to Halford's account, after hearing of this breach in the wall, "His Royal Highness perceived at once, that a doubtful point in History might be cleared up by opening this vault," specifically, whether or not the regicides had permitted a proper burial for Charles I.[60] After they found a coffin with the inscription, "King Charles, 1648," the king looked on as his attendants pried it open and then unwrapped its "cere-cloth" with great difficulty. The corpse's distinctive face and beard convinced all the onlookers that, despite "disfigurement, the countenance did bear a strong resemblance to the coins, the busts, and especially to the pictures of King Charles I by Vandyke, by which it had been made familiar to us."[61] Sir Henry dramatically concludes his tale from the crypt by stating that "When the head had been entirely disengaged from the attachments which confined it, it was found to be loose, and without any difficulty, was taken up and held to view," and he speculates that the dark liquid oozing from it was the royal blood of King Charles.[62]

Cruikshank's "Meditations Amongst the Tombs" makes a splendid mockery of this grisly inquest (figure 42).[63] On the left, Sir Henry Halford manhandles the corpse of Henry VIII as he prepares to cut off some of the dead king's whiskers. The Prince Regent wants to add these to his own to "make me a prime pair of Royal *Whiskers*" because "great Harry . . . got rid of many wives, whilst I, poor soul, can't get *rid* of one." George's difficulties with his wife were a source of mortification throughout his regency. He had submitted to his marriage to Caroline of Brunswick with the greatest reluctance in 1795, and he left her the next year, demanding a formal separation. His animosity toward her only increased when public sympathy turned her way and against him. George's unpopularity had many sources, and Cruikshank's caricature depicts another in the figure on the right. The man shown standing behind the regent with the P.P.P on his sash is Colonel John McMahon, Secretary to the Regent and Prince's Privy Purse. His sinecure and salary provoked parliamentary protest and popular outrage, including an anonymous letter from "an enemy of the damned Royal Family" threatening George with assassination.[64] In Cruikshank's picture, McMahon directs George's attention to Charles I as the dead king holds his own head aloft, remarking "How queer King Charley looks without his Head, doesn't he?!!! Faith & sure & I wonder how *we* should look without our Heads?!!" Fears of regicide haunted the reigns of George III and IV after the

FIGURE 42

George Cruikshank, "Meditation Amongst the Tombs"

By permission of the British Library; MS. Addl. 6306

execution of Louis XVI, and, in a later caricature entitled "Radical Reformer, a Neck or Nothing Man" (1819), Cruikshank shows the regent and his ministers fleeing a guillotine come to life.[65] Meanwhile, in "Meditations Amongst the Tombs," the smiling devil suggests that a fate worse than death or a miserable marriage may await the Prince of Wales in the afterlife.

George survived the threats and embarrassments of his regency, but his struggle with his wife, Caroline, reached its nadir in 1820 after his accession to the throne. She had decamped for a comfortable "exile" on the Continent in 1814, but when George III died, she returned to England to reclaim her prerogative as queen. Once again, popular opinion favored her over her husband. Enthusiastic crowds greeted her, and opposition politicians took up her cause. The government retaliated by launching divorce proceedings in the House of Lords. Charges of adulterous intimacies with her Italian valet were plausible enough, but her persecution by a promiscuous husband proved another public relations disaster. Government prosecutors had vainly tried to keep the king's name out of the proceedings, but before the fiasco ended, Henry Brougham, one of the queen's principal defenders, demanded to know their client's identity. Met with evasions, Brougham snidely replied, "I know nothing about this shrouded, this mysterious being—this retiring phantom, this uncertain shape," capping the insult by quoting John Milton's description of Death in *Paradise Lost*:

> If shape it might be called that shape had none
> Distinguishable in member, joint, or limb,
> Or substance might be called that shadow seemed,
> For each seemed either; . . . what seemed his head
> The likeness of a kingly crown had on.
>
> (2.666–673)

The king was mortally offended, but his response to the comparison simply betrayed his obtuse vanity; Brougham reports that George said, "I might have spared him the attack on his shape. . . . He thought that everybody allowed whatever faults he might have, his legs were not as I described them."[66]

The government dropped the divorce trial, but Caroline's triumph was short-lived, and the struggle ended ignominiously for both sides. She was excluded from the coronation despite her efforts to crash the event, and the doors of Westminster were slammed in her face. Some in the crowd even jeered her appearance later that day at a theater in Drury Lane. Shaken by these setbacks, Queen Caroline fell ill and died within months. Her death revived the popular image of Caroline as a martyr and victim, and her funeral was marked by renewed demonstrations of grief and outrage. Brougham recorded that the widespread mourning "was such as I can never forget or reflect upon without emotion. The multitudes assembled from all parts of the country were immense."[67] Yet, because he was eager to regain favor in the new regime, Brougham insisted that it was "very well known that through the whole business he had never been very much for the Queen!"[68] William Hazlitt was an astute critic of politics as well as poetry, and, disgusted by the whole affair, he condemned the cynical hypocrisy of friends like these and the fickle sympathies of the general public. His contempt for "the wretched, helpless, doating, credulous, meddlesome people" recalls Milton's condemnation of the "Image-doting rabble" in Eikonoklastes (CPW 3:601), and both writers hated the hypocrisy of "Presbyterian parsons" who, as Hazlitt says, "knelt to kiss the hand of their royal mistress."[69] Hazlitt was also revolted by those flocking to the queen's side during the divorce trial: "Here were all the patriots and Jacobins of London and Westminster, who scorned and hated the King, going to pay their homage to the queen, and ready to worship the very rags of royalty. . . . The world must have something to admire, and the more worthless and stupid their idol is, the better. . . . We in modern times have got from the *dead* to the *living* idol, and bow to hereditary imbecility."[70]

In Hazlitt's hyperbolic account, "modern times" have brought no progress because we continue to idolize living kings and queens rather than graven images. Yet despite his pessimism, few of his contemporaries actually believed in kingship's sanctity, and this made genuine civil idolatry harder to sustain. Fickle sentiment proved too feeble a prop for sacred kingship, and satiric scorn too strong a solvent. Caroline was soon forgotten, and George IV remained the butt of satires even after his ascent to the throne. The new king's coronation in 1821 was a magnificent ceremony, but William Hone honored the occasion with a mocking tract entitled *The Right Divine of Kings to Govern Wrong*. Hone's title is taken from Alexander Pope's *Dunciad* (4:188), and his verse and commentary, adapted from Daniel Defoe's *Jure Divino*, pours scorn on despotic pretensions.[71] George Cruikshank's title page (figure 43) shows the coronation of a grotesque madman grasping implements of torture and terror as he is anointed by a fat bishop and crowned by a thin one. As Cruikshank's caricatures of royal burials and coronations amply demonstrate, by the beginning of the nineteenth century, the "cease of majesty" inspired little pity or terror, and the "divinity [that] doth hedge a king" had lost most of its sanctity.

Nevertheless, the civil idolatry so deplored by John Milton and William Hazlitt has not completely faded away even in our own time. In his provocative study of the modern British monarchy, *The Enchanted Glass*, Tom Nairn argues that England's ruling class carefully preserved this archaic institution in order to suppress the democratic and egalitarian prospects of republican rule, and he concludes that in England today, "most of society's instincts can still be channeled upwards into adoration of the Crown."[72] In a country that continues to call itself the United Kingdom, many still believe that the royal family represents, in the words of a *London Times* editorial, the *"inner spiritual essence of our national life."*[73] Such quasi-mystical claims recall those made by Tudor propagandists for royal supremacy when they described Henry VIII as "the soul of the whole kingdom."[74] Each makes the royal presence into a real presence incarnating and binding the corporate body into a unified whole. The same equation may still hold. According to Nairn, coronations, visitations, and walkabouts, as well as royal weddings and funerals, still provide the nation with "orgasmic moments of communion."[75]

In England's recent history, few events have aroused such strong feelings of communal intensity or civil idolatry as the funeral of Diana, Princess of Wales, in 1997. Her death inspired a degree of grief and hagiography that evoked older traditions of sacred kingship. Images of Diana as martyr, saint, and healer coalesced into something like a devotional cult, and many saw the huge crowds, floral tributes, and homemade shrines as portents of a profound, almost sacramental

THE

RIGHT DIVINE OF KINGS TO GOVERN WRONG!

Dedicated to the holy Alliance

BY THE AUTHOR OF

THE POLITICAL HOUSE THAT JACK BUILT.

" The devil will not have me damn'd, lest the *oil* that is in me should set hell on fire."
SHAKSPEARE.

LONDON:

PRINTED FOR WILLIAM HONE,
45, LUDGATE-HILL.

1821.

Eighteenpence.

FIGURE 43
George Cruikshank, *The Right Divine of Kings to Govern Wrong*, title page
Copyright: Bodleian Library, University of Oxford; 270d58 (9)

alteration of state.[76] Writing immediately after her death, the otherwise sober historian David Cannadine embraces this point of view: "And who can doubt that the events of this week have marked the beginning of the myth of Diana as saint and martyr. . . . From this perspective, her funeral will conclude and consolidate a public relations triumph far surpassing anything she achieved in life: we shall always remember the day she died and the day she was buried, her grave will soon become a place of national and international pilgrimage, the vacant plinth at the north-west corner of Trafalgar Square need no longer lack a statue, and biographies will cascade from the presses with haunting, bitter-sweet pictures. Diana, Princess of Wales, is dead; but Diana, Queen of Hearts, yet lives."[77] Now, just a few years later, a less exalted legacy seems likelier. The first noteworthy posthumous biography, authored by her private secretary and serialized in the *Sunday Times*, describes Diana as a scheming, malicious, and unstable neurotic with a "pathological craving for victimhood."[78] The number of visitors to the grave at her family home has dropped, contributions to her memorial fund have taken a "nosedive," and the third anniversary of her death drew small crowds and no public tributes.[79]

From a less enraptured perspective, Diana's legend acquires a more prosaic dimension. The marital miseries of Charles and Diana recall those of an earlier Prince and Princess of Wales, and many of the same mood swings in the tabloid and popular response are discernible.[80] The bitter estrangement, adulterous affairs, and adversarial maneuvers of George and Caroline provoked a similar blend of scandalized sanctimony, salacious mockery, and prurient fascination. In each case, the royal household's efforts to shut the woman out backfired badly, and the aggrieved wife deliberately exploited her advantage.[81] Although the highly publicized improprieties of each woman threatened her reputation, death inflamed popular sympathy to extremes that alarmed the surviving dynasty. Nevertheless, despite huge demonstrations at each funeral, the intense grief displayed subsided fairly quickly. An apparent resurgence of sacramental devotion was soon supplanted by sentimentality, skepticism, and relative indifference.

Contemporary attitudes toward monarchy remain ambivalent. Although few still believe in sacred kingship, the fall of princes—and princesses—can still have an exceptional emotional and social impact, as the reaction to Diana's death shows. Even the demise of one who "in story only rules" often elicits widespread and genuine grief. Yet the intensity of these feelings does not last long, and civil idolatry in our own time has proven shallow and ephemeral. Without a belief in divine right rule, royal alterations of state lack cosmic significance or profound historical consequence. At the same time, the death of royalty can still stir up desires for a lost real presence, only briefly allayed by collective "moments of communion." The literature of the English Reformation offers significant insight into the origins of these ambivalent feelings. The enduring power of "sad stories of the death of kings" by Shakespeare and his contemporaries can help us understand our abiding distress at "the cease of majesty." Moreover, they provide us with something more substantive than a real or royal presence. In the words of William Hazlitt, the great works of Skelton and Shakespeare, Milton and Marvell all allow us a relation to a reality as vivid and "as real as our own thoughts."

Notes

PREFACE

1. John Bossy, *Christianity in the West: 1400–1700* (Oxford: Oxford University Press, 1985), 145, and "The Mass as a Social Institution, 1200–1700," *Past and Present* 100 (1983): 59.

2. John Phillips, *The Reformation of Images: Destruction of Art in England, 1535–1660* (Berkeley: University of California Press, 1973), 204–205. Eamon Duffy, *The Stripping of the Altars: Traditional Religion in England, 1400–1580* (New Haven: Yale University Press, 1992), 566 and 580.

3. Paul Kléber Monod, *The Power of Kings: Monarchy and Religion in Europe, 1589–1715* (New Haven: Yale University Press, 1999), 47. Despite the opposition of many reformers, European monarchs still promoted their sacral pretensions through "rituals, ceremonies, paintings, and literature" in an enlarged "public sphere" (84) in what Monod calls "the theatre of royal virtue" (81–141).

4. John Milton, *Eikonoklastes*, in *The Complete Prose Works of John Milton*, ed. Don M. Wolfe, 8 vols. (New Haven: Yale University Press, 1959), 3:343; all references to Milton's prose are to this edition and hereafter cited in the text.

5. J. A. Sharpe, *Early Modern England: A Social History, 1550–1760* (1987; reprint, London: Edward Arnold, 1990), 1–2.

6. Thomas Dekker, *The Wonderful Year*, in *Non-Dramatic Works*, ed. Alexander B. Grosart, 5 vols. (London, 1884), 1:88.

7. Caroline Bingham, *James I of England* (London: Weidenfeld and Nicolson, 1981), 32.

8. William Shakespeare, *Hamlet*, ed. Harold Jenkins (London: Methuen, 1982), 3.3.15 and 1.5.196. All references to Shakespeare's plays and poems are from the Arden editions, hereafter cited in the text.

9. Cf. G. Wilson Knight, who says that "This fine speech, in the style of *Troilus and Cressida*, cannot be written off as sheer flattery" in *The Wheel of Fire: Interpretations of Shakespearean Tragedy* (1930; reprint, New York: Meridian, 1958), 318.

10. Laertes describes himself in the same way when he offers to open his arms to his late father's true friends and "like the kind life-rend'ring pelican,/Repast them with my blood" (4.5.146–147).

11. Ernst Kantorowicz, *The King's Two Bodies: A Study in Medieval Political Theology* (1957; reprint, Princeton: Princeton University Press, 1981), 196 and 206. For a probing critique of Kantorowicz's mystical, quasi-totalitarian conception of kingship and nostalgia for a lost world of "sacramental unity" (341), see David Norbrook, "The Emperor's New Body? *Richard II,* Ernst Kantorowicz and the Politics of Shakespeare Criticism," *Textual Practice* 10 (1996): 329–357. Norbrook notes the principled opposition to the pretensions of sacred kingship throughout the early modern period, and he objects to criticism that makes Shakespeare into an absolutist. While my own reading of *Hamlet* emphasizes the disturbing impact of "the cease of majesty," I also show how the play undermines a belief in the "divinity [that] doth hedge a king" even as it invokes it.

12. Michel Foucault, *The Order of Things: An Archaeology of the Human Sciences* (1970; reprint, New York: Vintage, 1973), 4. Cf. Franco Moretti: "As the one who, himself in equilibrium, provides the point of equilibrium for the social order, the sovereign is the missing person, the impossible being in Shakespearean tragedy" (*Signs Taken for Wonders: Essays in the Sociology of Literary Forms,* trans. Susan Fischer, David Forgacs, and David Miller [London: Verso, 1983], 68).

13. Foucault, 4 and 308. For a discussion of the ways in which *Las Meninas* is "structured like a representation of a court play which was attended by many, but intended for the king who was present both as a spectator and participant in the drama," see Jonathan Brown, *Velasquez: Painter and Courtier* (New Haven: Yale University Press, 1986), 303 and 259.

14. Foucault, *History of Sexuality,* trans. Robert Hurley, 2 vols. (New York: Pantheon, 1978), 1:88–89.

15. The Eucharist became the "focus of more theological controversy in the sixteenth century than any other item of Christian confession or practice" according to Christopher Elwood, *The Body Broken: The Calvinist Doctrine of the Eucharist and the Symbolization of Power in Sixteenth-Century France* (New York: Oxford University Press, 1999), 3–4. See also Euan Cameron, *The European Reformation* (Oxford: Clarendon Press, 1991), 161.

16. Brian A. Gerrish, "Eucharist," in *The Oxford Encyclopedia of the Reformation,* ed. Hans Hillerbrand, 4 vols. (New York: Oxford University Press, 1996), 2:76. See also Thomas J. Davis, *The Clearest Promises of God: The Development of Calvin's Eucharistic Teaching* (New York: AMS Press, 1993), 29–30.

17. Jaroslav Pelikan, *The Christian Tradition: A History of the Development of Doctrine; Reformation of Church and Dogma, 1300–1700,* 5 vols. (Chicago: University of Chicago Press, 1984), 4:186 and 192–193. See also Kilian McDonnell,

John Calvin, the Church, and the Eucharist (Princeton: Princeton University Press, 1967), 224–225, and Brian A. Gerrish, *Grace and Gratitude: The Eucharistic Theology of John Calvin* (Minneapolis: Fortress Press, 1993), 104–106 and 140–145. Calvin's efforts at mediation were not wholly successful for, as Gerrish says, he sometimes "seemed to stumble between the rival opinions of Luther and Zwingli rather than to harmonize them" (10).

18. Pelikan, 4:201. Stephen Greenblatt cites this same passage in his fascinating account of the importance of Eucharistic doctrine for *Hamlet*, but he suggests that both Beza and Calvin conclude that transubstantiation and trope are the "only two possibilities," whereas they and most other reformers were intent on finding a third alternative; Catherine Gallagher and Stephen Greenblatt, *Practicing New Historicism* (Chicago: University of Chicago Press, 2000), 146. See also Greenblatt's *Hamlet in Purgatory* (Princeton: Princeton University Press, 2001), 241–244.

19. Joseph C. McLelland, *The Visible Words of God: An Exposition of the Sacramental Theology of Peter Martyr Vermigli A.D. 1500–1562* (Grand Rapids, MI: Eerdmans Press, 1957), 16.

20. Ibid., 20. See also Peter Martyr Vermigli, *The Oxford Treatise and Disputation on the Eucharist, 1549*, trans. and ed. Joseph C. McClelland (Kirksville, MO: Truman State University Press, 2000), 151.

21. John Calvin, *Short Treatise of the Lord's Supper* (1541), in *Theological Treatises*, trans. J. K. S. Reid (Philadelphia: Westminster Press, 1954), 59.

22. *Apologia Prima*, in *Contra Claude de Sainctes* (1567), 298, cited in Jill Raitt, *The Eucharistic Theology of Theodore Beza: Development of the Reformed Doctrine* (Chartersburg, PA: American Academy of Religion, 1972), 39.

23. Beza, *De Controversius*, in *Coena Domini* (1593), 38, in Raitt, 64–65.

24. Greenblatt, *Practicing New Historicism*, 151.

25. Paul de Man, *Rhetoric and Romanticism* (New York: Columbia University Press, 1984), 239 and 242–243.

26. Geoffrey Hartman, *Criticism in the Wilderness: The Study of Literature Today* (New Haven: Yale University Press, 1980), 167.

27. Hartman, *The Fatal Question of Culture* (New York: Columbia University Press, 1997), 181 and 111.

28. Stephen Greenblatt, *Shakespearean Negotiations: The Circulation of Social Energy in Renaissance England* (Chicago: University of Chicago Press, 1988), 1. The idea of literature and literary studies as magical practices continues to inform *Hamlet in Purgatory*, where Greenblatt describes Shakespeare as a "conjurer" (3) and his theater as "a cult of the dead that I and the readers of this book have been serving" (257). *Conjurer* was a loaded term in

early modern England, for, as Keith Thomas explains, "In the reign of Elizabeth I . . . the term 'conjurer' came to be a synonym for recusant priest";
Protestants repeatedly accused Catholic clergy of resorting to necromancy
and conjuring in their efforts to consort with dead or demonic spirits; see *Religion and the Decline of Magic* (New York: Scribners, 1971), 68.

29. Greenblatt, *Shakespearean Negotiations*, 1.

30. Leah Marcus, "Renaissance/Early Modern Studies," *Redrawing the
Boundaries: The Transformation of English and American Literary Studies*, ed.
Stephen Greenblatt and Giles Gunn (New York: Modern Language Associa-
tion, 1992), 45. These same premises are reemphasized by Gallagher and
Greenblatt in *Practicing New Historicism*, 51–56; here too, "a humanist faith in
historical understanding" is treated with somewhat patronizing skepticism
(56), whereas the "quasi-magical effect" of "conjuring" is enthusiastically endorsed (37).

31. Francesco Petrarca, *Letters on Familiar Matters XVII–XXIV*, trans. Aldo S.
Bernardo (Baltimore: Johns Hopkins University Press, 1985), 350. Thomas
Greene's discussion of this letter and Petrarch's complex conception of conti-
nuity with the past is especially illuminating; see *The Light in Troy: Imitation and
Discovery in Renaissance Poetry* (New Haven: Yale University Press, 1982), 29–45.

32. Links between *Richard II* and the Essex revolt are discussed in the
Arden edition of *Richard II* edited by Peter Ure (1956; reprint, London:
Methuen, 1989), lvii–lxii; cf. Leeds Barroll, who says that these connections
have "become something of a cliché" for new historicism ("A New History
for Shakespeare and His Time," *Shakespeare Quarterly* 39 [1988]: 442). *Hamlet's*
cryptic reference to "the late innovation" as a source of trouble for the players is also seen as a glance at the Essex revolt; see Harold Jenkins in the
Arden *Hamlet*, 470–472.

33. See my " 'Thou Idol Ceremony': Elizabeth I, *The Henriad*, and the
Rites of the English Monarchy," in *Urban Life in the Renaissance*, ed. Susan
Zimmerman and Ronald F. E. Weissman (Newark: University of Delaware
Press, 1989), 240–266.

I. REAL PRESENCE TO ROYAL PRESENCE

1. Calvin objects to Catholic notions of Christ's "local presence" in the
sacrament, "to be touched by the hands, to be chewed by the teeth, and to
be swallowed by the mouth" in *Institutes of the Christian Religion* (IV.xvii.12),

trans. Ford Lewis Battles, ed. John T. McNeill (Philadelphia: Westminster Press, 1960), 2:1374.

2. Thomas Becon, *The Jewel of Joy*, in *The Catechism . . . with other works written in the Reign of Edward VI*, ed. A. J. Ayre, Parker Society Publications, vol. 3 (Cambridge: Cambridge University Press, 1844), 413. A chaplain to Cranmer and a prolific author, Becon was imprisoned for the first year of Mary's reign, sought refuge in Strassburg, and returned to England with other Marian exiles after Elizabeth's accession.

3. Becon 3:414.

4. Christopher Haigh, *English Reformations: Religion, Politics, and Society Under the Tudors* (1993; reprint, Oxford: Clarendon Press, 1995), 191. While I use the conventional singular, capitalized *Reformation* in my title and elsewhere because it permits a broad overview, I agree with Haigh's revisionist account of England's slow and conflicted conversion to Protestantism and refer to its erratic reformations in the lower case.

5. Francis Clark, S. J., *Eucharistic Sacrifice and the Reformation* (Westminster, MD: The Newman Press, 1960), 103–104 and 140.

6. Jonathan Z. Smith, *To Take Place: Toward Theory in Ritual* (Chicago: University of Chicago Press, 1987), 104.

7. Claude Lévi-Strauss, *The Savage Mind* (1962; reprint, Chicago: University of Chicago Press, 1966), 10.

8. John Bossy, *Christianity in the West: 1400–1700* (Oxford: Oxford University Press, 1985), 145.

9. Carlos M. N. Eire, *War Against the Idols: The Reformation of Worship from Erasmus to Calvin* (Cambridge: Cambridge University Press, 1986), 1.

10. Jaroslav Pelikan, *The Christian Tradition: A History of the Development of Doctrine; The Growth of Medieval Theology, 600–1300*, 5 vols. (Chicago: University of Chicago Press, 1978), 3:159, 185. Pelikan notes that, during the Middle Ages, the Eucharist supplanted Baptism, which had been deemed the central sacrament of the earlier Patristic era (3:205).

11. Eamon Duffy, *The Stripping of the Altars: Traditional Religion in England, 1400–1580* (New Haven: Yale University Press, 1992), 92.

12. Pelikan, 303–304. See also E. Schillebeeckx, *The Eucharist*, trans. N. D. Smith (New York: Sheed and Ward, 1968), 30–31, 40–41, and 55–56. On the other hand, Gary Macy qualifies Pelikan's claims for a definitive formulation of this doctrine at the Lateran Council by describing three different theories of sacramental change, at least two of which were accepted as orthodox. See "The Dogma of Transubstantiation in the Middle

Ages," *Journal of Ecclesiastical History* 45 (1994): 11–41; Macy concludes that "'transubstantiation' itself did not have a fixed meaning" (40).

13. C. W. Dugmore, *The Mass and the English Reformers* (London: Macmillan, 1958), 25 and 55–56. See also V. A. Kolve, *The Play Called Corpus Christi* (Stanford: Stanford University Press, 1966), 44–45.

14. Duffy, 36.

15. *Memoirs of a Renaissance Pope: The Commentaries of Pius II* (abridged), trans. Florence A. Gragg, ed. Leona C. Babel (New York: Capricorn, 1959), 268. I am grateful to Joseph Connors for this reference.

16. Erwin Panofsky, *Albrecht Dürer*, 2 vols. (Princeton: Princeton University Press, 1948), 1:216. See Friedrich Winkler, *Die Zeichnungen Albrecht Dürers*, 7 vols. (Berlin: Deutscher Verein für Kunstwissenschaft, 1936), 2:138–139.

17. Roger Jones and Nicholas Penny, *Raphael* (New Haven: Yale University Press, 1983), 60.

18. Ibid.; cf. Panofsky's discussion of the "dematerialization" of the basilica of St. Peter's in his picture of the Mass of St. Gregory (1:137). Dürer's engraving was made in 1511, but Panofsky sees an incipient sympathy for Protestant spiritualism, which would eventually lead Dürer to convert to Lutheranism (1:198–199).

19. Leopold D. and Helen S. Ettlinger, *Raphael* (Oxford: Phaidon, 1987), 107.

20. Ann Eljenholm Nichols, *Seeable Signs: The Iconography of the Seven Sacraments, 1350–1544* (Woodbridge: Boydell, 1994), 9–11. Cf. Robert Whiting, *The Blind Devotion of the People: Popular Religion and the English Reformation* (Cambridge: Cambridge University Press, 1989), 17.

21. *English Works*, 127, 110–111, cited in Nichols, 6. See also Richard Rex, *The Theology of John Fisher* (Cambridge: Cambridge University Press, 1991), 132–134.

22. See the description of the sermon, miracle, and recantation in Margaret Aston, *Faith and Fire: Popular and Unpopular Religion, 1350–1600* (London: Hambledon, 1993), 41. See also J. C. T. Oates, "Richard Pynson and the Holy Blood of Hayles," *The Library*, 5th Series, 13 (1958): 269–277.

23. Croxton, *Play of the Sacrament: Non-Cycle Plays and Fragments*, ed. Norman Davis, *Early English Text Society*, s.s. 1 (London, 1970), 58–89. Cecilia Cutts was the first to pursue this approach in "The Croxton Play: An Anti-Lollard Piece," *Modern Literature Quarterly* 5 (1944): 45–60, and she provides a thorough summary of Eucharistic miracles and legends of the period. Richard L. Homan agrees with her interpretation in "Devotional Themes in the Violence and Humor of the *Play of the Sacrament*," *Comparative Drama* 20 (1986–87): 339, as does Victor I. Scherb in "Violence and the Social Body in the Croxton *Play of the Sacrament*," *Violence in Drama: Themes in Drama* 13, ed.

James Redmond (Cambridge: Cambridge University Press, 1991), 71. Ann El-jenholm Nichols disputes Cutts's reading, distinguishing the play's affirmation of Eucharistic piety from "a reaction to anti-Eucharistic heresy" in "The Croxton *Play of the Sacrament*: A Re-Reading," *Comparative Drama* 22 (1988): 117, but she also acknowledges that the play includes many technical terms of Lollard controversy in "Lollard Language in the Croxton *Play of the Sacrament*," *Notes and Queries* 36 (1989): 23–25.

24. K. B. McFarlane, *John Wycliffe and the Beginnings of English Nonconformity* (London: English University Press, 1972), 167–168.

25. Skepticism toward such Eucharistic miracles may be the inevitable reaction in a system in which the "miracle itself was already disturbingly dependent on doubt," as Stephen Greenblatt notes in "The Wound in the Wall," in *Practicing New Historicism* (Chicago: University of Chicago Press, 2000), 100.

26. Martin Luther, *The Babylonian Captivity of the Church*, trans. A. T. W. Steinhauser, rev. by Frederick C. Ahrens and Abdel Ross Wentz, in *Luther's Works: Word and Sacrament*, ed. Abdel Ross Wentz and Helmut T. Lehman, 54 vols. (Philadelphia: Fortress, 1959), 36:35–36.

27. Martin Luther, *Ein Sermon von dem heillegen hochwirdigen Sacrament der Tauffe* (Leipzig, 1520); Folger 218–319q. For a discussion of Luther's sacramental theology, see Robert Herndon Fife, *The Revolt of Martin Luther* (New York: Columbia University Press, 1957), 459–461.

28. Ulrich Zwingli, *Exposition of Faith* (1530), cited in G. R. Potter, "Zwingli and Calvin," in *The Reformation Crisis*, ed. Joel Hurstfield (New York: Harper and Row, 1965), 34.

29. G. R. Potter, *Zwingli* (Cambridge: Cambridge University Press, 1978), 325–331.

30. Brian J. Gerrish, "Eucharist," in *The Oxford Encyclopedia of the Reformation*, ed. Hans Hillerbrand, 4 vols. (New York: Oxford University Press, 1996), 2:79; Gerrish still emphasizes Cranmer's determination "to press against the limits of the Zwinglian position" and establish a "true presence" (78–79). Gregory Dix, *The Shape of the Liturgy* (London: Dacre, 1945), 656–659, and Cyril Richardson, *Zwingli and Cranmer on the Eucharist* (Evanston, IL: Seabury-Western, 1949) emphasize Cranmer's affinities with Zwingli, but Peter Brooks, *Thomas Cranmer's Doctrine of the Eucharist: An Essay in Historical Development* (New York: Seabury, 1965), 35–37 and 51–71, and Diarmaid MacCulloch, *Thomas Cranmer* (New Haven: Yale University Press, 1996), 378–405 demonstrate Cranmer's debt to more moderate reformers such as Martin Bucer and Peter Martyr Vermigli.

31. St. Thomas More, *Responsio Ad Lutheram*, in *The Complete Works*, trans. Sister Scholastica Mandeville, ed. John M. Headley, 15 vols. (New Haven: Yale University Press, 1969), 5:1 and 2:687.

32. Pelikan, 4:257.

33. Haigh, 153.

34. Henry VIII, *Assertio Septem Sacramentorum or a Defence of the Seven Sacraments Against Martin Luther*, trans. T. W. (Dublin, 1766), 71–72.

35. Diarmaid MacCulloch, *The Later Reformation in England*, 2nd ed. (London: Palgrave, 2001), 1.

36. Haigh, 167.

37. Eustace Chapuys to the Emperor (December 6, 1529), *Calendar of State Papers, Spanish*, Henry VIII, 1529–30, ed. Pascual de Gayangos (London, 1879), 4:349–350.

38. Susan Brigden, *London and the Reformation* (Oxford: Oxford University Press, 1989), 353. Cf. Christopher Elwood, *The Body Broken: The Calvinist Doctrine of the Eucharist and the Symbolization of Power in Sixteenth-Century France* (New York: Oxford University Press, 1999), 75: "The social order lost its sacred ground."

39. *The Supplication of Souls*, *The Complete Works of St. Thomas More*, ed. Frank Manley, Germain Marc'Hardour, Richard Marius, and Clarence H. Miller, 15 vols. (New Haven: Yale University Press, 1990): 7:161. In More's view, the "specyall poynt and foundacyon of all Luthers heresyes" is this attack on the link between the priesthood's sacramental powers and the ecclesiastical community of faith that the sacraments sustain (7:154).

40. Bossy, 153–154.

41. J. J. Scarisbrick, *Henry VIII* (Berkeley: University of California Press, 1968), 275–276.

42. *The Tudor Constitution: Documents and Commentary*, ed. G. R. Elton (Cambridge: Cambridge University Press, 1962), 344. See also S. J. Gunn, *Early Tudor Government, 1485–1558* (New York: St. Martin's, 1995), 164–165. Thomas Cromwell is credited by Elton as the coordinator of the propaganda and legislative campaign promoting royal supremacy ("Propaganda," in *Policy and Police: The Enforcement of the Reformation in the Age of Thomas Cromwell* [Cambridge: Cambridge University Press, 1972], 171–216), but John Guy concludes that "Cranmer is a better candidate than Cromwell as agent of this new direction" in "Thomas Cromwell and the Intellectual Origins of the Henrician Revolution," in *Reassessing the Henrician Age: Humanism, Politics and Reform: 1500–1550*, ed. Alistair Fox and John Guy (Oxford: Blackwell,

1986), 156. For a discussion of the ideas informing this propaganda campaign, see Franklin Le Van Baumer, *The Early Tudor Theory of Kingship* (New York: Russell & Russell, 1966), 41–49; W. Gordon Zeeveld, *Foundations of Tudor Policy* (Cambridge: Harvard University Press, 1948); and Quentin Skinner, *The Foundations of Modern Political Thought*, 2 vols. (Cambridge: Cambridge University Press, 1978), 1:52–65 and 2:84–108.

43. See Richard Rex on the early Tudor "obsession with obedience" in *Henry VIII and the English Reformation* (Basingstoke: Macmillan, 1993), 25–26.

44. G. R. Elton, *Studies in Tudor and Stuart Politics and Government*, 2 vols. (Cambridge: Cambridge University Press, 1974), 1:105.

45. Scarisbrick, 386.

46. See the discussion of Henry VIII's "reorientation" of traditional "sacral kingship" in Rex, 28–29.

47. Dale Hoak, "The Iconography of the Crown Imperial" in *Tudor Political Culture*, ed. Dale Hoak (Cambridge: Cambridge University Press, 1995), 54–103; see also Fritz Kern, *Kingship and Law in the Middle Ages*, trans. S. B. Chrimes (1948; reprint, Westport, CT: Greenwood, 1985), 48–49 and 54–56.

48. Ernst Kantorowicz, *The King's Two Bodies: A Study in Medieval Political Theology* (1957; reprint, Princeton: Princeton University Press, 1981), 206.

49. Marc Bloch, *The Royal Touch: Sacred Monarchy and Scrofula in England and France*, trans. J. E. Anderson (London: Routledge, 1973).

50. "Treatise on Royal Power," PRO SP 1/238, f. 245, cited in Scarisbrick, 386, and BL Lansdowne MSS. 97, Plut LXXV, E 13, ff. 148–153, cited in Baumer, *The Early Tudor Theory of Kingship*, 86.

51. Scarisbrick, 386.

52. Most recent scholarship disputes the view of Foxe as an exponent of apocalyptic nationalism and royalism advanced by William Haller in *Foxe's Book of Martyrs and the Elect Nation* (London: J. Cape, 1963). Citing Aylmer's marginal notation, "God is English," Haller argues that the church "appeared now as one with the nation, and for many, besides the champions of a still more perfect reformation, the nation itself assumed something of the nature of a mystical communion of chosen spirits" embodied in the monarchy (245), but most now see Foxe as more internationalist and less apocalyptic and argue that his support for the Tudor monarchy was conditional. See William M. Lamont, *Godly Rule: Politics and Religion, 1603–60* (London: Macmillan, 1969), 23–25 and 34; V. Norskov Olsen, *John Foxe and the Elizabethan Church* (Berkeley: University of California Press, 1973), 191–195;

Richard Bauckham, *Tudor Apocalypse: Sixteenth-Century Apocalypticism, Millenarianism, and the English Reformation* (Oxford: Sutton Courtenay Press, 1978), 71–73 and 87; K. R. Firth, *The Apocalyptic Tradition in Reformation Britain 1530–1645* (Oxford: Clarendon Press, 1979), 107–108; and Peter Lake, "The Significance of the Elizabethan Identification of the Pope as Antichrist," *Journal of Ecclesiastical History* 31 (1980): 161–178.

53. Edward Hall, *Chronicle of the History of England* (1809; reprint, New York: AMS Press, 1965), 865–866.

54. MacCulloch, *Thomas Cranmer*, 348. See also Diarmaid MacCulloch, "Henry VIII and the Reform of the Church" in *The Reign of Henry VIII: Politics, Policy, and Piety*, ed. Diarmaid MacCulloch (New York: St. Martin's, 1995), 175.

55. Frances Yates, *Astraea: The Imperial Theme in the Seventeenth Century* (London: Routledge & Kegan Paul, 1975), and John King, *Tudor Royal Iconography* (Princeton: Princeton University Press, 1989).

56. John Foxe, *Actes and Monuments* (London, 1563), B1r.

57. Roy Strong, *The Cult of Elizabeth* (Berkeley: University of California Press, 1977).

58. Sir Thomas Smith, *De Republica Anglorum*, ed. Mary Dewar (Cambridge: Cambridge University Press, 1982), 88. For all his reverence toward the sovereign, Smith remains an advocate of England's mixed rule of crown and parliament rather than absolute monarchy (52–55).

59. Yates, 59.

60. Christopher Haigh describes this period as a "reformation reversed" (152–167).

61. Elaine V. Beilin, Introduction to *The Examinations of Anne Askew*, ed. Elaine V. Beilin (New York: Oxford University Press, 1996), xxvii.

62. Susan Wabuda, "The Woman with the Rock: The Controversy on Women and Bible Reading," *Belief and Practice in Reformation England*, ed. Susan Wabuda and Caroline Litzenberger (Aldershot: Ashgate, 1998), 56. See also Thomas Betteridge, *Tudor Histories of the English Reformations, 1530–83* (Aldershot: Ashgate, 1999), 101–102; Maria Dowling, "Anne Boleyn and Reform," *Journal of English History* 35 (1984): 30–46; E. W. Ives, "Anne Boleyn and the Early Reformation: The Contemporary Evidence," *Historical Journal* 32 (1994): 389–400; John King, "Patronage and Piety: The Influence of Catherine Parr," in *Silent But for the Word: Tudor Women as Patrons, Translators, and Writers of Religious Works*, ed. Margaret Hannay (Kent: Ohio State University Press, 1985), 43–60; Janel Mueller, "A Tudor Queen Finds Voice: Katherine Parr's *Lamentation of a Sinner*," in *The Historical Renais-*

sance: New Essays on Tudor and Stuart Literature and Culture, ed. Heather Dubrow and Richard Strier (Chicago: University of Chicago Press, 1988), 15–47.

63. Beilin, xxviii.

64. *The Examinations of Anne Askew*, 150. Henry Howard, Earl of Surrey, similarly paraphrases Ecclesiastes in a poem describing his own perilous situation near the end of Henry's reign; see Beilin, xxxii. Beilin argues that "Far from being an indictment of Henry VIII," this passage "is an apocalyptic vision of the usurpation of Scriptural Justice by the Pope" in *Redeeming Eve: Women Writers of the English Renaissance* (Princeton: Princeton University Press, 1987), 45; however, the disappointment expressed in these lines suggests that they apply to a ruler from whom "Justyce" was actually expected: i.e., Henry rather than the pope.

65. *The Examinations of Anne Askew*, 102.

66. John Foxe, *Acts and Monuments*, ed. George Townsend, 8 vols. (1843–49?; reprint, New York: AMS Press, 1965), 5:537. Hereafter cited in the text. A British Academy Research Project, under the direction of Professor David Loades, is currently preparing a new scholarly edition of Foxe's *Acts and Monuments* to replace the highly unreliable nineteenth-century amalgam, but until it is available, the Cattley-Townsend edition remains the most accessible reference.

67. Diarmaid MacCulloch finds additional evidence for "a tilt toward an evangelical direction" in Martin Bucer's description of Henry's plans for "a further instauration [i.e., renovation] of the churches" in "Henry VIII and the Reform of the Church" (180).

68. Paul Christianson, *Reformers and Babylon: English Apocalyptic Visions from the Reformation to the Eve of the Civil War* (Toronto: University of Toronto Press, 1978), 41–45, and Betteridge, 186. Betteridge contrasts the more spiritual and apocalyptic emphasis of the 1570 edition of Foxe's *Acts and Monuments* with the more worldly focus of the 1563 edition. However, Betteridge points out that, even though Foxe shared in the optimism that that greeted Elizabeth's accession, he criticized Tudor rule in both editions (176–177). Foxe and the other Reformation historians treat the monarch as a means to godliness and seek to dissociate the Reformation from any merely royal agenda (213).

69. Patrick Collinson, "If Constantine, Then Also Theodosius: St. Ambrose and the Integrity of the Elizabethan *Ecclesia Anglicana*," in *Godly People: Essays on English Protestantism and Puritanism* (London: Hambledon, 1983), 113.

2. SACRED SPACE:
JOHN SKELTON AND WESTMINSTER'S
ROYAL SEPULCHER

1. H. Maynard Smith, *Pre-Reformation England* (1938; London: Macmillan, 1963), 7.

2. W. R. Lethaby, *Westminster Abbey Re-examined* (London: Duckworth, 1925), 167.

3. See Jocelyn Perkins, *Westminster Abbey: Its Worship and Ornaments*, 3 vols. (London: Oxford University Press, 1938), 2:2 for a comparison of the ground plans "as completed by Henry VIII" and "as intended by the founder." According to Perkins, Henry VI was supposed to be placed in the chapel directly behind the altar and Henry VII's tomb placed in the choir, but Henry VIII buried his parents behind the altar instead.

4. Bertram Wolffe, *Henry VI* (London: Methuen, 1981), 4–6 and 351–357; Sydney Anglo, "Henry VI: The Lancastrian Saint," in *Images of Tudor Kingship* (London: Seaby, 1992), 61–73; John W. McKenna, "Piety and Propaganda: The Cult of Henry VI" in *Chaucer and Middle English Studies*, ed. Beryl Rowland (Kent: Kent State University Press, 1974), 72–88; Dale Hoak, "The Iconography of the Crown Imperial," *Tudor Political Culture*, ed. Dale Hoak (Cambridge: Cambridge University Press, 1995), 74.

5. Brian Spencer, "King Henry of Windsor and the London Pilgrim" in *Collectanea Londiniensia*, ed. J. Bird, H. Chapman, and J. Clark (London: London and Middlesex Archaeological Society, 1978), 235–264. Richard III moved the body from Chertsey Abbey to Windsor in 1484, placing it in a tomb across from that of his brother, Edward IV.

6. Francis Bacon, *The History of the Reign of King Henry VII* in *The Works of Francis Bacon*, ed. James Spedding, Robert Leslie Ellis, and Douglas Denon Heath, 15 vols. (London, 1861), 6:233. See also S. J. Gunn, *Early Tudor Government, 1485–1558* (New York: St. Martin's, 1995), 196–198.

7. Cf. Polydore Virgil, who concedes, even as he criticizes the king's stinginess, that Henry "was the most ardent supporter of our faith, and daily participated with great piety in religious services" in S. B. Chrimes, *Henry VII* (Berkeley: University of California Press, 1972), 299. According to Anthony Goodman, Henry's piety was essential to his "renewal of the religious authority of kingship"; see "Henry VII and Christian Renewal," in *Religion and Humanism*, ed. Keith Robins, *Studies in Church History* 17 (Oxford: Blackwell; Ecclesiastical History Society, 1981), 117 and 122; see also R. L. Storey, *The Reign of Henry VII* (New York: Walker, 1968), 63.

8. Peter Brown, *The Cult of the Saints: Its Rise and Function in Latin Christianity* (Chicago: University of Chicago Press, 1981), 86–88 and 105.

9. Ibid., 37.

10. Patrick J. Geary, *Living with the Dead in the Middle Ages* (Ithaca: Cornell University Press, 1994), 170.

11. Wilhelm Busch, *England Under the Tudors: King Henry VII*, trans. Alice M. Todd (1895; reprint, New York: Burt Franklin, 1965), 312, and J. J. Scarisbrick, *The Reformation and the English People* (Oxford: Blackwell, 1984), 58. Pope Julius II was trying to corner the market on indulgences as part of his fund-raising campaign for rebuilding St. Peter's.

12. *The Will of King Henry VII*, ed. T. Astle (London, 1775), 3; hereafter cited in the text.

13. Perkins, 2:47, and Frank Barlow, *Edward the Confessor* (Berkeley: University of California Press, 1970), 277–284.

14. Frank Barlow, "The King's Evil," *English Historical Review* 95 (1980): 25. On the abbey's importance to the monarchy as a coronation and burial site and stable center for a "once itinerant monarchy," see Paul Binski, *Westminster Abbey and the Plantagenets: Kingship and the Representation of Power: 1200–1400* (New Haven: Yale University Press, 1995), 5–6, and Barbara Harvey, *Westminster Abbey and Its Estates in the Middle Ages* (Oxford: Clarendon Press, 1977), 25.

15. According to one biography, Edward the Confessor had a miraculous vision of the Christ child in the host in Westminster, and the king "to Jesus bows and prays / With joy of spirit weeps / . . . As long as lasted the Mass"; see Binski, 146. Henry VII's coronation ordo has him "groveling afore the high aulter" and receiving the sacrament "wt a great devocion"; see Leopold G. Wickham Legg, *English Coronation Records* (Westminster: A. Constable, 1901), 220–239. Henry VIII also revered the Eucharist, but the Reformation he launched gradually eroded this devotion.

16. See Jacques Le Goff, *The Birth of Purgatory*, trans. Arthur Goldhammer (Chicago: University of Chicago Press, 1984). Stephen Greenblatt gives a vivid account of purgatorial beliefs and practices in *Hamlet in Purgatory* (Princeton: Princeton University Press, 2001).

17. Eamon Duffy, *The Stripping of the Altars: Traditional Religion in England, 1400–1580* (New Haven: Yale University Press, 1992), 161–162. Henry's devotion to his patron saints is evident in his funerary iconography. At his funeral procession, the banners of four of his "avowries" were carried at each corner of his coffin. His will specified "as many of the Ymagies of our said advouries, as the said table wol receive" carved on the chapel's main

altar (*Will*, 33), and the magnificent sarcophagus includes images of twelve of his patron saints. Alan Darr notes that the iconography of the English king's tomb was more traditionally religious than those of his papal contemporaries, which depicted regal virtues and the liberal arts; see "The Sculptures of Torrigiano: The Westminster Abbey Tombs," *The Connoisseur* 200 (1979): 183.

18. Thomas Aquinas cited in Le Goff, 275. See also Duffy, who says that "charity is the life of Purgatory" (344).

19. Ibid., 349–350.

20. Joyce Youings, *The Dissolution of the Monasteries* (London: Allen and Unwin, 1971), 188–190, and A. Kreider, *English Chantries: The Road to Dissolution* (Cambridge: Harvard University Press, 1979), 119–120.

21. Hugh Latimer, *Sermons and Remains*, ed. George Elwes Corrie, 2 vols. (Cambridge: Cambridge University Press, 1845; Parker Society Publications, vols. 33–34), 2:249.

22. Anglo, *Images of Tudor Kingship*, 100.

23. Edmund Dudley, *Tree of Commonwealth* (Manchester, 1859), 24.

24. Desiderius Erasmus, *Correspondence of Erasmus*, in *The Collected Works of Erasmus*, trans. R. A. B. Mynors and D. F. S. Thomson, ed. Wallace K. Ferguson (Toronto: University of Toronto Press, 1974), 1:197.

25. William Nelson gives the most complete account of Skelton's court career in *John Skelton: Laureate* (New York: Columbia University Press, 1939); for Skelton's appointment as *orator regius*, see 122–124. Greg Walker treats Skelton as a more marginal and opportunistic courtier with only a precarious hold on royal and aristocratic patronage in *John Skelton and the Politics of the 1520s* (Cambridge: Cambridge University Press, 1988).

26. Arthur F. Kinney, *John Skelton: Priest as Poet* (Chapel Hill: University of North Carolina Press, 1987), 119.

27. David R. Carlson includes them among "Writings Dubiously Attributable to Skelton in *The Latin Writings of John Skelton*," *Studies in Philology* 88 (1991): 59–60; he still argues for Skelton's authorship (121).

28. William Camden, *Reges, Reginae, Nobiles . . . in Westmonasterii sepulti* (London, 1606), 21–23; John Weever, *Ancient Funerall Monuments* (London, 1631), 476; Henry Keepe, *Monumenta Westmonasteriensa* (London, 1683), 287; Jodocus Crull, *The Antiquities of . . . Westminster* (London, 1711), 80–81.

29. Carlson includes the originals and translations of both eulogies (46–48 and 50–52).

30. "*Hac sub mole latet regis celeberrima mater/Henrici magni, quem locus iste fovet,/Quem locus iste sacer celebri celebrat poliandro*": "Beneath this pile lies the

celebrated mother of the king, the mighty Henry, whom this place also enshrines, whom this holy place celebrates with a celebrated tomb" (Carlson, 51–52).

31. Skelton's aggressive energy and ingenuity have received renewed attention. His verses' blend of braggadocio, ridicule, and abuse, coupled with their shortened meter and multiple rhymes, leads Allen Ginsberg to cite *Elynour Rummynge* as a model for contemporary rap lyrics and "poetry slams." See Henry Louis Gates, Jr., "Downtown Chronicles: Sudden Def," *The New Yorker* (June 19, 1995): 34–42. Ginsberg says that "Rap poetry, then evokes a very ancient, classical style, the style of toasts and boasts—hyperbole, exaggeration, the exchange of insults on a verbal, symbolic level that's used to siphon off aggression and to make political statements. It's important to remember that the humorless one always loses in the contest of bards" (40).

32. *The Complete English Poems*, ed. John Scattergood (Harmondsworth: Penguin, 1983), 305, lines 1044–1045; hereafter cited by line in the text.

33. Nelson, 134–135.

34. Susan Brigden, *London and the Reformation* (1989; reprint, Oxford: Oxford University Press, 1991), 82–84.

35. *Rites of Durham*, ed. J. T. Fowler (Durham: Surtees Society, 107, 1903), 26. The anonymous author of this late sixteenth-century compilation reports that the corporal was eventually burned by the wife of the dean of the cathedral in contempt "of all auncyent & goodly reliques" (28). In 1513, the Bishop of Durham reports on the banner's presence at the battle of Flodden Field and says that all believe that victory was "wrought by the intercession of St. Cuthbert" in *Letters and Papers, Foreign and Domestic (Henry VIII)*, ed. R. H. Brodie (London, 1920): 1.2.2283, page 1021. Reports on the Earl of Surrey's plan to carry the banner into battle in 1523 are included in *Letters and Papers, Foreign and Domestic (Henry VIII)*, ed. J. S. Brewer (London, 1867), 3.2:3481–2, page 1448.

36. Robert S. Kinsman and Theodore Yonge assume that it describes an actual event in their dating of the poem in *John Skelton: Canon and Census* (Renaissance Society of America: Bibliographies and Indexes, 4, 1967), 13; however, as Scattergood notes, the hunting, hawking priest is a comic stereotype of rustic clerical buffoonery, familiar from Chaucerian fabliaux (*Complete English Poems*, 400). As for tone, Arthur Kinney reads it as a didactic allegory of the soul of man allured by Christ's flesh, with the delinquent priest as "holy fool" (92–93), whereas Richard Halpern sees Skelton exulting in "the violation of boundaries" in *The Poetics of Primitive Accumulation: English Renaissance Culture and the Genealogy of Capital* (Ithaca: Cornell University Press, 1991), 112; Stanley Fish concludes that the poem has "no clear moral

focus" to indicate whether it is a product of "personal pique, . . . burlesque of an abused discipline, or . . . straightforward indictment" in *John Skelton's Poetry* (1965; reprint, Hamden, CT: Archon, 1976), 97.

37. This vitality is the subject of the major revisionist histories of the English Reformation, notably Duffy and Christopher Haigh, *English Reformations: Religion, Politics, and Society Under the Tudors* (1993; reprint, Oxford: Clarendon Press, 1995). See especially Duffy on the combination of farce and learning in religious drama (68), the sacred and profane in almanacs (50), and piety and marvels in popular romances (173).

38. Halpern, 116.

39. Mikhail Bakhtin, *Rabelais and His World*, trans. Helene Iswolsky (Cambridge: MIT Press, 1968), 379.

40. Ibid., 287.

41. William Butler Yeats, "Crazy Jane Talks with the Bishop," *Collected Poems* (New York: Macmillan, 1966), 255; Crazy Jane sounds like a spiritual and poetic descendant of Skelton's Elynour Rummynge.

42. Carolyn Walker Bynum, *The Resurrection of the Body in Western Christianity, 200–1336* (New York: Columbia University Press, 1995), 113.

43. Desiderius Erasmus, *A Pilgrimage for Religion's Sake*, in *The Colloquies*, trans. and ed. Craig R. Thompson (Chicago: University of Chicago Press, 1965), 308.

44. Haigh, 191.

45. Geoffrey Chaucer, *The Canterbury Tales*, in *Chaucer's Major Poetry*, ed. Albert C. Baugh (New York: Appleton-Century Crofts, 1963), 491 and 500.

46. Tyndale says that Wolsey "made by craft of necromancy, graven imagery to bear upon him, wherewith he bewitched the king's mind, and made the king to dote upon him more than ever he did on any lady or gentlewoman" in *The Practice of Prelates*, in *The Works of the English Reformers: William Tyndale and John Frith*, ed. Thomas Russell (London, 1831), 4:452–453; see also John Foxe, *Actes and Monuments* (London, 1563), 4:590.

47. Jerome Barlowe and William Roye, *Rede Me and Be Not Wrothe*, ed. Douglas H. Parker (Toronto: University of Toronto Press, 1992). John Anstis attributes *Rede Me* to Skelton in *Typographical Antiquities* (London, 1790), 3:1539. The mock-requiem was an increasingly popular Reformation genre, often aimed at sectarian adversaries; cf. the one for Bishop Bonner, which renders *Phyllyp Sparrow's* opening echo of the requiem Mass even more ridiculous by reducing it to nonsense: "*Placebo. Bo. Bo. Bo. Bo. Bo.*" (*A Commemoration or Dirige of Bastarde Edmonde Boner, alias Sauage, usurped Bisshope of London,* compiled by Lemeke Auale, 1569). Skelton reduces his heretics to comparable

nonsense in his *Replycacion*: "Se where the heretykes go, / Wytlesse wandring to and fro! / With, 'Te he, ta ha, bo ho bo ho!' " (73–75).

48. Edward Hall, *Chronicle of the History of England* (1809; reprint, New York: AMS Press, 1965), 719 and Foxe, 4:657.

49. Simon Fish, *Supplication for Beggars*, ed. Edward Arber (London, 1880), 12–13. The tract was supposedly recommended to the king by Anne Boleyn; see Foxe, 4:657–658. See also W. A. Clebsch, *England's Earliest Protestants, 1520–1535* (New Haven: Yale University Press, 1964), 243–244, and Maria Dowling, "The Gospel and the Court: Reformation under Henry VIII," *Protestantism and the National Church in Sixteenth-Century England*, ed. Peter Lake and Maria Dowling (London: Croom Helm, 1987), 51–52.

50. Thomas More, *Supplication of Souls*, in *Complete Works*, ed. Frank Manley, Germain Marc'Hadour, Richard Marius, and Clarence H. Miller (New Haven: Yale University Press, 1990), 7:111–112; hereafter cited in text.

51. For a discussion of their theological position see J. F. Davis, "The Trials of Thomas Bilney and the English Reformation," *Historical Journal* 24 (1981): 775–790, and Diarmaid MacCulloch, *The Later Reformation in England 1547–1603*, 2nd ed. (London: Palgrave, 2001), 67–69.

52. Greg Walker accuses Skelton of becoming an opportunistic "mouthpiece of the crown" (192) near the end of his career, but though his submission to Wolsey is new, devotion to the crown is not.

53. Thomas More, *A Dialogue Concerning Heresies*, in *The Complete Works*, ed. Thomas M. C. Lawler, Germain Marc'Hadour, and Richard C. Marius (New Haven: Yale University Press, 1981), 6:97.

54. Ibid., 261 and 423.

55. As Scattergood explains, swallowing a fly was the proverbial equivalent of infection by heresy (518–519).

56. Foxe, 4:642 and 620.

57. Ibid., 7:550.

58. The poem is bound as the BL Ms. Lansdowne 794. Alexander Dyce includes it in *The Poetical Works of John Skelton* (1843; reprint, New York: AMS Press, 1965) among "Poems attributed to Skelton" (2:413–447) but notes that internal evidence indicates that it was written after his death (413). Peter Le Neve, an eighteenth-century owner of the work, records the attribution to Skelton by his colleague, Thomas Hearne, on the title page. John Leland was an early owner, and John Bale may have been the first to attribute the work to Skelton, since he was a Protestant admirer of Skelton who worked with Leland's collection. See Leslie Fairfield, *John Bale: Mythmaker for the English Reformation* (West Lafayette, IN: Purdue University Press, 1976), 90 and 97.

59. Dyce, 2:414, 429, and 434. Hereafter cited by page number in the text.

60. Records of the debates are included in appendix 5 of Francis Adrian Gasquet and Edmund Bishop, *Edward VI and the Book of Common Prayer* (London, 1891), 395–443.

61. W. K. Jordan, *Edward VI: The Young King: The Protectorship of the Duke of Somerset* (London: Allen and Unwin, 1968), 135–140; see also Charles H. Herford, *Studies in the Literary Relations of England and Germany in the Sixteenth Century* (Cambridge, 1886), 50; and "Preparations for the First Prayer Book of Edward VI: Some Scarce Published Works of 1547–9," *Church Quarterly Review* XXXV (1892): 36–68; Dickie Spurgeon's introduction to *Three Tudor Dialogues* (Delmar, NY: Scholars' Facsimiles, 1978), v–xx; and John King, *English Reformation Literature: The Tudor Origins of the Protestant Tradition* (Princeton: Princeton University Press, 1982), 258–270 and 284–289. Patrick Collinson shows how "rituals of inversion, or 'misrule' " were used to advance a "cultural revolution" in *The Birthpangs of Protestant England: Religious and Cultural Change in the Sixteenth and Seventeenth Centuries* (New York: St. Martin's Press, 1988), 107 and 112–114.

Once Protestant authority was securely established, its tolerance for satire diminished, as Collinson points out in his discussion of the suppression of the Marprelate tracts in "Ecclesiastical Vitriol: Religious Satire in the 1590s and the Invention of Puritanism," in *The Reign of Elizabeth: Court and Culture in the Last Decade*, ed. John Guy (Cambridge: Cambridge University Press, 1995), 150–170. Natalie Zemon Davis notes a similar tendency among Calvinists who initially welcomed and then denounced the "insolent masquerades" of Mardi Gras in *Society and Culture in Early Modern France* (Stanford: Stanford University Press, 1975), 117–120. Such appropriations of carnival's exuberant misrule show how, despite Bakhtin's claim that "no dogma, no authoritarianism, no narrow-minded seriousness can coexist with Rabelaisian images" (3), such satire is often used for sectarian polemical purposes, as Rabelais's texts were. Bakhtin acknowledges this but insists that Rabelaisian images remain independent of didactic purpose (63–64). For an account of Protestant Rabelaisianism, see Samuel Kinser, *Rabelais's Carnival: Text, Context, Metatext* (Berkeley: University of California Press, 1990), 129–130.

62. *"In clero pleraque videbat mala, . . . Cum quibusdam mendicantium fratrum blateronibus, precipue Dominicanis, continuum gerebat bellum."* John Bale, *Index Britanniae Scriptorum*, ed. Reginald Lane Poole and Mary Bateson (Oxford: Clarendon Press, 1902), 253. My translation. See also *Merie Tales, newly imprinted and made [by] Master Skelton, poet-laureat, (1566–67)*, ed. W. Carew Hazlitt (London, 1866). In one tale, Skelton agrees to Wolsey's request for a funeral

tribute only "if it shall like your Grace to creepe into thys tombe whiles you be alyue, . . . for I am sure that you when you be dead you shall neuer haue it" (12–13) and in another, he shits on a pesky mendicant (16–18). Comparably ribald and anticlerical stories were published in 1526 by John Rastell, Thomas More's brother-in-law. Rastell also printed More's antiheretical tracts but eventually converted to Protestantism, according to Foxe, confirming More's apprehensions regarding the dangers of clerical satire. See *A Hundred Merry Tales and Other English Jestbooks of the Fifteenth and Sixteenth Centuries*, ed. Paul Zall (Lincoln: University of Nebraska Press, 1963), 134–135, and Albert J. Geritz and Amos Lee Laine, *John Rastell* (Boston: Twayne, 1982), 12–14 and 46–47.

63. "*Lucas Opilio . . . poeta ualde facetuserat, qui in poematibus ac rhythmis Skeltono non inferior*"; John Bale, *Scritptorvm Illustrium Maioris Brytannias*, 2 vols. (Basel, 1557–59), 2:109. My translation.

64. *John Bon and Mast Person* (1547), n.p.

65. [Luke Shepherd], *Pathose, or an inward passion of the pope for the losse of hys daugther the masse* (London, 1548), and *The Upcheringe of the Masse* (London, 1547).

66. Anonymous, "The Ruins of Walsingham," in *The New Oxford Book of Sixteenth-Century Verse*, ed. Emrys Jones (Oxford: Oxford University Press, 1991), 551.

67. *Confutation of Tyndale's Answer* (1532), in St. Thomas More, *Complete Works*, ed. Louis A. Schuster, Richard Marius, James Lusardi, and Richard J. Schoeck (New Haven: Yale University Press, 1973), 8:179.

68. Gardiner's letter is included in John Strype, *Memorials of the Most Reverend Father in God Thomas Cranmer*, 2 vols. (Oxford, 1812), 2:789–780.

69. Diarmaid MacCulloch, *Thomas Cranmer* (New Haven: Yale University Press, 1996), 617. For a less sympathetic account of the tragic irony of Cranmer's fall, see Gregory Dix, *The Shape of the Liturgy* (London: Dacre, 1945), 673.

70. *Letters and Papers, Foreign and Domestic (Henry VIII)*, ed. James Gardiner and R. H. Brodie (London: HMSO, 1910), 21:2, 320. Henry maintained in his *King's Book*, his conservative revision of Cranmer's *Bishop's Book*, that Christians ought "to pray for one another, both quick and dead, and to commend one another in their prayers to God's mercy, and to cause other to pray for them also, as well in masses and exequies." See *Formularies of Faith . . . During the Reign of Henry VIII*, ed. C. Lloyd (Oxford, 1825), 375–376.

71. Pamela Tudor-Craig says that Henry contracted to pay Torrigiano £1,500 for his parents' tomb and £2,000 for his own in "The Medieval Monuments and Chantry Chapels," in *Westminster Abbey*, ed. Christopher Wilson, Pamela Tudor-Craig, John Physick, and Richard Gem (London: Bell

and Hyman, 1986), 136–137. Clement VII granted the papal bull in 1525; see Herbert Francis Westlake, *Westminster Abbey*, 2 vols. (London: Philip Allan, 1923), 2:479.

72. William Sessions contends that Edward's shrine and cult remained inviolable for Henry VIII and that the tomb was not destroyed until the reign of Edward VI; see *Henry Howard The Poet Earl of Surrey* (Oxford: Oxford University Press, 1998), 273 and 395. However, J. G. O'Neilly and I. E. Tanner say that the general belief was that, while Henry "may well have hesitated to desecrate the bones of a royal saint, the golden feretory which contained the body of the saint was plundered either in whole or part, and the body itself was quietly buried beneath or on the site of the shrine" during Henry's reign; see "The Shrine of Edward the Confessor," *Archaeologia* 100 (1966): 129–154.

73. *Letters and Papers (Henry VIII)*, 21:2634, 320.

74. Nigel Llewellyn, "The Royal Body: Monuments to the Dead, For the Living," in *Renaissance Bodies: The Human Figure in English Culture, c. 1540–1660*, ed. Lucy Gent and Nigel Llewllyn (London: Reaktion Books, 1991), 235; and Jennifer Woodward, *The Theatre of Death: Ritual Management of Royal Funerals in Renaissance England* (Woodbridge: Boydell, 1997), 132. See also the discussion and sketches of tombs planned for Henry VIII and Edward VI in Hoak, 96–103. Henry planned to use materials purchased by Wolsey for his tomb.

75. *Letters and Papers (Henry VIII)*, 21:2634, 320.

76. Cited in A. G. Dickens, *The English Reformation* (New York: Schocken, 1964), 230 and 243.

77. Scarisbrick, 497; Robert Parsons, the scandal-mongering Jesuit, was one source of these rumors.

78. Woodward attributes the failure to complete this grandiose monument during Elizabeth's reign to its extravagant cost and its design's "incompatibility with the Reformation" (132).

79. Perkins, 2:167–168.

3. RITES OF MEMORY:
SHAKESPEARE AND THE ELIZABETHAN COMPROMISE

1. *The Diary of Henry Machyn*, ed. J. G. Nichols (Camden Society 42; London, 1848), 130. See also Jocelyn Perkins, *Westminster Abbey: Its Worship and Ornaments*, 3 vols. (London: Oxford University Press, 1938), 2:81–87.

2. Cited in Arthur Penrhyn Stanley's *Historical Memorials of Westminster* (London, 1868), 614–615.

3. Norman L. Jones, *Faith by Statute: Parliament and the Settlement of Religion, 1559* (London: Royal Historical Society, 1982), 83; cf. William Haugaard, who contends that Elizabeth was not rejecting monastic superstition but simply giving precedence to her own choristers in *Elizabeth and the English Reformation: The Struggle for a Stable Settlement of Religion* (Cambridge: Cambridge University Press, 1968), 82. Nevertheless, the vernacular service and hostile sermon accurately signaled a bleak future for a monastery that would be once again dissolved by July 1559. Feckenham and his monks might have been allowed to stay had they taken the oath of supremacy and conformed to the new liturgy, but he refused to do so and was sent to the Tower in 1560; see David Knowles, *The Religious Orders in England*, 3 vols. (Cambridge: Cambridge University Press, 1948–59), 3:433–434.

4. David M. Loades, *Mary Tudor: A Life* (Oxford: Blackwell, 1989), 310. For a description of Mary's requiem Mass, see Machyn, 183–184.

5. Owen Oglethorpe, Bishop of Carlisle, had been celebrating Christmas Mass when Elizabeth ordered him not to elevate the host. When he replied "that thus he had learnt the mass, and that she must pardon him as he could not do otherwise," she walked out after the gospel and replaced him at the next day's service with her own royal chaplain. Il Schifanoya to Ottaviano Vivaldino (31 December 1558), *Calendar of State Papers, Venetian* (1558–1580), ed. Rawdon Brown and G. Cavendish Bentinck (London, 1890), 7:2.

6. Il Schifanoya reported on January 23, 1559 that "the Bishop of Carlisle commenced the coronation according to the Roman ceremonial, neither altering nor omitting anything but the outward forms"; *CSP, Venetian*, 7:17. For a discussion of the confusion surrounding Elizabeth's coronation, see my " 'Thou Idol Ceremony': Elizabeth I, *The Henriad*, and the Rites of the British Monarchy," in *Urban Life in the Renaissance*, ed. Susan Zimmerman and Ronald F. E. Weissman (Newark: University of Delaware Press, 1989), 240–266 and also my " 'The Wonderfull Spectacle': The Civic Progress of Elizabeth I and the Troublesome Coronation," in *Coronations: Medieval and Early Modern Monarchic Ritual*, ed. Janos M. Bak (Berkeley: University of California Press, 1990), 217–227.

7. *The Quenes Maiesties Passage through the Citie of London to Westminster the Day before her Coronacion*, ed. James M. Osborn (New Haven: Yale University Press, 1960), 28.

8. Lawrence M. Bryant, *The King and the City in the Parisian Royal Entry Ceremony: Politics, Ritual, and Art in the Renaissance* (Geneva: E. Droz, 1986), 103.

9. On the suppression of the Corpus Christi feast under Elizabeth see Eamon Duffy, *The Stripping of the Altars: Traditional Religion in England, 1400–1580* (New Haven: Yale University Press, 1992), 566 and 579–580.

10. See chapter 1, 18–19.

11. Il Schifanoya to the Castellan of Mantua (23 January 1559), *CSP, Venetian*, 7:11.

12. Paolo Tiepolo to the Doge and Senate (19 March 1559), *CSP, Venetian*, 7:53.

13. C. G. Bayne, "The Coronation of Queen Elizabeth," *English Historical Review* 24 (1909): 322–323; A. F. Pollard, "The Coronation of Queen Elizabeth," *English Historical Review* 25 (1910): 125–126.

14. de Feria to Philip (29 April 1559), *Calendar of State Papers, Spanish*, ed. Martin A. S. Hume (London, 1892–99), 11:29, 62.

15. Guzman de Silva to Philip (9 October 1564), *CSP, Sp.*, 1:270; 387.

16. Cf. Norman Jones, who says that the "genius of the Elizabethan Settlement was its vagueness" in the introduction to *Belief and Practice in Reformation England*, ed. Susan Wabuda and Caroline Litzenberger (Aldershot: Ashgate, 1998), 13. In *Faith by Statute*, Jones sees Elizabeth's remarks to foreign emissaries as part of a diplomatic and "political smokescreen" providing cover for more radical reform (58) and Diarmaid MacCulloch sees a determination to conceal her intentions throughout these early maneuvers (*The Later Reformation in England*, 2nd ed. [London: Palgrave, 2001], 28), whereas William Haugaard sees them as evidence of genuine conservatism (185–186), as does Patrick Collinson in "Windows in a Woman's Soul: Questions about the Religion of Queen Elizabeth I," in *Elizabethan Essays* (London: Hambledon, 1994), 87 and 111.

17. BL Cotton Julius F. VI f. 161. This document is reprinted and discussed in Henry Gee, *The Elizabethan Prayer-Book and Ornaments* (London: Macmillan, 1902), and his page references are included in the text. See discussions by Haugaard, 80; Jones, 16–17, 22–26, 47–49 *et passim.*; John Guy, *Tudor England* (Oxford: Oxford University Press, 1988), 259–260, MacCulloch, 29–30. J. E. Neale downplays the importance of the "Device" in "The Elizabethan Acts of Supremacy and Uniformity," *English Historical Review* 65 (1950): 304–332.

18. *The Boke of the Common Praier* (Worcester, 1549), clxiv.

19. *The Boke of Common Praier* (London, 1552), n.vii.r.

20. *Boke of Common Praier* (1552) o.ii.r; for a discussion of these changes, see A. G. Dickens, *The English Reformation* (New York: Schocken, 1964), 243, 280–283; and Christopher Haigh, *English Reformations: Religion, Politics, and Society Under the Tudors* (1993; reprint, Oxford: Clarendon Press, 1995), 179–181.

21. Ibid., 292.

22. Alexandra Walsham, *Church Papists: Catholicism, Conformity and Confessional Polemic in Early Modern England* (Woodbridge: Boydell, 1993), 1–2, 46–47, and 19.

23. *The Book of Common Prayer 1559: The Elizabethan Prayer Book*, ed. John E. Booty (Charlottesville: University of Virginia Press; Folger Shakespeare Library, 1976), 273. See also Patrick Collinson, *The Elizabethan Puritan Movement* (Berkeley: University of California Press, 1967), 34.

24. Article 31 in Edgar C. S. Gibson, *The Thirty-Nine Articles of the Church of England*, 2 vols. (London: Methuen, 1906), 2:687; article 24 repudiates services "in a tongue not understood of the people" (581).

25. Duffy, 578.

26. *Liturgies and Occasional Forms of Prayer Set Forth in the Reign of Queen Elizabeth*, ed. William Keating Clay (Cambridge, 1847), 433–434. See also G. J. Cuming, *A History of Anglican Liturgy* (London: Macmillan, 1969), 124–125 and 368–369.

27. Cited in Haugaard, 113–115.

28. John Jewel to Peter Martyr (14 April 1559), *The Zurich Letters . . . during the Reign of Queen Elizabeth*, ed. Hastings Robinson, 3 vols. (Cambridge, 1842), 1:55.

29. Ibid., 1:55. Patrick Collinson discusses the distress of the Marian exiles in *The Elizabethan Puritan Movement*, 31, as does Margaret Aston in *The King's Bedpost: Reformation and Iconography in a Tudor Group Portrait* (Cambridge: Cambridge University Press, 1993), 97–102; Aston notes that many were still angry in 1585 about "that foule Idoll the Crosse" on "the altar of abhomination" (102).

30. Francis Procter and Walter Howard Frere, *A New History of the Book of Common Prayer* (London: Macmillan, 1958), 124, and Haugaard, 116. The requiem communion service and the commendation of benefactors were eliminated from the 1571 prayer book according to Cuming, 124.

31. *An Admonition to Parliament*, in *Puritan Manifestoes*, ed. W. H. Frere and C. E. Douglas (London: Church Historical Society, 1952), 21. Both the queen's chapel and cathedral churches are denounced as "popishe dennes" (30).

32. "Of Ceremonies, Why Some Be Abolished, and Some Retained," in *Book of Common Prayer* (1549), f33r.

33. *Thirty-Nine Articles*, 2:716.

34. Patrick Collinson, "Ecclesiastical Vitriol: Religious Satire in the 1590s and the Invention of Puritanism" (150–170), and John Guy, "The Elizabethan Establishment and the Ecclesiastical Polity" (126–149), in *The Reign of Elizabeth I:*

Court and Culture in the Last Decade, ed. John Guy (Cambridge: Cambridge University Press, 1995). As both Collinson and Guy point out, Richard Bancroft mounted the fiercest counterattack on the Marprelate pamphlets and eventually succeeded Whitgift as Archbishop of Canterbury in 1604, intensifying "the conformist drive for hierarchy and order" in the Stuart regime (Guy, 148).

35. Cf. "An exhortation concerning good Order, and obedience to *Rulers and Magistrates*" (1:69–77) and "An Homily against disobedience and wilfull rebellion" (2:275–322) in *Certaine Sermons or Homilies Appointed to be Read in Churches in the Time of Queen Elizabeth I*, 2 vols. (London, 1623), ed. Mary Ellen Rickey and Thomas B. Stroup (Gainesville, FL: Scholars' Facsimiles, 1968).

36. John Whitgift, *Works*, ed. John Ayre, 3 vols. (Cambridge: Cambridge University Press, 1853; Parker Society Publications, vols. 46–48), 3:593, 591, and 586–588.

37. Ibid., 586. Paul Kléber Monod contends that "it was courtiers, not clerics, who gave shape to the amazing 'cult of Elizabeth,'" noting that Archbishop Edmund Grindal insisted on the subordination of "all princes . . . to the Son of God" in *The Power of Kings: Monarchy and Religion in Europe, 1589–1715* (New Haven: Yale University Press, 1999), 64. This overlooks the fact that Grindal was disgraced and suspended for his Puritan sympathies and replaced by Whitgift, who set a more adulatory tone for the remainder of Elizabeth's reign.

38. Helen Hackett, *Virgin Mother, Maiden Queen: Elizabeth and the Cult of the Virgin Mary* (New York: St. Martin's, 1995), 110.

39. John Howson, *A Sermon preached . . . in defence of the Festivities of the Church of England, and namely that of her Maiesties Coronation* (Oxford, 1602), sig. D1r–D2v. Howson criticizes not only Puritans but also Erasmus for opposing feast days and the cult of the saints. He deems Elizabeth worthy of canonization and *latria*, "a vertue morall, & not intellectual" scorned only by those who "gad vp & downe to hear the word preached." Thus he revives the scholastic distinctions used by Skelton in his attack on Bilney's heretical promulgation of "disorder" (see above, 53–54). Howson would prosper as bishop of Oxford and Durham under James and Charles.

40. Frances Yates, *Astraea: The Imperial Theme in the Seventeenth Century* (London: Routledge & Kegan Paul, 1975), 100.

41. "Tale of Hemetes the Hermit," in Sir William Segar, *Honour, Military and Ciuill* (1602), 197–200.

42. Sir Philip Sidney, *Miscellaneous Prose of Sir Philip Sidney*, ed. Katherine Duncan-Jones and Jan Van Dorsten (Oxford: Clarendon Press, 1973), 31. I discuss the resistance of Sidney and others to the cult of Elizabeth in *The Rites*

of Knighthood: The Literature and Politics of Elizabethan Chivalry (Berkeley: University of California Press, 1989), 55–78.

43. The parson's deposition is included in the *Royal Commission on Historical Manuscripts*, 8th Report (London, 1881), Appendix, part 2. The account of the ecclesiastical commission headed by John Aylmer is included in John Strype, *The Life and Acts of John Aylmer* (Oxford, 1821), 54–57, and John Strype, *Annals of the Reformation*, 4 vols. (Oxford, 1824), 3:2, 228–237.

44. Thomas Holland, *Panegyros* (Oxford, 1601), sig. H4v.

45. See my discussion of the earl's chivalric performances and political and military ambitions in *The Rites of Knighthood*, 79–102.

46. Wallace T. MacCaffrey, *Elizabeth I: War and Politics: 1588–1603* (Princeton: Princeton University Press, 1992), 532–533.

47. D. Harris Willson, *King James VI and I* (London: Jonathan Cape, 1956), 152. See also G. V. Akrigg, *Jacobean Pageant or the Court of King James* (London: Hamish Hamilton, 1962), 36–38.

48. J. E. Neale, *Queen Elizabeth I* (1937; reprint, New York: Doubleday, 1957), 385.

49. Stuart M. Kurland, *"Hamlet* and the Scottish Succession?" *Studies in English Literature* 34 (1994): 279–300, and Steven Mullaney, "Mourning and Misogyny: *Hamlet, The Revenger's Tragedy*, and the Final Progress of Elizabeth I, 1600–1607," *Shakespeare Quarterly* 45 (1994): 147; see also Mark Thornton Burnett's brief discussion of "secrets and succession" in "The 'heart of my mystery': *Hamlet* and Secrets," in *New Essays on Hamlet*, ed. Mark Thornton Burnett and John Manning (New York: AMS Press, 1994), 37–39.

50. Patrick Collinson, "The Elizabethan Exclusion Crisis and the Elizabethan Polity," *Proceedings of the British Academy* 84 (1994): 51–92, and *Elizabethan Essays* (London: Hambledon, 1994), 69–70.

51. On an "Elizabethan Settlement [that] settled nothing, or at least left much unsettled," see Collinson, "The Religion of Elizabethan England and of its Queen" in *Giordano Bruno, 1583–1585: The English Experience*, ed. Michele Cilibreto and Nicholas Mann (Florence: Leo S. Olschki, 1997), 5.

52. MacCulloch, 6.

53. Stephen Greenblatt, *Hamlet in Purgatory* (Princeton: Princeton University Press, 2001), 252.

54. The play's ambiguous views of spirits and the afterlife have been the subject of much critical controversy, focusing primarily on the provenance and credibility of the ghost; is it actually Hamlet's father's spirit or a demon from hell? See, among others, Roy W. Battenhouse, *Shakespearean Tragedy: Its Art and Its Christian Premises* (Bloomington: Indiana University Press,

1969), 237–240; Sister Miriam Joseph, "Discerning the Ghost in *Hamlet*," *PMLA* 76 (1961): 493–502; Eleanor Prosser, *Hamlet and Revenge* (Stanford: Stanford University Press, 1971), 136–137; Robert H. West, *The Invisible World: A Study of Pneumatology in Elizabethan Drama* (Athens: University of Georgia Press, 1939), 162–200, and *Shakespeare and the Outer Mystery* (Lexington: University of Kentucky Press, 1968), 56–68; Arthur McGee, *The Elizabethan Hamlet* (New Haven: Yale University Press, 1987), 112; and J. Dover Wilson, *What Happens in Hamlet* (Cambridge: Cambridge University Press, 1967), 62 and 184–185. Paul N. Siegel provides an excellent review of these arguments in "'Hamlet, Revenge!': The Uses and Abuses of Historical Criticism," *Shakespeare Survey* 45 (1993): 15–26.

55. Dover Wilson discusses the play's requiem (298–299), as does Roland Mushat Frye, *Renaissance Hamlet: Issues and Responsibilities in 1600* (Princeton: Princeton University Press, 1984), 306.

56. See my "A Wedding and Four Funerals: Conjunction and Commemoration in *Hamlet*," *Shakespeare Survey* 54 (2001): 122–139. See also Michael Neill, who says that "No play is more obsessively concerned with funeral proprieties than *Hamlet*" in *Issues of Death: Mortality and Identity in English Renaissance Tragedy* (Oxford: Clarendon Press, 1997), 300; and David Bevington, " 'Maimed Rites': Violated Ceremony in *Hamlet*," *Critical Essays on Shakespeare's* Hamlet, ed. David Scott Kastan (New York: G. K. Hall, 1995), 126–138.

57. Battenhouse, 250 and Robert N. Watson, *The Rest Is Silence: Death as Annihilation in the English Renaissance* (Berkeley: University of California Press, 1994), 88–89.

58. Ralph Houlbrooke, *Death, Ritual and Bereavement* (London: Routledge, 1989), 40–42. In *Death, Religion, and the Family in England 1480–1750* (Oxford: Clarendon Press, 1998), Houlbrooke still speaks of a "gap left by the abolition of Catholic intercessory rites" but concedes that "private rites of commemoration" involving "personal mementoes" help fill the void (374).

59. Fortinbras launches a surprise attack on Elsinore and topples the statue of old Hamlet in *Hamlet*, dir. Kenneth Branagh, Castle Rock Entertainment, 1996, and his acquisition of the Denmark corporation is announced as a hostile corporate takeover in *Hamlet*, dir. Michael Almereyda, Miramax Films, 2000.

60. *The Letters of John Keats 1814–1821*, ed. Hyder Edward Rollins, 2 vols. (Cambridge: Harvard University Press, 1958), 1:193.

61. Norman Rabkin, *Shakespeare and the Common Understanding* (New York: Free Press, 1967), 10.

62. Cf. Stephen Greenblatt, who advances a notion of Shakespearean

"equivocality" that does not "simply locate us in a disenchanted world of natural causes" because "murky currents of invisible agency" are still perceptible, in "The Eating of the Soul," *Representations* 48 (1994): 110–111.

63. William Kerrigan, *Hamlet's Perfection* (Baltimore: The Johns Hopkins University Press, 1994), 58–59.

64. "Form and cause" is an example of *hendiadys*, a figure of speech combining two proximate substantive nouns that abounds in *Hamlet*, as George T. Wright points out in "Hendiadys and *Hamlet*," in *Critical Essays on Shakespeare's Hamlet*, ed. David Scott Kastan (New York: G. K. Hall, 1995), 79–109, but, as Wright notes, all the play's conjunctions "mask deeper disjunctions" (95). "Form and cause conjoined" recalls—and might even recover—Hamlet's image of his father as a "combination and a form indeed/Where every god did seem to set his seal/To give the world assurance of a man" (3.4.60–62).

65. According to F. C. Coppleston, these terms were adapted from Aristotle by St. Bonaventure, who claimed that "almost all natural forms, at any rate corporal forms, are actualized through the action of a particular finite efficient cause"; see *A History of Medieval Philosophy* (New York: Harper & Row, 1972), 164.

66. Rosemond Tuve, *Elizabethan and Metaphysical Imagery* (1947; reprint, Chicago: University of Chicago Press, 1968), 12n7 and 24–26.

67. *The Geneva Bible: A Facsimile of the 1560 Edition* (Madison: University of Wisconsin Press, 1969); hereafter cited in the text.

68. C. H. McIlwain, *The Political Works of King James I* (Cambridge: Cambridge University Press, 1918), 272.

69. Edmund Plowden, *The Commentaries or Reports*, 2 vols. (London, 1816), 1:238. Sir John Hawkins was the first to suggest that Shakespeare knew Plowden, suggesting that the jurist's summary of the tortuous intricacies of "Crowner's Quest Law" was an influence on the gravedigger scene (5.1.22); see *A New Variorum Edition of Shakespeare: Hamlet*, ed. Horace Howard Furness, 2 vols. (1877; reprint, New York: Dover, 1963) 1:376–377.

70. See Preface, xv–xvi.

71. Richard Hooker, *Of the Law of Ecclesiastical Polity, Book V*, ed. W. Speed Hill, 7 vols. (Cambridge: Belknap/Harvard University Press, 1977), 2:234.

72. I find little evidence of the "holy peace" that Dover Wilson believes to be conferred by the ghost's "spiritual presence" (255).

73. Watson, 5.

74. Jacques Lacan, "The Art of Mémoires," quoted in Marjorie Garber, *Shakespeare's Ghost Writers: Literature as Uncanny Causality* (New York: Methuen, 1987), 172.

75. Beza, *Coena Domini* (1593), cited in Jill Raitt, *The Eucharistic Theology of Theodore Beza: Development of the Reformed Doctrine* (Chartersburg, PA: American Academy of Religion, 1972), 64–65.

76. Neill, 225.

77. Ibid., 240 and 303.

78. Critical opinion is again divided. Barbara Hardy says that Horatio "makes an intelligent, accurate, and fairly comprehensive summary of external events, and his capacity to tell is guaranteed by the preview" in "Figure of Narration in *Hamlet*," in *A Centre of Excellence: Essays Presented to Seymour Betsky*, ed. Robert Druce (Amsterdam: Costerus Rodopy, 1987), 14. By contrast, Terence Hawkes says that Horatio's oration cannot possibly comprehend "the subtleties, the innuendoes, the contradictions, the imperfectly realized motives and sources for action that have been exhibited to us" in "*Telmah*," in *Shakespeare and the Question of Theory*, ed. Patricia Parker and Geoffrey Hartman (New York: Methuen, 1985), 311.

79. Anthony B. Dawson's discussion of theater as a "conduit for 'social memory' " (55) is pertinent here, as is his account of the struggle between Fortinbras and Hamlet's ghost in this last scene, especially in its emphasis on how "the performance of memory . . . ignites a struggle for control of interpretation"; see "The Arithmetic of Memory: Shakespeare's Theatre and the National Past," *Shakespeare Survey* 52 (1999): 54–67.

80. Roland Mushat Frye discusses parallels between Hamlet and King James, including their obligation to avenge their fathers' murders (31–37) as well as the adulterous liaisons of their mothers with the murderers (102–111) in *Renaissance Hamlet*, but he does not consider parallels between James and Fortinbras or the possibility that James might want to avenge his mother.

81. Howard Nenner, *The Right to Be King: The Succession to the Crown of England* (Chapel Hill: University of North Carolina Press, 1995), 95.

82. In Ingmar Bergman's production, Fortinbras has Horatio shot at the end of the play; *Hamlet*, dir. Ingmar Bergman, Brooklyn Academy of Music, 1988.

83. Thomas Dekker, *The Wonderful Year*, in *Non-Dramatic Works*, ed. Alexander B. Grosart, 5 vols. (London, 1884), 1:97.

84. M. Handover, *The Second Cecil: The Rise to Power, 1563–1604, of Sir Robert Cecil, later, first Earl of Salisbury* (London: Eyre and Spottiswoode, 1959), 235–240. James initially demanded that Elizabeth "give out a plain declaration, which must be enacted in her own records, that I am untouched in any action or practice that hath ever been intended against her, especially in this last [the Essex revolt]," and he reminded her of her "old promise, that

nothing shall be done by her, in her time, in prejudice of my future right"; James to the Earl of Mar and Edward Bruce (8 April 1601), *The Secret Correspondence of Sir Robert Cecil with James VI of Scotland*, ed. David Dalrymple (Edinburgh, 1766), 5–6. Cecil, in turn, urged James to forego "needless expostulations" and "generall acclamation"; *The Correspondence of King James of Scotland with Sir Robert Cecil and others*, ed. John Bruce (London: 1861), 7.

85. Lord Henry Howard to Edward Bruce (4 December 1601), *Secret Correspondence*, 46.

86. Lords of the Privy Council to James (8 April 1603), *Historical Manuscripts Commission, Salisbury*, ed. M. S. Giuseppi (London: HMSO, 1930), 15:39–40.

87. James to the Earl of Mar and Edward Bruce (12 April 1603), ibid., 15:44. See also Willson, 166. Cecil traveled to York to greet his new sovereign on April 18 and remained in the royal entourage until April 25 (Handover, 299–300). Even as he hastened to join his new master, Cecil remained concerned with his duties to his old mistress, writing to the Privy Council that "if his Majesty should hold on his journeys thither with such speed as he has begun, he would be near London before the funerals, or at the very time. So as the State could not attend both the performance of that duty to our late Sovereign, and of this other of this Majesty's reception" (18 April 1603), *HMC Salisbury*, 15:53.

88. (12 April 1603), ibid., 15:44.

89. Julia M. Walker, "Reading the Tombs of Elizabeth I," *English Literary Renaissance* 26 (1996): 510–530.

90. James I to Dean of Peterborough (September 28, 1612), *Letters of Kings of England*, ed. J. O. Halliwell-Phillipps, 2 vols. (London, 1846), 2:119.

91. Walker, 515–516.

92. For a discussion of Stuart efforts to propagate this patriarchal image, see Jonathan Goldberg, "Fatherly Authority: The Politics of Stuart Family Images," in *Rewriting the Renaissance: The Discourses of Sexual Difference in Early Modern Europe*, ed. Margaret W. Ferguson, Maureen Quilligan, and Nancy J. Vickers (Chicago: University of Chicago Press, 1986), 3–32.

93. Woodward, 136; Walker, 523–524.

94. Woodward attributes this not to a lack of funds, arguing instead that the continued display of James's funeral effigy as well as other posthumous portraits and statues precluded the need for a memorial (202–203).

95. Bishop Goodman cited in Akrigg, 17.

96. See Thomas Cogswell, *The Blessed Revolution: English Politics and the Coming of War, 1621–1624* (Cambridge: Cambridge University Press, 1989).

97. For a discussion of this chivalric nostalgia, see my "Old English Honour in an Evil Time: Aristocratic Principle in the 1620s," in *The Stuart Court and Europe: Essays in Politics and Political Culture*, ed. Malcolm Smuts (Cambridge: Cambridge University Press, 1996), 133–155.

98. Roy Strong, *Henry, Prince of Wales and England's Lost Renaissance* (London: Thames & Hudson, 1986), 72 and 222–224.

99. Joseph Mead to Sir Martin Stuteville (30 March 1622 and 25 January 1623), *The Court and Times of James I*, ed. Thomas Birch, 2 vols. (London, 1848), 2:301, 360. As David Norbrook points out, George Buchanan was not only a proponent of republican resistance theory but also the "tutor to James VI [who] 'whipped the arse of the Lord's anointed.'" See "The Emperor's New Body? *Richard II*, Ernst Kantorowicz and the Politics of Shakespeare Criticism," *Textual Practice* 10 (1996): 343.

100. "The Coppie of a Libell put into the hand of Queen Elizabeth's statue in Westminster by an unknown person, Anno dni 1610 [corrected to]—1621. Ultimo die Martii. 1623" [Bod. Malone 23/32]. "This copie was founde in the hand of Queen Elizabeths tombe at West. February [erased] 22 of june 1623" [Folger MS V.a.275, Commonplace book of George Turner]. Alastair Bellany has transcribed this petition, which appears in different versions in several ballad collections and commonplace books of the 1620s and reappears in 1642. I am very grateful to Professor Bellany for alerting me to its existence and kindly sharing his transcription with me. Elizabeth's reply combines admonitions to subject and sovereign, warning that "Princes are gods on earth, and subjects' eyes/Upon their actions must not stand like spies," while condemning the dispersal of the "revenues of the Crown . . . to favourite or friend."

101. Ibid.

102. Thomas Dempster, *History of the Scottish Church*, 2 vols. (N.p., 1627), 2:464.

103. James refused to have the Earl of Northampton's florid epitaphs describing his mother as a martyr for her faith placed on her tomb; see James Emerson Phillips, *Images of a Queen: Mary Stuart in Sixteenth-Century Literature* (Berkeley: University of California Press, 1964), 226–227.

104. Thomas Fuller, *The Church History of Britain* (Oxford, 1845), 5:258. This image of Elizabeth's tomb is included in Henry Holland's *Heruuologia* (1620), a collection of portraits of "reformers and opponents of the papacy"; there are several engravings of Prince Henry as well as various Elizabethan heroes (Dudley, Leicester, Walsingham, Drake, Essex, Grenville, etc.) and early Tudor martyrs (Tyndale, Latimer, Ridley, Cranmer, etc.); see Arthur

M. Hind, *Engraving in England in the Sixteenth and Seventeenth Centuries*, 3 vols. (Cambridge: Cambridge University Press, 1955), 2:115–116.

105. Walter Benjamin, *Illuminations*, trans. Harry Zohn, ed. Hannah Arendt (New York: Harcourt, Brace, 1969), 222–223.

106. Stephen Greenblatt, *Shakespearean Negotiations: The Circulation of Social Energy in Renaissance England* (Chicago: University of Chicago Press, 1988), 127–128.

107. William Hazlitt, *The Complete Works*, ed. P. P. Howe, 21 vols. (London: J. M. Dent, 1930), 4:232.

4. IDOLIZING KINGS: JOHN MILTON AND STUART RULE

1. *HMC Salisbury Mss*, 15:11, cited in G. V. Akrigg, *Jacobean Pageant or the Court of King James* (London: Hamish Hamilton, 1962), 16.

2. Sir Roger Wilbraham, *Journal (1593–1616)*, ed. Harold Spencer Scott (London: Royal Historical Society, 1902), 54.

3. Francis Bacon to Lord Ellesmere (2 April 1605), "A letter to the Lord Chancellor, Touching the History of Britain," in *The Works of Francis Bacon*, ed. James Spedding, Robert Leslie Ellis, and Douglas Denon Heath, 15 vols. (London, 1861), 10:250. Bacon's letter begins by addressing the king's proposal "for the erection of a tomb or monument for our late sovereign Lady Queen Elizabeth" (249).

4. James I, *True Law of Free Monarchies* and *Basilikon Doron*, ed. Daniel Fischlin and Mark Fortier (Toronto: Centre for Reformation and Renaissance Studies, 1996), 80. See also *Basilikon Doron*: "But if God give you not succession, defraud never the nearest by right, whatsoever conceit ye have of the person. For kingdoms are ever at God's disposition and in that case we are but live-renters, [it] lying no more in the king's nor people's hands to dispossess the righteous heir" (142–143).

5. Howard Nenner, *The Right to Be King: The Succession to the Crown of England* (Chapel Hill: University of North Carolina Press, 1995), 95 and 59. See also D. Harris Willson, *King James VI and I* (London: Jonathan Cape, 1956), 140–141; James was the grandson of Henry VII.

6. C. H. McIlwain, *The Political Works of King James I* (Cambridge: Cambridge University Press, 1918), 272. Cf. Dudley Digges, who argues in *The Unlawfulness of Subjects Taking Up Arms Against their Sovereign* (n.p., 1643) that the king is "husband and father, not to single persons, but to the Commonwealth"; consent initially "joynd man and wife, King and people, but divine

ordinance continues this union; marriages and governments are both rati-
fied in heaven. *Qua Deus coniunixit, homo ne separet"* (150).

7. Speech to Parliament on 21 March 1610 in James I, *Works* (London:
1616), 529–531. See also his *True Law of Free Monarchies*, 51 and 54. See also *Political Works of King James I*, 3 and 307.

8. Conrad Russell, "Divine Rights," *Public Duty and Private Conscience in
Seventeenth-Century England*, ed. John Morrill, Paul Slack, and Daniel Woolf
(Oxford: Clarendon Press, 1993), 117–118.

9. Sir Thomas Craig, *The Right of Succession To the Kingdom of England:
Against the Sophisms of Parsons the Jesuite (Doleman)* (London, 1703), 122. See
also Sir John Hayward's "defence, both of the present authoritie of Princes,
and of succession according to proximitie of bloud," in *An Answer to the First
Part of a Certaine Conference concerning Svccession, pvblished not long since vnder
the name of R. Dolman* (London, 1603), sig. A3v. As Hayward's title indicates,
they are responding to the radically subversive claims made by Robert Parsons; under the pseudonym Doleman, Parsons says that "propinquity of
Birth or Blood alone, without other circumstances, is not sufficient to be
preferred to a crown"; see *A Conference about the Next Succession to the Crown
of England* (1594; reprint, London, 1681), 1. Even Peter Wentworth, who was
sent to the Tower for urging Elizabeth to consult Parliament on the succession, attacked Parsons for subordinating a God-given hereditary right to parliamentary prerogative in *A Discourse containing the Author's opinion of the true
and lawful successor to her Majesty* (1598), 262–263.

10. Robert Brady, *Great Point of Succession* (1681), 1–2 and 36, cited in Nenner, 107 and 110; recoiling from such hyperbole, the great Whig historian,
Lord Macaulay, allowed that hereditary right was a reasonably "good political institution" but still complained that "bigoted and servile theologians
had turned it into a religious mystery almost as awful and incomprehensible
as transubstantiation itself" (Nenner 260n24).

11. See Debora Shuger, *Habits of Thought in the English Renaissance: Religion, Politics, and the Dominant Culture* (Berkeley: University of California
Press, 1990), 124; Graham Parry, *The Golden Age Restor'd: The Culture of the
Stuart Court, 1603–42* (Manchester: Manchester University Press, 1981), 239;
Malcolm Smuts on "the religion of monarchy" in *Court Culture and the Origins of the Royalist Tradition in Early Stuart England* (1987; reprint, Philadelphia: University of Pennsylvania Press, 1999), 230–238; and Jennifer Woodward, *The Theatre of Death: Ritual Management of Royal Funerals in Renaissance
England* (Woodbridge: Boydell, 1997), 127–128.

12. John King, *A Sermon at Paules Crosse, on behalfe of Paules Church* (London, 1620), 43, 34, and 37, cited in Vaughan Hart, *Art and Magic in the Court of the Stuarts* (London: Routledge, 1994), 44 and 127.

13. Ibid., 172–173.

14. See Julius S. Held, *The Oil Sketches of Peter Paul Rubens: A Critical Catalogue*, 2 vols. (Princeton: Princeton University Press, 1980), 2:139–158; and Charles Scribner, *Triumph of the Eucharist: Tapestries Designed by Rubens* (Ann Arbor, MI: UMI Research, 1982).

15. Rubens's paintings depict James as a Solomonic judge, uniting England and Scotland in their devotion to the infant Charles in one painting and presiding over a Golden Age of Peace and Plenty with War while banishing Rebellion and Discord in another. The centerpiece shows him ascending into heaven with the aid of Justice, Religion, and Faith; see Held, 1:185–190. For discussions of the political agenda behind the reconstruction and decoration of Whitehall, see Per Palme, *Triumph of Peace: A Study of the Whitehall Banqueting House* (London: Thames and Hudson, 1957); Oliver Millar, *Rubens: The Whitehall Ceiling* (London: Oxford University Press, 1958); and Roy Strong, *Britannia Triumphans: Inigo Jones, Rubens, and the Whitehall Palace* (London: Thames and Hudson, 1980).

16. Ben Jonson, "The Dedication of the Kings New Cellar to Bacchus," in *The Complete Poetry of Ben Jonson*, ed. William B. Hunter, Jr. (New York: Norton, 1963), 204.

17. Stephen Orgel, *The Illusion of Power: Political Theater in the English Renaissance* (Berkeley: University of California Press, 1975), 8. Orgel's evocative title conveys the paradoxically illusory yet powerful qualities of the masque; see his discussion of the court's "faith in the power of idealization" (40–52).

18. William Davenant, *Salmacida Spolia*, in *The Dramatic Works*, 5 vols. (1872–74; reprint, New York: Russell and Russell, 1964), 2:326.

19. Charles to Archbishop Abbot, Tanner MSS, 71, 42, cited in Charles Carlton, *Charles I: The Personal Monarch* (1983; reprint, London: Routledge, 1995), 161. See also Kevin Sharpe, *The Personal Rule of Charles I* (New Haven: Yale University Press, 1992), 209–235 and 275–292.

20. *Works of King Charles* (1662), 1:98, cited in Julian Davies, *The Caroline Captivity of the Church: Charles I and the Remoulding of Anglicanism* (Oxford: Clarendon Press, 1992), 15. See also Sharpe, 328–345.

21. Kenneth Fincham and Peter Lake, "The Ecclesiastical Policies of James I and Charles I," in *The Early Stuart Church, 1603–1642*, ed. Kenneth Fincham (Stanford: Stanford University Press, 1993), 44. See also Judith Richards, " 'His Nowe Majestie' and the English Monarchy: The Kingship of Charles

I before 1640," *Past and Present* 113 (1986): 70–96; Richards sees the king's activities as an "assiduous 'stroker' for the king's evil" as belated compensation for the earlier lack of popular access (93). According to Arthur Wilson, James had reluctantly endured the practice because he knew that it was "a *Device*, to aggrandize the *Virtue* of Kings, when *Miracles* were in fashion; but he let the World believe it, though he smiled at it, in his own *Reason*, finding the strength of the *Imagination* a more powerfull *Agent* in the *Cure*"; *The History of Great Britain: Being the Life and Reign of King James the First* (1653), 289.

22. Fincham and Lake, 49.

23. Anthony Van Dyck's sketch of "Charles I and the Knights of the Garter in Procession" is one indication of the importance the king assigned to these ceremonies. It was associated with a scheme for four tapestries depicting the history of the Order to be placed on the walls of the Banqueting House; see Palme, 124–135 and 282–288, and Roy Strong, *Charles I on Horseback* (New York: Viking, 1972), 59–63. See also Sharpe, 219–222.

24. C. V. Wedgewood, *A Coffin for King Charles: The Trial and Execution of Charles I* (New York: Macmillan, 1964), 222.

25. Cited in Peter Lake, "The Laudian Style: Order, Uniformity and the Pursuit of the Beauty of Holiness in the 1630s," in Fincham and Lake, 168.

26. Joseph Mede, *The Reverence of God's House* (1638), 11. As I've noted in chapter 2, Sir Thomas Smith demands the same reverence for the cloth of state in the presence chamber; see *De Republica Anglorum*, ed. Mary Dewar (Cambridge: Cambridge University Press, 1982).

27. Lake, "The Laudian Style," 171–173.

28. William Laud, *Works*, ed. William Scott and James Bliss, 7 vols. (Oxford, 1847–60), 6:57.

29. Fulke Robarts, *Gods Holy House and Service* (1639), 44–45. Robarts distinguishes between two types of holiness, the essential and original as opposed to the accidental and derivative (1), but then blurs his own distinction by writing that the latter sort can be "immediate." In the Folger Library's copy, one reader maintains the distinction by crossing out "im" in "immediate" and crossing out "to be" and replacing it with "where was" in the discussion "Of the Holy Place" (3–5). The same reader also replaces the word *Church* in the sentence "men were begotten in the Church faith" with the less institutional term *Christian* (8).

30. Derek Hirst, *Authority and Conflict: England 1603–1658* (Cambridge: Harvard University Press, 1986), 196.

31. *Constitutional Documents of the Puritan Revolution, 1625–1660*, ed. Samuel Rawson Gardiner, 3rd ed. (Oxford: Clarendon Press, 1902), 140–141.

32. Jocelyn Perkins, *Westminster Abbey: Its Worship and Ornaments*, 3 vols. (London: Oxford University Press, 1938), 2:167–168.

33. Ibid.

34. Charles was buried in Henry's tomb at Windsor, though one of his loyal attendants was initially reluctant to place him there because Charles "would upon occasional Discourse express some dislike in King *Harry's* Proceedings, in misimploying those vast Revenues the suppressed Abbeys, Monasteries, and other religious Houses were endowed with, and by demolishing those many beautiful and stately Structures (which both expressed the Greatness of their Founders, and preserved the Splendour of the Kingdom)"; Sir Thomas Herbert, *Memoirs of the Last Two Years of the Reign of King Charles I* (London, 1839), 201. In *A Messenger From the Dead, or Conference . . . Between the Ghost of Henry the 8. And Charls the First* (London, 1658), Henry VIII, disturbed by the arrival of a new body in his tomb, complains that "I commanded also that a more sumptuous Monument should be provided for me, then was euer raised of any of my Predecessors, and as yet I have no Monument at all," even as he realizes that he is reviled by all for destroying monastic "Monuments of Learning" (15).

35. Henry Spelman, *History and Fate of Sacrilege* (London, 1698), 259 and 182. Writing in 1632, Spelman not only claims that the Stuarts "had no hand in the like degradation of the Monasteries and Churches" but also adds that the late King James said "that if he had found the Monasteries standing he would not have pulled them down; not meaning to continue them in their superstitious Uses, but to employ them, as *Chorah's* censers to some godly purposes" (192).

36. Margery Corbett, "The Title Page and Illustrations to the *Monasticon Anglicanum* 1655–1673," *The Antiquaries Journal* 67 (1987): 102–110. For a discussion of the antiquarians' renewed enthusiasm for monasteries, see Graham Parry's *The Trophies of Time: English Antiquarians of the Seventeenth Century* (Oxford: Oxford University Press, 1995), 10–11, 227–236, 271–273.

37. John Morrill, *The Nature of the English Revolution* (London: Longman, 1993), 21. See also Patricia Crawford, " 'Charles Stuart, That Man of Blood,' " *Journal of British Studies* 16 (1977): 41–61.

38. Cited in Barry Coward, *The Stuart Age: England 1603–1714* (1980; reprint, London: Longman, 1994), 236.

39. *Eikon Basilike: The Portraiture of His Sacred Majesty in His Solitudes and Sufferings*, ed. Philip A. Knachel (Ithaca: Cornell University Press, 1966), 142; cf. the horror registered at the "breaking of church windows, . . . pulling down of crosses, . . . defacing of the monuments and inscriptions of the dead," and other acts of iconoclastic vandalism (126); hereafter cited in the

text. There were 35 English editions in the first year as well as 3 Latin, 7 Dutch, 7 French, 2 German and 1 Danish edition. The actual author is probably John Gauden, a Presbyterian clergyman rewarded with a bishopric after the Restoration (xxv–xxxii). For a vivid account of the book's authorship and impact, see H. R. Trevor-Roper, *"Eikon Basiliké*: The Problem of the King's Book," in *Historical Essays* (New York: Harper Torchbooks, 1957), 211–220.

40. Ann Eljenholm Nichols, *Seeable Signs: The Iconography of the Seven Sacraments, 1350–1544* (Woodbridge: Boyell, 1994), 9–11; see chapter 1.

41. John Quarles, *Regale Lectum Miseriae: or A Kingly Bed of Miserie* (1649), 41 and 100.

42. "John Cleveland," *Monumentum Regale: or a Tombe, Erected for . . . Charles I* (1649), 40 and 45.

43. [Peter Du Moulin], *Regii Sanguinis Clamor ad Coelum* (Cry of the Royal Blood unto Heaven), trans. Paul W. Blackford, in John Milton, *Complete Prose Works*, ed. Don M. Wolfe (New Haven: Yale University Press, 1966), 4.2.1067.

44. *A Miracle of Miracles: wrought by the blood of King Charles the First . . . upon a Mayd at Detford* (London, 1649), 3–6.

45. Ibid., 6–7.

46. [Du Moulin], 1070. Du Moulin, an Anglican priest, attacks the churchmen of the Commonwealth for "creating that very election their own office; for they call none elect save those whom they elect," adding that "no sacraments are administered by these men, and wisely so, for they are endowed with no faculty for administering them; but it is impious that they order the sacraments to be omitted as not at all necessary, unmindful that there is no greater necessity than to obey God's commandments" (1070).

47. *Princely Pellican* (1649), 5.

48. Ibid., title page and 2–3.

49. Lois Potter, *Secret Rites and Secret Writing: Royalist Literature, 1641–1660* (Cambridge: Cambridge University Press, 1989), 175. Potter notes Abraham Wright's poem on a copy of *Eikon Basilike* "in a Cover coloured with His Blood" (175).

50. [Robert Brown], *The Subjects Sorrow or Lamentations Upon the Death of Britains Josiah, King Charls* (1649), 23–24.

51. Cf. Stanley Fish's critique of *Areopagitica's* veneration of books as "the purest efficacie and extraction of that living intellect that bred them" and claim that censorship "kills reason itselfe, kills the Image of God, as it were in the eye" (492) as a form of reification and idolatry, in "Driving from the Letter: Truth and Indeterminacy in Milton's *Areopagitica*," in *Re-Membering Milton: Essays on the Texts and Traditions*, ed. Mary Nyquist and Margaret

Ferguson (New York: Methuen, 1987), 235–236. As Fish notes, Milton's lapse into literalism does not last.

52. Richard Helgerson, "Milton Reads the King's Book: Print, Performance, and the Making of a Bourgeois Idol," *Criticism* 29 (1987): 1–25. See also Bruce Boehrer, "Elementary Structures of Kingship: Milton, Regicide, and the Family," *Milton Studies* 23 (1987): 97–117; Steven N. Zwicker, "The King's Head and the Politics of Literary Property: The *Eikon Basilike* and *Eikonoklastes*," in *Lines of Authority: Politics and English Literary Culture, 1649–1689* (Ithaca: Cornell University Press, 1993), 37–59; Laura Blair McKnight, "Crucifixion or Apocalypse? Refiguring the *Eikon Basilike*," in *Religion, Literature and Politics in Post-Reformation England, 1540–1688*, eds. Donna Hamilton and Richard Strier (Cambridge: Cambridge University Press, 1996), 138–160.

53. *The Scotch Souldiers Lamentation upon the Death of the most Glorious and Illustrious Martyr, King Charles* (1649), 3.

54. [Du Moulin], 1068.

55. For some, the *Eikon Basilike* was great literature. David Hume regarded it as "the best prose composition which at the time of its publication was to be found in the English language," whereas Thomas Carlyle considered it "one of the paltriest pieces of vapid, shovel-hatted, clear-starched immaculate falsity and cant I have ever read"; cited in Richard Ollard, *The Image of the King: Charles I and Charles II* (New York: Atheneum, 1979), 25 and 194.

56. "On the New Forcers of Conscience under the Long Parliament," in *Complete Poems and Major Prose*, ed. Merritt Y. Hughes (New York: Odyssey, 1957), 144–145; all references to Milton's verse are to this edition and are hereafter cited in the text. In Milton's mockery of the material grossness of Presbyterian priestcraft in the *Tenure of Kings*, there are echoes of the Skeltonic satires of the Tudor period; cf. the anticlerical and antipapal jibes of Milton's "*In Quintum Novembris*," (On the Fifth of November) and *An Apology for Smectymnuus*.

57. See Kevin Sharpe, " 'An Image Doting Rabble': The Failure of Republican Culture in Seventeenth-Century England," in *Refiguring Revolution: Aesthetics and Politics from the English Revolution to the Romantic Revolution*, ed. Kevin Sharpe and Steven N. Zwicker (Berkeley: University of California Press, 1998), 25–56.

58. Bulstrode Whitelock, *Memorials of the English Affairs* (London, 1862), 491–492, cited in Roy Sherwood, *Oliver Cromwell: King in All But Name* (Stroud, Gloucestershire: Sutton, 1997), 4.

59. Ibid., 3–4.

60. Ibid., 102. Sherwood's earlier study, *The Court of Oliver Cromwell* (London: Croom Helm, 1977), discusses Cromwell's royal style.

61. Woodward, 199–201; David Norbrook, *Writing the English Republic: Poetry, Rhetoric and Politics 1627–1660* (Cambridge: Cambridge University Press, 1999), 380.

62. See A. H. Woolrych, "Milton and Cromwell: 'A Short but Scandalous Night of Interruption,'" in *Achievements of the Left Hand*, ed. Michael Lieb and John Shawcross (Amherst: University of Massachusetts Press, 1974), 185–218.

63. William Riley Parker, *Milton: A Biography*, 2 vols. (Oxford: Clarendon Press, 1968), 1:567–570.

64. John Richardson in ibid., 1:577.

65. Mary Ann Radzinowicz, "The Politics of *Paradise Lost*," in *The Politics of Discourse: The Literature and History of Seventeenth-Century England*, ed. Kevin Sharpe and Steven N. Zwicker (Berkeley: University of California Press, 1987), 205.

66. Nicholas von Maltzahn, "The First Reception of *Paradise Lost* (1667)," *Review of English Studies* 47 (1996): 481.

67. Ibid., 483.

68. Ibid., 482–483.

69. Cf. Eve's comparable attachment to her "native soil" (11:270) and Michael's rejoinder that wherever her husband henceforth "abides, think there thy native soil" (292).

70. See Jon Whitman on the conclusion's "radical displacements" (27) in "Losing a Position and Taking One: Theories of Place and *Paradise Lost*," *Milton Studies* 29 (1993): 21–33.

71. *Christian Doctrine* 15:395–397, cited by Stanley Fish, *Surprised by Sin: The Reader in* Paradise Lost, 2nd ed. (1967; reprint, Cambridge: Harvard University Press, 1997), 276. Cf. Carey's translation in *CPW* 6:472: "Here *substance* means that we are persuaded that *the things hoped for* will be ours, just as firmly as if they not only already existed but were actually in our possession."

72. Joseph C. McLelland, *The Visible Words of God: An Exposition of the Sacramental Theology of Peter Martyr Vermigli A.D. 1500–1562* (Grand Rapids, MI: Eerdmans Press, 1957), 166–167.

73. Ibid., 166n19.

74. "This day have I begot whom I declare / My only son, and on this holy Hill / Him have anointed" (5:603–605). God's announcement makes it sound like the Son was begotten and exalted after the Angels were created, but Abdiel later rebukes Satan for assuming that to be the case and ignoring the Son's role in their creation (5:835–837).

75. William Myers, *Milton and Free Will: An Essay in Criticism and Philosophy* (London: Croom Helm, 1987), 201.

76. Ibid., 212.

77. McLelland, 76.

78. Ashraf H. A. Rushdy, "On *Paradise Regained*: the Interpretation of Career," *Milton Studies* 24 (1988): 254. See also Arnold Stein, *Heroic Knowledge: An Interpretation of "Paradise Regained" and "Samson Agonistes"* (Minneapolis: University of Minnesota Press, 1957). See also Mary Ann Radzinowicz, "*Paradise Regained* as Hermeneutic Combat," *University of Hartford Studies in Literature* 16 (1984): 99–107; Roger H. Sundell, "The Narrator as Interpreter in *Paradise Regained*," *Milton Studies* 2 (1970): 83–10; and Stanley Fish on the rejection of signs altogether in his "Preface to the Second Edition," in *Surprised by Sin*, xxxv.

79. McLelland, 187, 107.

80. Jeffrey B. Morris, "Disorientation and Disruption in *Paradise Regained*," *Milton Studies* 26 (1990): 233. Morris's discussion of the poem's "spatial disjointedness" (225) is also pertinent to my own emphasis on displacement. Cf. Irene Samuel's emphasis on the Son's "common bond with all humanity" (123) and "likeness to other men" (131) as the basis of his victory in "The Regaining of Paradise," in *The Prison and the Pinnacle*, ed. Balachandra Rajan (Toronto: University of Toronto Press, 1973), 111–134.

81. Milton's distinction between a union in substance and difference in essence of the Father and Son in *Christian Doctrine* (*CPW* 6:220) is pertinent to the somewhat blurred vision of the Son as "true Image of the Father" in *Paradise Regained*. For discussion of the ambiguous relation of the Father and the Son in Milton, see W. B. Hunter, "Milton on the Incarnation," in *Bright Essence: Studies in Milton's Theology* (Salt Lake City: University of Utah Press, 1971), 132–141; Barbara Lewalski, *Milton's Brief Epic: The Genre, Meaning, and Art of* Paradise Regained (Providence: Brown University Press, 1966), 156–163; Hugh MacCallum, *Milton and the Sons of God: The Divine Image in Milton's Epic Poetry* (Toronto: Toronto University Press, 1986), 212–225; and C. A. Patrides, *Milton and the Christian Tradition* (Hamden, CT: Archon, 1979), 16–25.

5. SACRAMENTAL TO SENTIMENTAL:
ANDREW MARVELL AND THE RESTORATION

1. Edmund Waller, "On the Statue of King Charles I at Charing Cross," in *The Poems*, ed. G. Thorn Drury (1893; reprint, New York: Greenwood Press, 1968), 203. Waller was a cavalier poet, banished for plotting to retake

London for the king in 1643. Pardoned by Parliament, he returned home and composed a tribute to Cromwell but subsequently welcomed the Restoration in verse of this sort. During the Civil War, in 1645, Milton and Waller were both published by the same man, Humphrey Mosely, who apparently regarded Waller as the superior poet; in his preface to Milton's verses, Mosely says he was encouraged by the reception of "most ingenious men" of "Mr. Wallers late choice pieces." See Louis Martz, "The Rising Poet," in *Poet of Exile: A Study of John Milton's Poetry* (New Haven: Yale University Press, 1980), 33–34; and Thomas Corns, "Milton's Quest for Respectability," *Modern Language Review* 77 (1982): 769–779 and "Ideology in the *Poemata*," *Milton Studies* 19 (1984): 195–203.

2. R. A. Beddard, "Wren's Mausoleum for Charles I and the Cult of the Royal Martyr," *Architectural History* 27 (1984): 40–44.

3. J. Douglas Stewart, "A Militant, Stoic Monument: The Wren-Cibber-Gibbons Charles I Mausoleum Project: Its Authors, Sources, Meaning, and Influence," in *The Restoration Mind*, ed. W. Gerald Marshall (Newark: University of Delaware Press, 1997), 22. Stewart also discusses the contributions of Grinling Gibbons and Caius Gabriel Cibber to the design (32–33 and 39).

4. Beddard, 45.

5. Barry Coward, *The Stuart Age: England, 1603–1714* (1980; reprint, London: Longman, 1994), 295.

6. John Spurr, *The Restoration Church of England, 1646–1689* (New Haven: Yale University Press, 1991), 344–346.

7. [Pete]R [Pet]T, *A Discourse Concerning Liberty of Conscience* (1661), 47–49, 55 cited in ibid., 219.

8. Gilbert Burnet, *History of My Own Times* (1723–24), 1:93, cited in J. A. I. Champion, *The Pillars of Priestcraft Shaken: The Church of England and its Enemies 1660–1730* (Cambridge: Cambridge University Press, 1992), 5.

9. Andrew Marvell, *An Account of the Growth of Popery and Arbitrary Government in England*, in *Complete Works in Verse and Prose*, ed. A. B. Grosart, 4 vols. (1875; reprint, New York: AMS, 1966), 4:248.

10. Jonathan Scott's probing analysis of the Exclusion Crisis in *Algernon Sidney and the Restoration Crisis, 1677–1683* (Cambridge: Cambridge University Press, 1991) treats it as a symptom of a more fundamental succession crisis, one that revived many of the fears surrounding earlier Tudor alterations of state (17–21). Algernon Sidney's devotion to the Protestant cause also recalls the fervor and martyrdom of his granduncle, Sir Philip Sidney (267–269 and 358). On the emergence of partisan divisions, see Mark Goldie, "The Roots of True Whiggism," *History of Political Thought* 1 (1980) and "Restoration Po-

litical Thought," in *The Reign of Charles II and James II*, ed. Lionel K. J. Glassey (Houndsmill, England: Macmillan, 1997), 12–35.

11. James I, *Basilikon Doron*, in *True Law of Free Monarchies* and *Basilikon Doron*, ed. Daniel Fischlin and Mark Fortier (Toronto: Centre for Reformation and Renaissance Studies, 1996), 143.

12. Howard Nenner, *The Right to Be King: The Succession to the Crown of England* (Chapel Hill: University of North Carolina Press, 1995), 95. See also Nenner, "Pretense and Pragmatism: The Response to Uncertainty in the Succession Crisis of 1689," in *The Revolution of 1688–89: Changing Perspectives*, ed. Lois Schworer (Cambridge: Cambridge University Press, 1992), 85.

13. John Miller, *The Glorious Revolution* (1983; reprint, Longman, 1987), 102.

14. Ibid.

15. Henry Coventry (1680), cited in J. R. Western, *Monarchy and Revolution: The English State in the 1680s* (Totowa, NJ: Rowman and Littlefield, 1972), 40.

16. Mark Kishlansky, *A Monarchy Transformed: Britain 1603–1714* (Harmondsworth: Penguin, 1996), 284.

17. Gilbert Burnet, *A Sermon Preached before the King and Queen, at White-Hall, On the 19th Day of October, 1690. Being the Day of Thanksgiving, for His Majesties Preservation and Success in Ireland* (London, 1690), 6–8, cited in Gerald Straka, "The Final Phase of Divine Right Theory in England, 1688–1702," *English Historical Review* 77 (1962): 656.

18. Francis Atterbury, "The Wisdom of Providence manifested in the Revolutions of Government. A Sermon Preach'd before the Honourable House of Commons" (29 May 1701), 1:251–252, cited in Straka, 645–646.

19. Nicholas von Maltzahn, "The First Reception of *Paradise Lost* (1667)," *Review of English Studies* 47 (1996): 481.

20. *A Vindication of Some Among Our Selves Against the False Principles of Dr. Sherlock* (1692), 7, cited in Helen W. Randall, "The Rise and Fall of a Martyrology: Sermons on Charles I," *Huntington Library Quarterly* 10 (1947): 153.

21. Straka, 657.

22. J. P. Kenyon, *Revolution Principles: The Politics of Party, 1689–1720* (Cambridge: Cambridge University Press, 1977), 29.

23. Robert Ferguson, cited in Nenner, "Pretense and Pragmatism," 92.

24. Scott, 210. In his *Discourses Concerning Government*, Sidney says that "Magistrates are distinguished from other men, by the power with which the law invests them for the public good" (Scott, 224–225).

25. John Miller, "Crown, Parliament and People," in *Liberty Secured?*

Britain Before and After 1688, ed. J. R. Jones (Stanford: Stanford University Press, 1992), 80.

26. Kishlansky, 316–317. In arguing for the continuation of a belief in sacred kingship into the eighteenth century, J. C. D. Clark calls "the practice of touching for the King's Evil . . . the crucial index of the persistence of a non-secular image of monarchy," but he concedes that while it stayed in some prayer books after 1714, it was "unused though not proscribed" in *English Society, 1688–1832* (Cambridge: Cambridge University Press, 1985), 162–163.

27. Cited in Coward, 407.

28. Champion, 196. On Anne as representative of a more secular "abstract concept of sovereign authority," see Paul Kléber Monod, *The Power of Kings: Monarchy and Religion in Europe, 1589–1715* (New Haven: Yale University Press, 1999), 295–296.

29. Kishlansky, 341.

30. Ibid., 316.

31. Linda Colley, *Britons: Forging the Nation: 1707–1837* (New Haven: Yale University Press, 1992), 233.

32. Ibid., 232.

33. John Barrell, "Sad Stories: Louis XVI, George III, and the Language of Sentiment," in *Refiguring Revolution: Aesthetics and Politics from the English Revolution to the Romantic Revolution*, ed. Kevin Sharpe and Steven N. Zwicker (Berkeley: University of California Press, 1998), 83.

34. "Found on the Church Door at White Hall, January 30th 1696," Bodleian Library, Rawlinson MS Poetry 169 f 9b, cited by Laura Knoppers, "Reviving the Martyr King: Charles I as Jacobite Icon," in *The Royal Image: Representation of Charles I*, ed. Thomas N. Corns (Cambridge: Cambridge University Press, 1999), 263.

35. Ibid., 263.

36. Miller, *The Glorious Revolution*, 30.

37. J. C. D. Clark maintains that the House of Hanover never abandoned their own hereditary claims to the English throne (127), but he concedes the greater advantage of providential arguments for the accession of George I and II since their hereditary claims were weaker than those of the Stuart pretenders (179).

38. Cf. Howard Erskine-Hill on the poems of Robert Burns, in which "the Cause of Heroic Loyalty" has become largely "sentimental" (60), in "Literature and the Jacobite Cause: Was There a Rhetoric of Jacobitism?" in *Ideology and Conspiracy: Aspects of Jacobitism, 1689–1759*, ed. Eveline Cruickshanks (Edinburgh: J. Donald, 1982), 49–69.

39. William Havard, *King Charles the First, An Historical Tragedy written in Imitation of Shakespeare* (London, 1737), sig. A3r. He also found it "a Story barren of Female Characters," and the epilogue gives the queen the last word; she condemns Cromwell and his cohort as "Rebels at once to Female Power, and Crown'd-heads!/But now—blest Change! Our Heroes give their Votes/ For Government of Kings, and Petticoats!" (62). Cromwell briefly feels pity for the king (7–8) but then sneers at Fairfax for giving in to it: "Shame on his pitying Heart! His Soul's unmann'd,/His Resolution dwindled to a Girl's" (16).

40. Ibid., 56 and 58.

41. Knoppers, 283. John Barrell discusses comparably pitiable engravings of Charles I and Louis XVI in the cottage of a patriotic rustic in George Crabbe's *The Parish Register*, published in 1807 ("Sad Stories," 91).

42. Blair Worden, "Andrew Marvell, Oliver Cromwell, and the Horatian Ode," in *The Politics of Discourse: The Literature and History of Seventeenth-Century England*, ed. Kevin Sharpe and Steven N. Zwicker (Berkeley: University of California Press, 1987), 150–151. See also David Norbrook's analysis of Marvell's ideological complexities in *Writing the English Republic: Poetry, Rhetoric and Politics 1627–1660* (Cambridge: Cambridge University Press, 1999), 243–298.

43. *Tom May's Death* (line 76), in *The Poems and Letters of Andrew Marvell*, ed. H. M. Margoliouth, 2 vols. (Oxford: Clarendon Press, 1971), 1:96; hereafter cited by line number in the text.

44. For a discussion of these prolific posthumous attributions, see Nicholas von Maltzahn, "Marvell's Ghost," in *Marvell and Liberty*, ed. Warren L. Chernaik and Martin Dzelzainis (London: Macmillan, 1999), 50–74.

45. "Introduction," in *Anthology of Poems on Affairs of State, Augustan Satirical Verse, 1660–1714*, ed. George deF. Lord (New Haven: Yale University Press, 1975), xviii.

46. Andrew Marvell, The Rehearsal Transpros'd and The Rehearsal Transpros'd, the Second Part, ed. D. I. B. Smith (Oxford: Clarendon Press, 1971), 135; hereafter cited in the text.

47. Marvell, *Account*, 4:250.

48. Annabel Patterson, *Marvell: The Writer in Public Life* (London: Longman, 2000), 76–78.

49. Warren L. Chernaik, *The Poet's Time: Politics and Religion in the Work of Andrew Marvell* (Cambridge: Cambridge University Press, 1983), 83.

50. Horace, *The Art of Poetry* (361), in *Satires, Epistles, Ars Poetica*, trans. H. Rushton Fairclough (1926; reprint, Cambridge: Harvard University Press,

1955), 480–481; and Sir Philip Sidney, *An Apology for Poetry*, ed. Geoffrey Shepherd (Manchester: Manchester University Press, 1973), 101.

51. Patterson, 81.

52. Horace, *Carmina* 3.2.13, in *The Odes and Epodes*, trans. C. E. Bennett (Cambridge: Harvard University Press, 1960), 174–175.

53. Patterson, 76.

54. Donald Friedman, "Rude Heaps and Decent Order," in Chernaik and Dzelzainis, eds., *Marvell and Liberty*, 140.

55. Peter Davidson, *Poetry and Revolution: An Anthology of British and Irish Verse, 1625–1660* (Oxford: Clarendon Press, 1998), lxx.

56. Ibid., lxx–lxxi.

57. John Nalson, *Impartial Collection of the Great Affairs of State, From the Beginning of the Scotch Rebellion In the year 1639 to the Murther of King Charles I* (London, 1683). The artist is Robert White, who also did a frontispiece for Richard Perrinchief's *The Royal Martyr: or, The Life and Death of King Charles I* (London, 1676) modeled even more closely on the allegorical portrait of Charles I of the *Eikon Basilike*. Ironically, White also engraved the portrait of John Milton for the title page of Jacob Tonson's 1688 edition of *Paradise Lost*. The portrait was part of that edition's attempt to present a more conservative image of Milton and to forge a rapprochement of Whigs and Tories; see von Maltzahn, "The Whig Milton, 1667–1700" in *Milton and Republicanism*, eds. David Armitage, Armand Himy, and Quentin Skinner (Cambridge: Cambridge University Press, 1998), 229–253.

58. "Commentary," in *The Poems and Letters of Andrew Marvell*, 256.

59. *The Satirical Etchings of James Gillray*, ed. Draper Hill (New York: Dover, 1976), plate 2; 103–104. Robert L. Patten, *George Cruikshank's Life, Times, and Art*, 2 vols. (New Brunswick: Rutgers University Press, 1992), 1:103–105.

60. Sir Henry Halford, *An Account of What Appeared on Opening the Coffin of King Charles the First in the Vault of King Henry the Eight in St. George's Chapel at Windsor on the First of April, 1813*, BL Addl. Ms. 8825, f. 7.

61. Ibid., ff. 8–9.

62. Ibid. Halford's handwritten account is certified by the stamped seal of the Prince Regent.

63. BL Addl. 6306, f. 83. For an explanation of the drawing see Mary Dorothy George, *Catalogue of Political and Personal Satires Preserved in the Department of Prints and Drawings in the British Museum (1811–19)*, 11 vols. (London: British Museum, 1949), 9:238–239 and 248–249. The episode inspired a

no less scathing poetic satire by Lord Byron entitled "Windsor Poetics," "composed on the occasion of H.R.H. the P[rinc]e R[e]g[en]t being seen standing betwixt the coffins of Henry 8 th and Charles 1st, in the Royal vault at Windsor."

> Famed for contemptuous breach of sacred ties,
> By Headless Charles, see heartless Henry lies;
> Between them stands another Sceptered thing,
> It moves, it reigns, in all but name—a King:
> Charles to his People, Henry to his Wife,
> —in him the double Tyrant starts to Life:
> Justice and Death have mixed their dust in vain,
> Each Royal Vampyre wakes to life again;
> Ah! What can tombs avail—since these disgorge
> The blood and dust of both—to mould a G[eor]ge.

This is the first of three versions; see Lord Byron, *The Complete Works*, ed. Jerome J. McGann, 7 vols. (Oxford: Clarendon Press, 1981), 3:86–87 and 424–425. I am grateful to my friend and colleague, Rachel Brownstein, for calling this poem to my attention.

64. Christopher Hibbert, *George IV, Regent and King, 1811–1830* (New York: Harper and Row, 1975), 21.

65. On this English obsession with the guillotine, see Marcus Wood, *Radical Satire and Print Culture, 1790–1822* (Oxford: Clarendon Press, 1994), 75, and Ronald Paulson, "The Severed Head: The Impact of French Revolutionary Caricatures on England," in *French Caricature and the French Revolution, 1789–1799* (Los Angeles: Grunwald Center for the Graphic Arts, UCLA/Chicago: University of Chicago Press, 1988), 55–66.

66. Hibbert, 178.

67. Edward Frederick Langley Russell, Baron Russell of Liverpool, *Caroline, The Unhappy Queen* (London: Hale, 1967), 163.

68. Flora Fraser, *The Unruly Queen: The Life of Queen Caroline* (New York: Knopf, 1996), 465.

69. William Hazlitt, "Common Places" (1823), in *The Complete Works*, ed. P. P. Howe, 21 vols. (London: J. M. Dent, 1930), 20:137. Hazlitt also notes the affinities of civil idolatry with religious idolatry, writing that those who joined Caroline's camp set up a veritable "rag-fair of royalty—every one carried his own paints and patches into the presence of the new Lady of Loretto" (137).

70. Hazlitt, "Conversations of James Northcote," in *The Complete Works*, II:240–241.

71. William Hone, *The Right Divine of Kings to Govern Wrong* (London: 1821), 8–9. In his commentary, Hone blames the English Reformation for preposterous notions of kingship's sanctity: "The tyrant Henry VIII, by making himself the head of the Church, clearly begat the *Right Divine*. . . . Before the Kings of England were heads of the church we hear little of *divine right*, and sometimes the Church itself was on the side of freedom; since that time, never" (33).

72. Tom Nairn, *The Enchanted Glass: Britain and Its Monarchy* (London: Radius, 1988), 183, 332, 357–358, 362, and 370.

73. Ibid., 56.

74. J. J. Scarisbrick, *Henry VIII* (Berkeley: University of California Press, 1968), 386.

75. Nairn, 91.

76. The religious dimensions of the event are discussed by Chris Harris, "Secular Religion and the Public Response to Diana's Death" (97–107) and by Jennifer Chandler, "Pilgrims and Shrines" (135–155), in *The Mourning for Diana*, ed. Tony Walter (Oxford: Berg, 1999), and Sara Maitland, "The Secular Saint," in *After Diana: Irreverent Elegies* (London: Verso, 1998), 63–73; see also *Diana, The Making of a Media Saint*, ed. Jeffrey Richards, Scott Wilson, and Linda Woodhead (London: I. B. Taurus, 1999). John A. Taylor argues that Diana's life and death reflect a profound transformation of British values in which self-interest finally trumps the public good and repressive constraints in *Diana, Self-Interest, and British National Identity* (Westport, CT: Praeger, 2000).

77. David Cannadine, "Diana, Princess of Wales," in *History in Our Time* (New Haven: Yale University Press, 1998), 81. Cannadine allows that the myth is "a partial version of the truth" but still expects it to prevail (81).

78. Patrick Jephson, *Shadows of a Princess* (New York: HarperCollins, 2000), 417.

79. Robert Mendick, "They Used to Cry in the First Two Years," *The Independent*, 31 Aug. 2000, 3; Adam Sherwin and Isabel Thomas, "Princess Diana's Fans Hold Anniversary Palace Vigil," *The London Times*, 1 Sept. 2000, 5. A more recent story notes an increase in sales of souvenirs and in television specials marking what would have been her fortieth birthday, but these trends are treated as commercial and media hype; see James Morrison, "The Long, Strange, and Highly Profitable Afterlife of the People's Princess," *The Independent*, 1 Jul. 2001, 3.

80. For a sympathetic account of the similarities between the two women, see Beatrix Campbell, *Diana, Princess of Wales: How Sexual Politics Shook the Monarchy* (London: The Women's Press, 1998), 15–20, 227–231; see also John Wolfe, "Royalty and Public Grief in Britain: An Historical Perspective 1817–1997," in Walter, *The Mourning for Diana*, 53–64.

81. Caroline admitted that she "derived great 'fun' from her 'warfare with the royal family,' keeping them 'in hot water,' 'teazing and worrying them' " (Hibbert, 40). Jephson describes Diana's tearful BBC television interview in 1995 as one of several tactical maneuvers against the royal family in "Diana's War," *Sunday Times*, 24 Sept. 2000, 15–17.

Index